ASTONISHING X-MEN

NORTHSTAR

ASTONISHING X-MEN VOL. 10: NORTHSTAR. Contains material originally published in magazine form as ASTONISHING X-MEN #48-51, NATION X #2 and ALPHA FLIGHT #106. First printing 2013. ISBN# 978-0-7851-6180-6. Published by MARVEL WORLDWIDE, INC., a subsidiary of MARVEL ENTERTAINMENT, LLC. OFFICE OF PUBLICATION: 135 West 50th Street, New York, NY 10020. Copyright © 1992, 2010, 2012 and 2013 Marvel Characters, Inc. All rights reserved. All characters featured in this issue and the distinctive names and likenesses thereof, and all related indicia are trademarks of Marvel Characters, Inc. No similarity between any of the names, characters, persons, and/or institutions in this magazine with those of any living or dead person or institution is intended, and any such similarity which may exist is purely coincidental. **Printed in the U.S.A.** ALAN FINE, EVP - Office of the President, Marvel Worldwide, Inc. and EVP & CMO Marvel Characters B.V.; DAN BUCKLEY, Publisher & President - Print, Animation & Digital Divisions; JOE QUESADA, Chief Creative Officer; TOM BREVOORT, SVP of Publishing; DAVID BOGART, SVP of Operations & Procurement, Publishing; RUWAN JAYATILLEKE, SVP & Associate Publisher, Publishing; C.B. CEBULSKI, SVP of Creator & Content Development; DAVID GABRIEL, SVP of Print & Digital Publishing Sales; JIM O'KEEFE, VP of Operations & Logistics; DAN CARR, Executive Director of Publishing Technology; SUSAN CRESPI, Editorial Operations Manager; ALEX MORALES, Publishing Operations Manager; STAN LEE, Chairman Emeritus. For information regarding advertising in Marvel Comics or on Marvel.com, please contact Niza Disla, Director of Marvel Partnerships, at ndisla@marvel.com. For Marvel subscription inquiries, please call 800-217-9158. **Manufactured between 1/9/2013 and 2/11/2013 by R.R. DONNELLEY, INC., SALEM, VA, USA.**

10 9 8 7 6 5 4 3 2 1

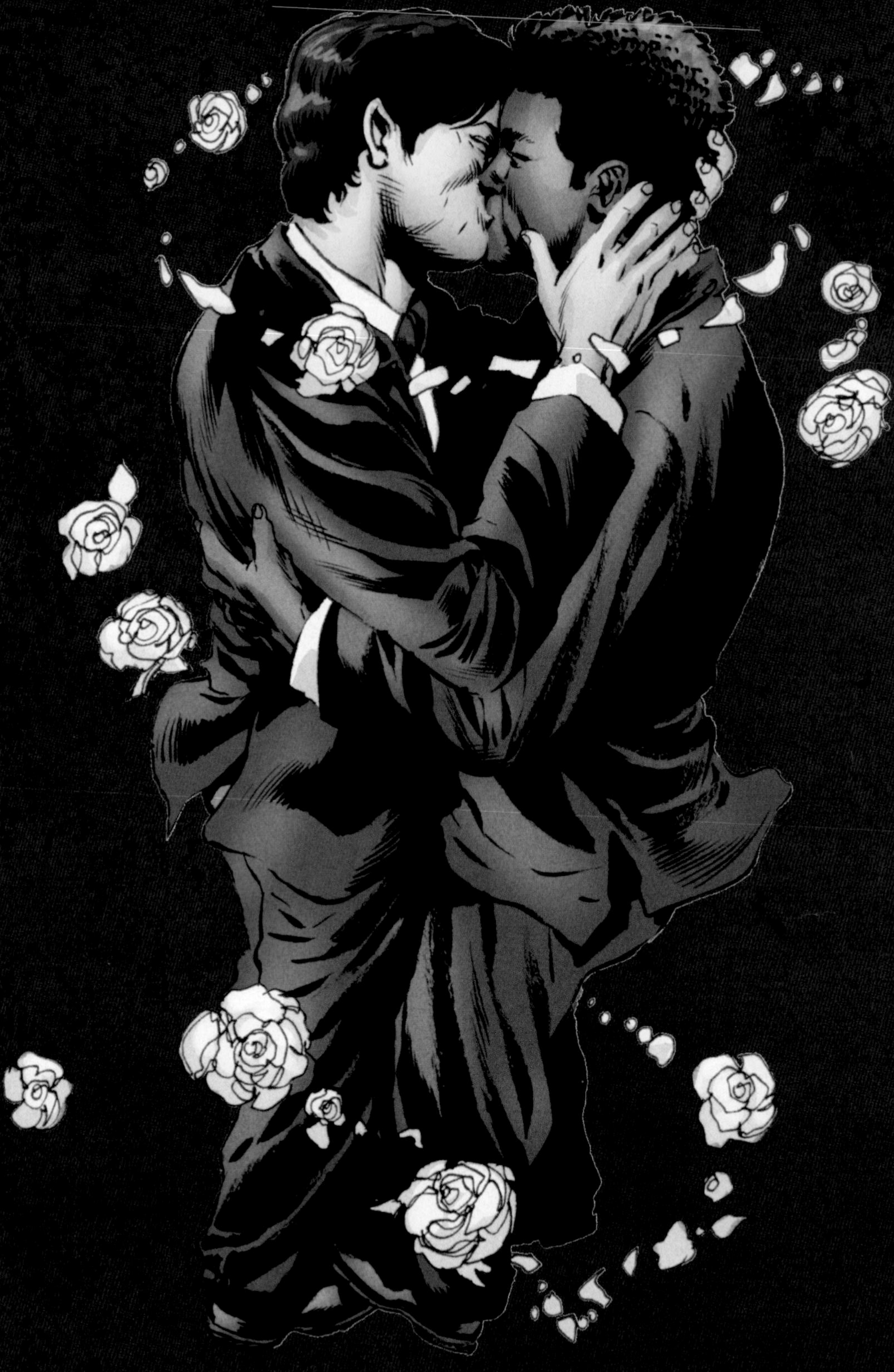

COLLECTION EDITOR: CORY LEVINE • ASSISTANT EDITORS: ALEX STARBUCK & NELSON RIBEIRO
EDITORS, SPECIAL PROJECTS: JENNIFER GRÜNWALD & MARK D. BEAZLEY • SENIOR EDITOR, SPECIAL PROJECTS: JEFF YOUNGQUIST
SVP OF PRINT & DIGITAL PUBLISHING SALES: DAVID GABRIEL

EDITOR IN CHIEF: AXEL ALONSO • CHIEF CREATIVE OFFICER: JOE QUESADA • PUBLISHER: DAN BUCKLEY • EXECUTIVE PRODUCER: ALAN FINE

ASTONISHING X-MEN

NORTHSTAR

Writer: **Marjorie Liu**

Artist: **Mike Perkins**

with **Andrew Hennessy** (Inker, Issue #51)

Color Artist: **Andy Troy**

with **Jim Charalampidis** and **Rachelle Rosenberg** (Issue #51)

Letterer: **VC's Joe Caramagna** with **Cory Petit** and **Clayton Cowles** (Issue #51)

Cover Art: **Dustin Weaver** with **Rachelle Rosenberg**

Associate Editor: **Daniel Ketchum**

Editor: **Jeanine Schaefer**

Group Editor: **Nick Lowe**

"LDR"
from *Nation X #2*
Writer & Artist: **Tim Fish**
Color Artist: **Tim Piotrowski**
Letterer: **Jared Fletcher**
Cover Art: **Dustin Weaver**
with **Morry Hollowell**
Editor: **Daniel Ketchum**

"THE WALKING WOUNDED"
from *Alpha Flight #106*
Writer: **Scott Lobdell**
Penciler: **Mark Pacella**
Inker: **Dan Panosian**
Colorist: **Bob Sharen**
Letterer: **Janice Chiang**
Cover Art: **Mark Pacella**
with **Bob McLeod**
Editor: **Bobbie Chase**

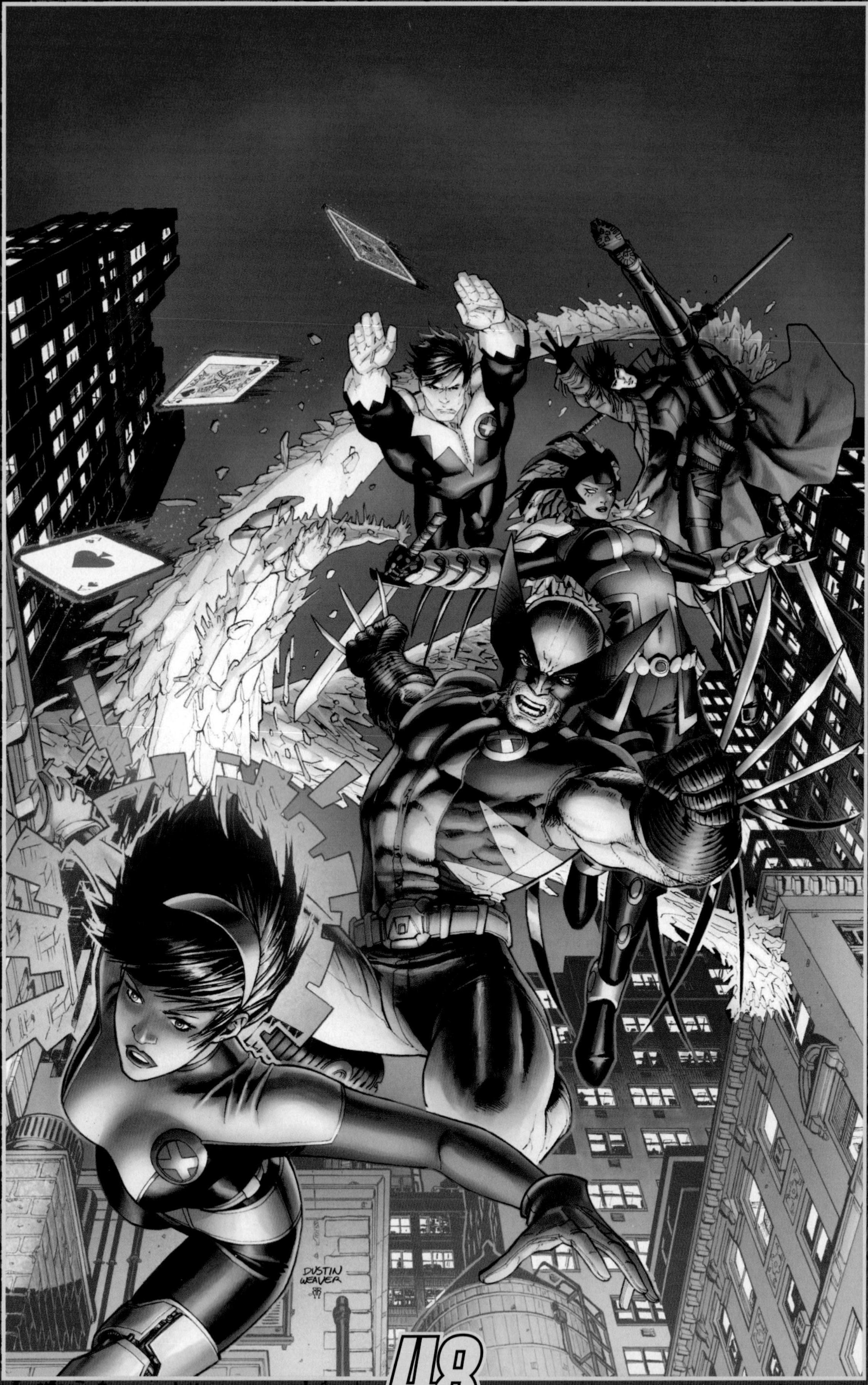
DUSTIN
WEAVER

48

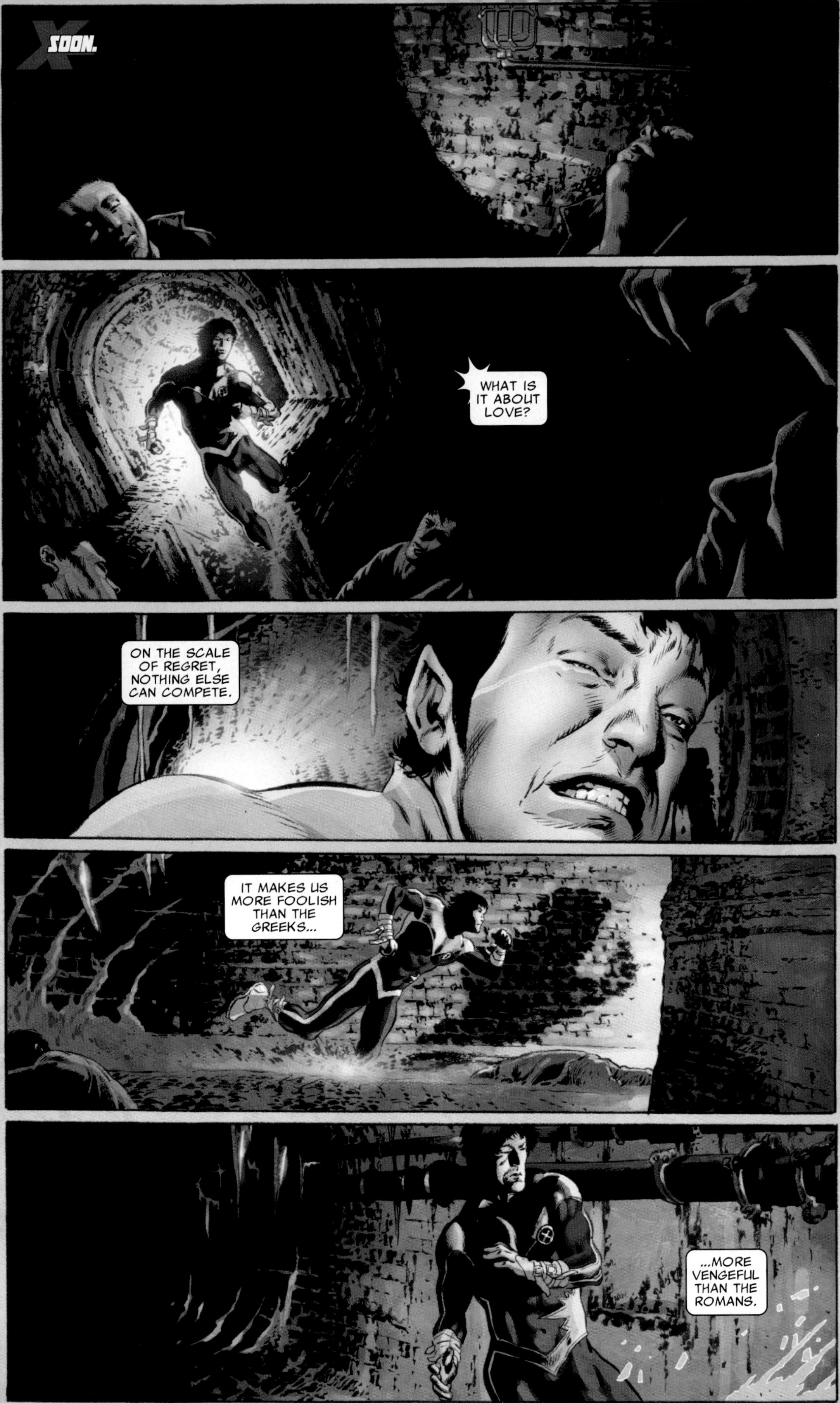
SOON.
WHAT IS IT ABOUT LOVE?
ON THE SCALE OF REGRET, NOTHING ELSE CAN COMPETE.
IT MAKES US MORE FOOLISH THAN THE GREEKS...
...MORE VENGEFUL THAN THE ROMANS.

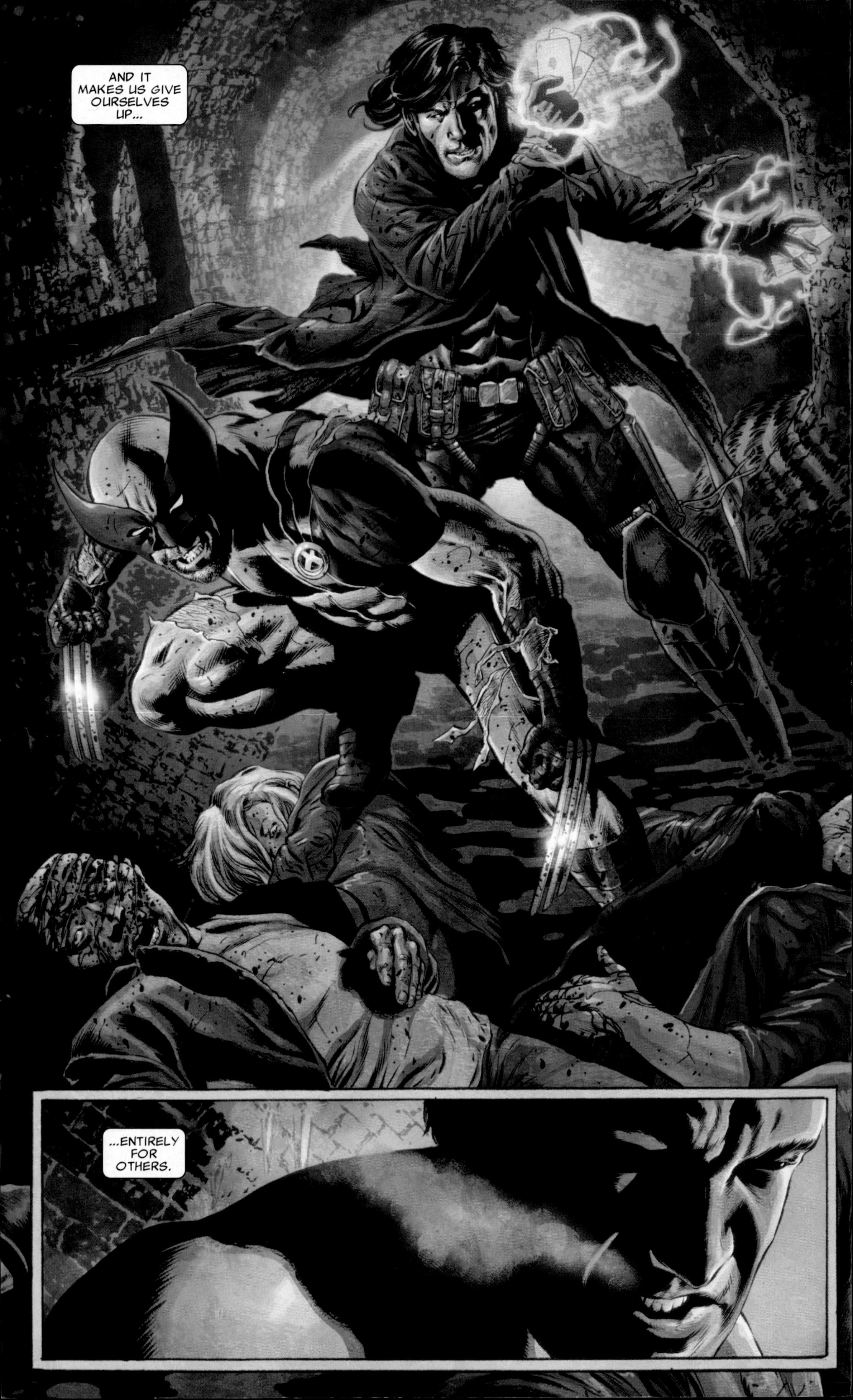
AND IT MAKES US GIVE OURSELVES UP...
...ENTIRELY FOR OTHERS.

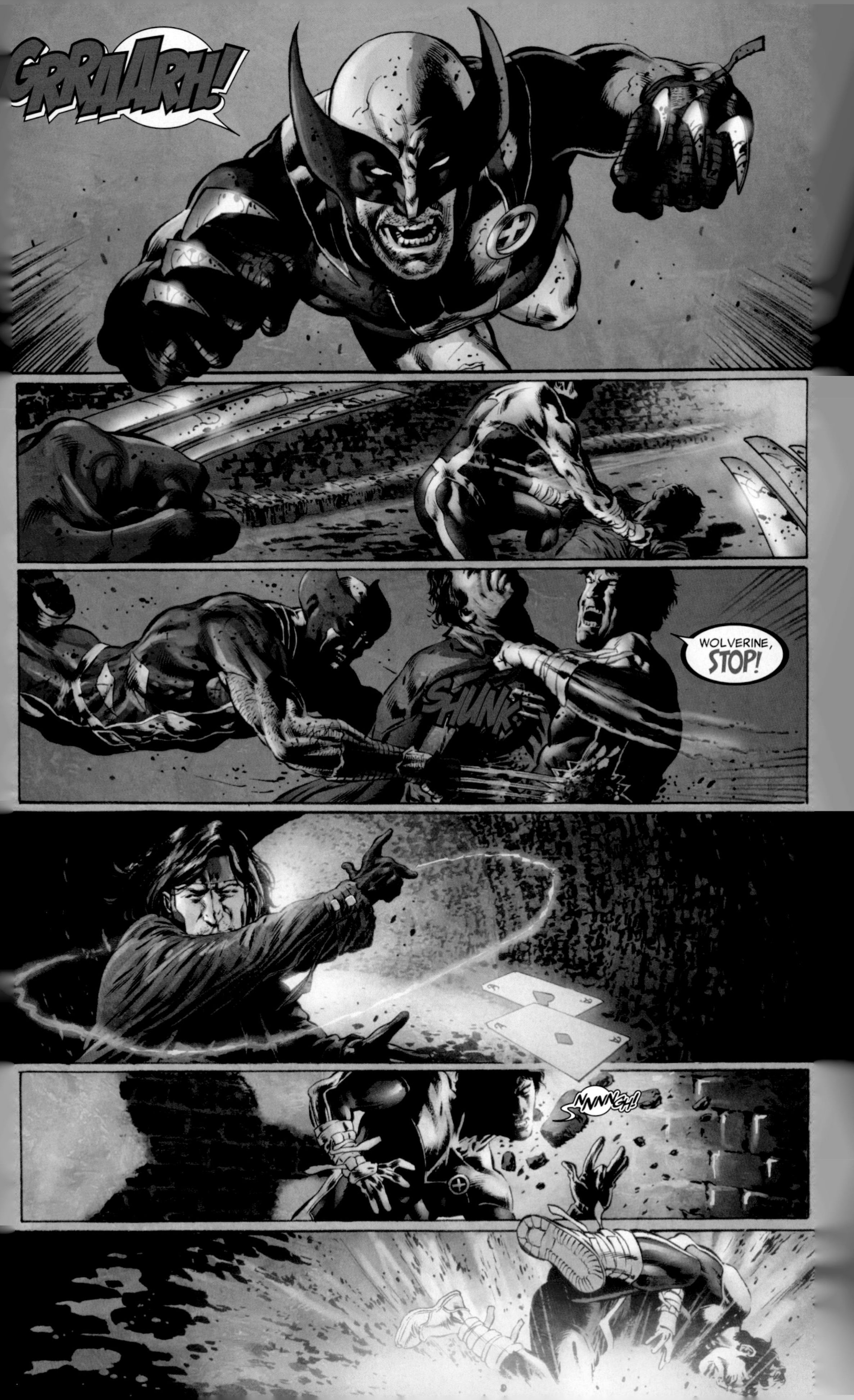
GRRAARH!
SHUNK
WOLVERINE, STOP!
NNNNGH!

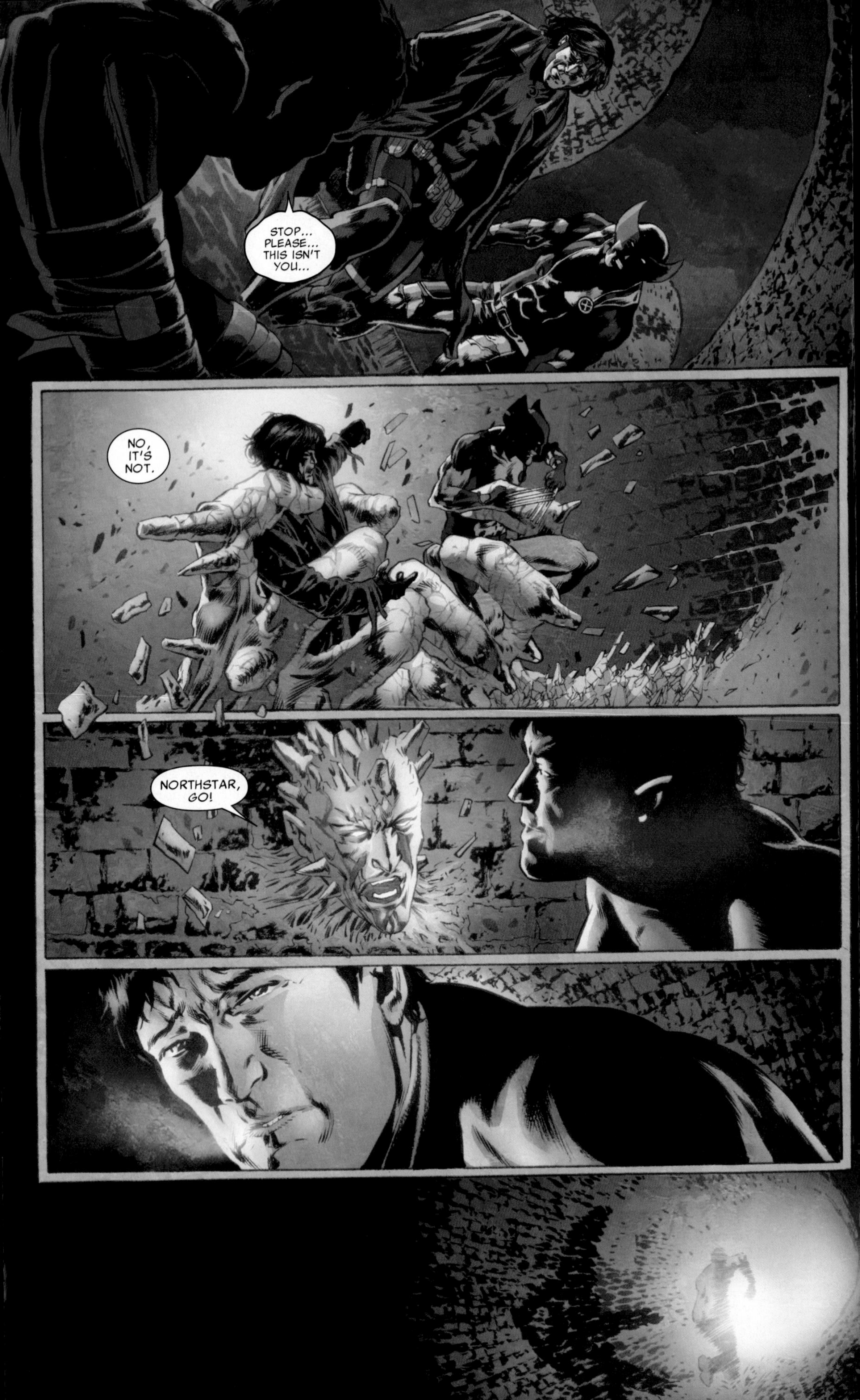
STOP... PLEASE... THIS ISN'T YOU...
NO, IT'S NOT.
NORTHSTAR, GO!

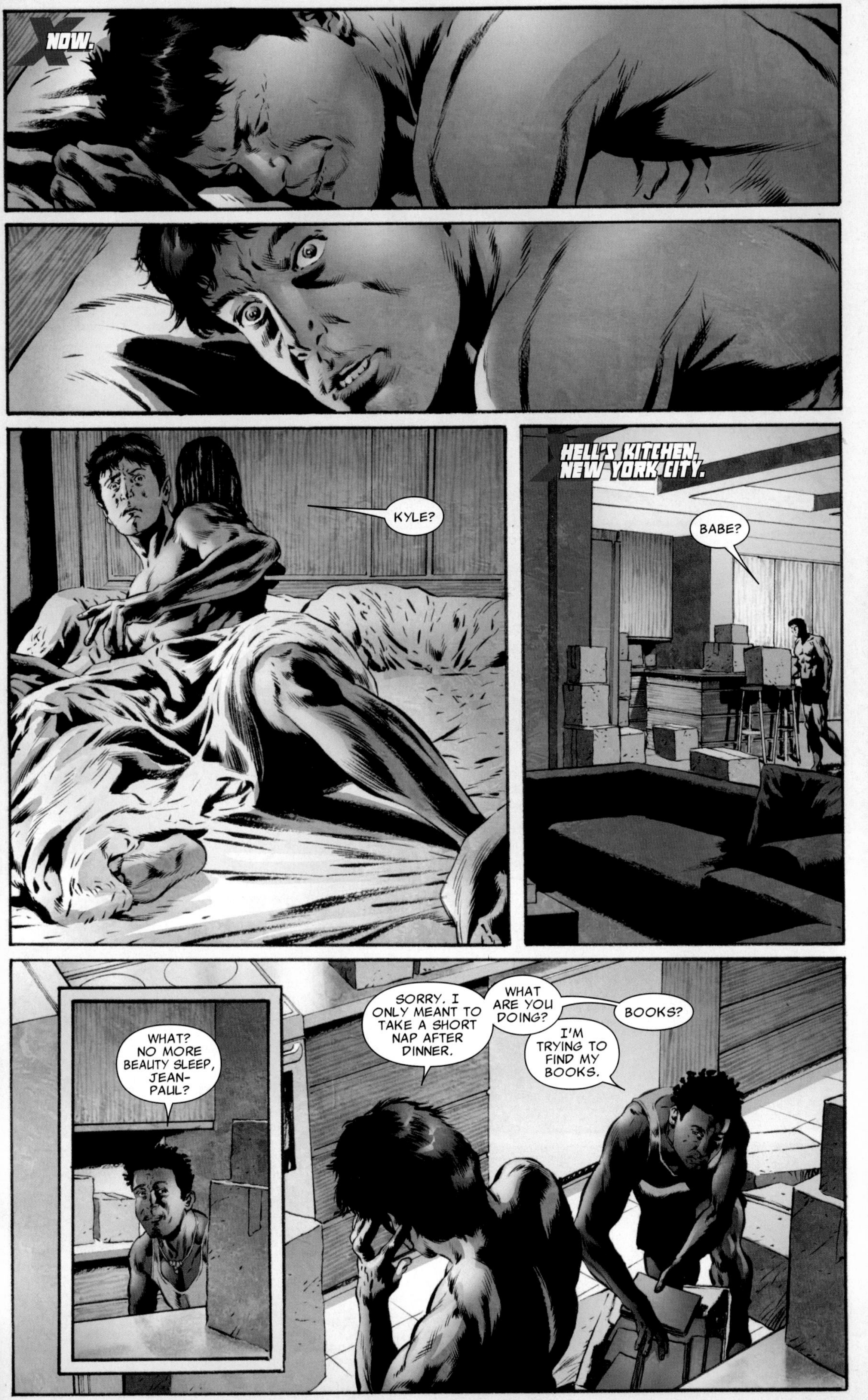
NOW.
HELL'S KITCHEN, NEW YORK CITY.
KYLE?
BABE?
WHAT? NO MORE BEAUTY SLEEP, JEAN-PAUL?
SORRY. I ONLY MEANT TO TAKE A SHORT NAP AFTER DINNER.
WHAT ARE YOU DOING?
I'M TRYING TO FIND MY BOOKS.
BOOKS?

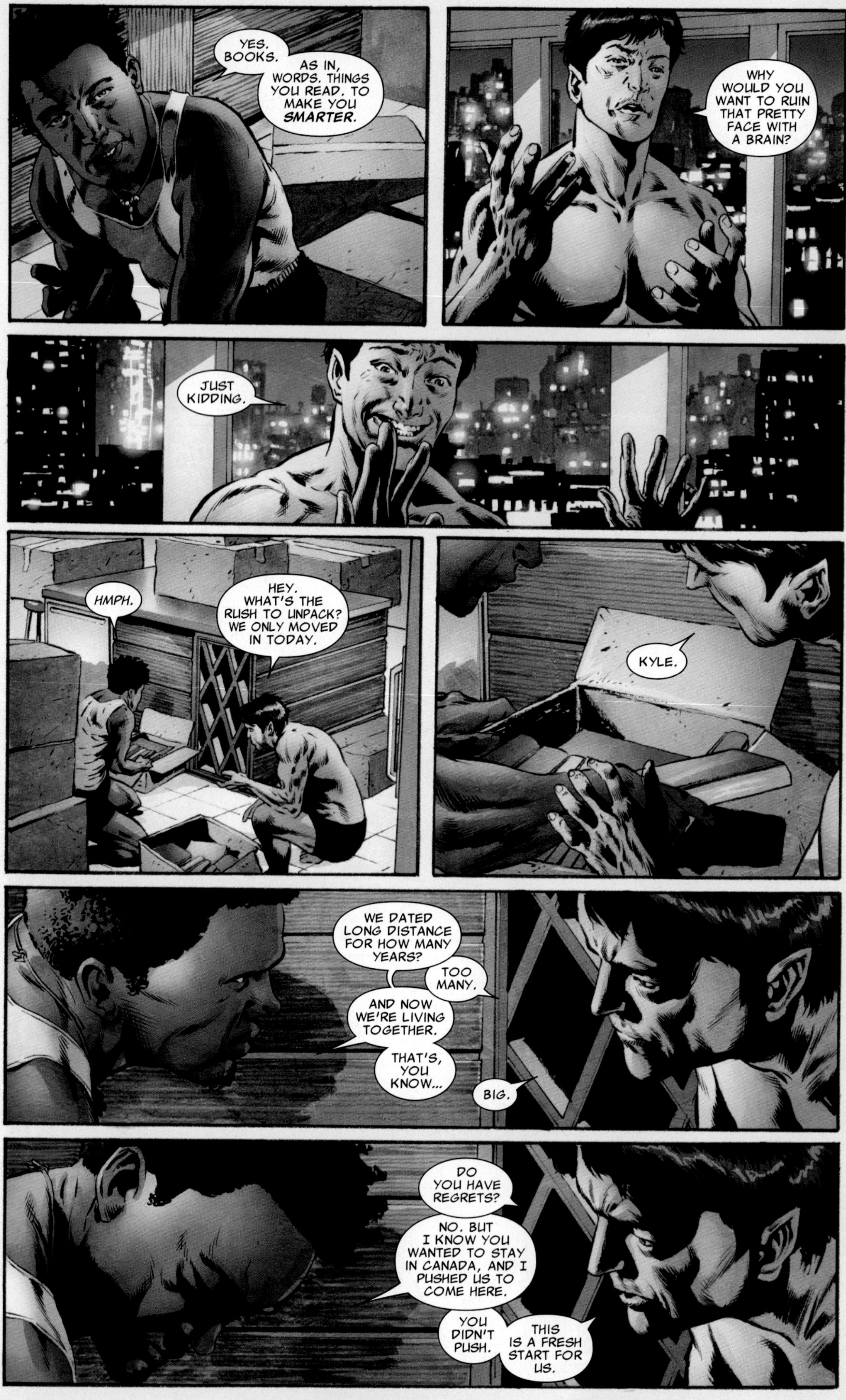
YES. BOOKS.
AS IN, WORDS. THINGS YOU READ. TO MAKE YOU SMARTER.
WHY WOULD YOU WANT TO RUIN THAT PRETTY FACE WITH A BRAIN?
JUST KIDDING.
HMPH.
HEY. WHAT'S THE RUSH TO UNPACK? WE ONLY MOVED IN TODAY.
KYLE.
WE DATED LONG DISTANCE FOR HOW MANY YEARS?
TOO MANY.
AND NOW WE'RE LIVING TOGETHER.
THAT'S, YOU KNOW...
BIG.
DO YOU HAVE REGRETS?
NO. BUT I KNOW YOU WANTED TO STAY IN CANADA, AND I PUSHED US TO COME HERE.
YOU DIDN'T PUSH.
THIS IS A FRESH START FOR US.

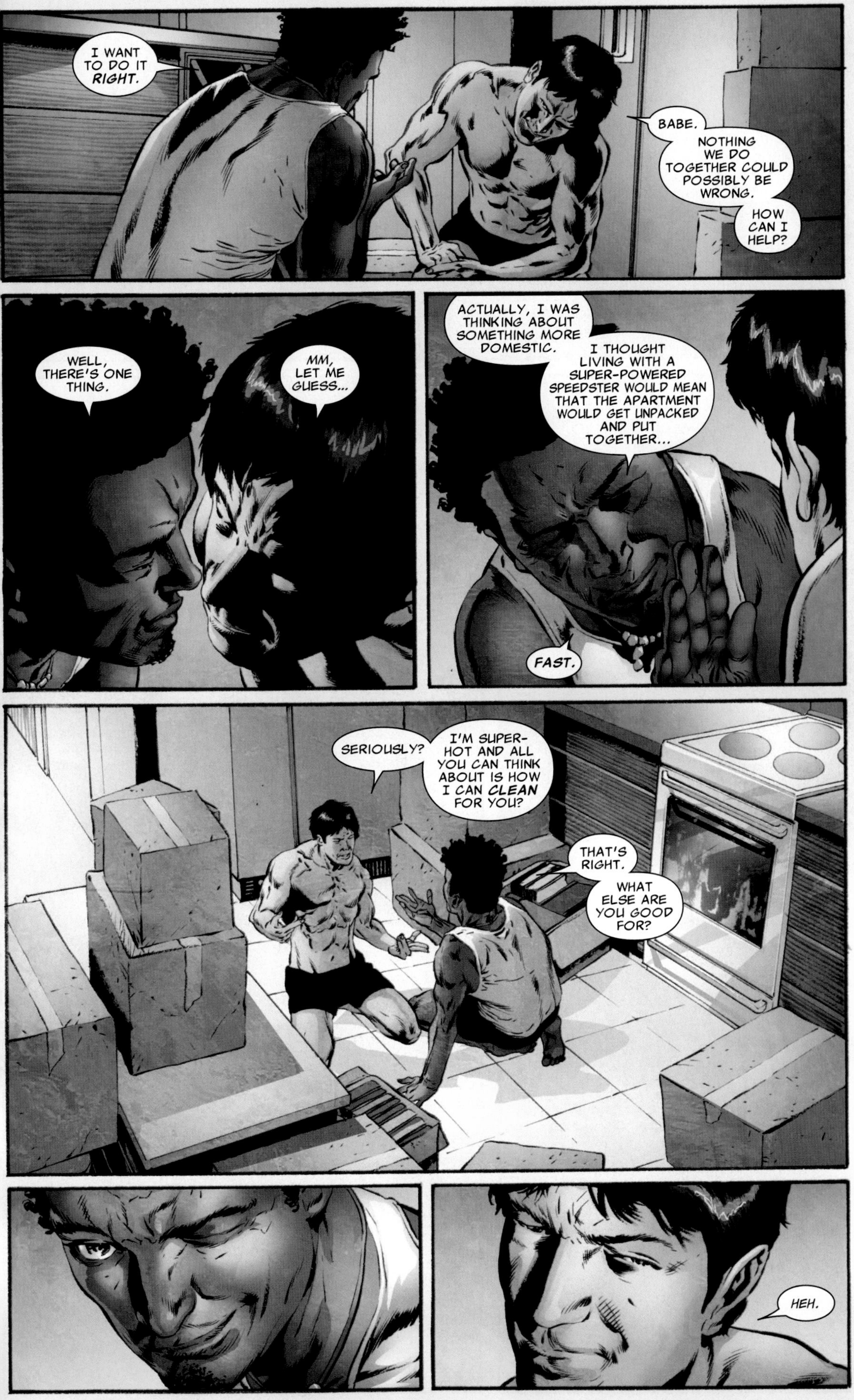
I WANT TO DO IT RIGHT.
BABE.
NOTHING WE DO TOGETHER COULD POSSIBLY BE WRONG.
HOW CAN I HELP?
WELL, THERE'S ONE THING.
MM, LET ME GUESS...
ACTUALLY, I WAS THINKING ABOUT SOMETHING MORE DOMESTIC.
I THOUGHT LIVING WITH A SUPER-POWERED SPEEDSTER WOULD MEAN THAT THE APARTMENT WOULD GET UNPACKED AND PUT TOGETHER...
FAST.
SERIOUSLY?
I'M SUPER-HOT AND ALL YOU CAN THINK ABOUT IS HOW I CAN CLEAN FOR YOU?
THAT'S RIGHT.
WHAT ELSE ARE YOU GOOD FOR?
HEH.

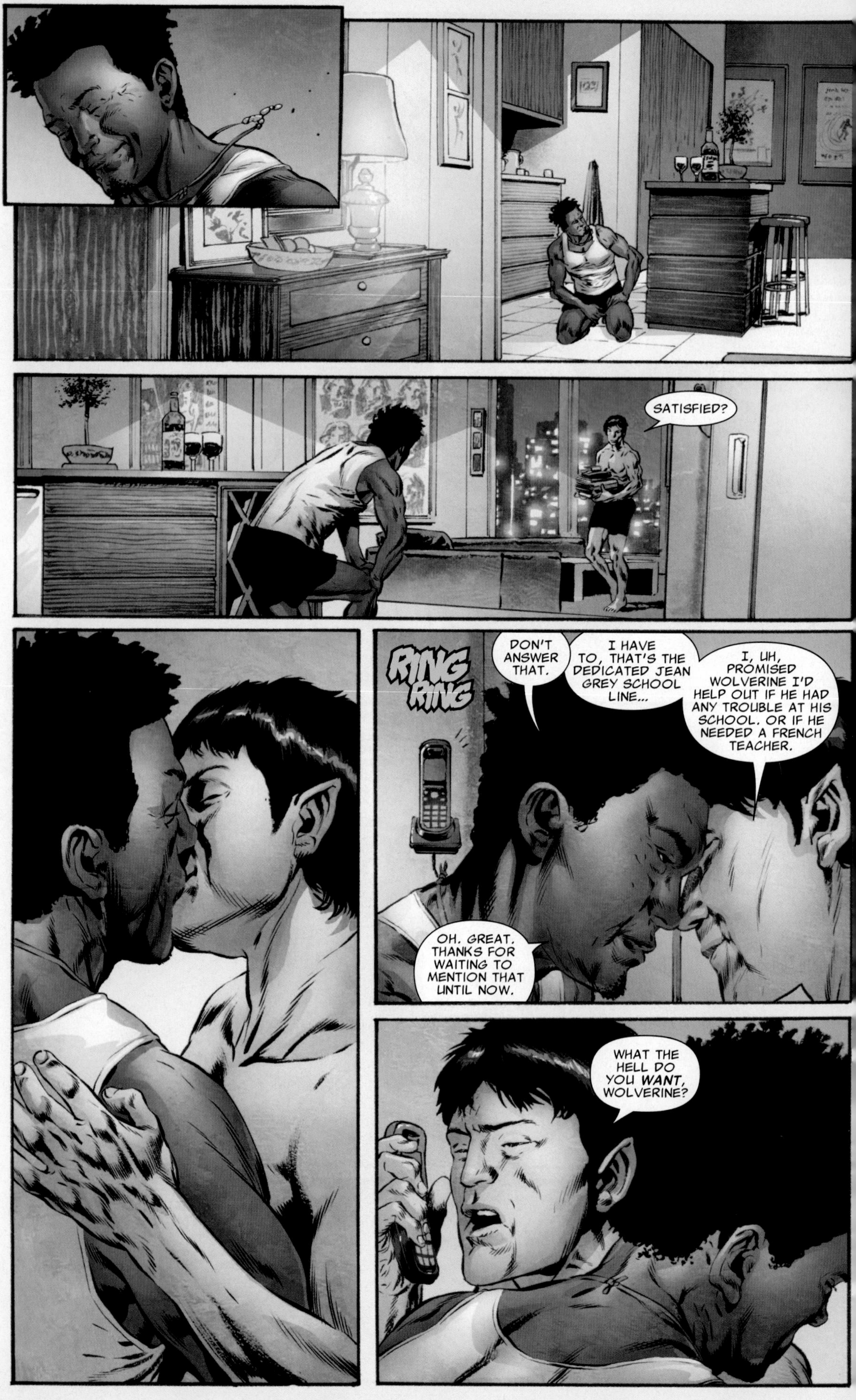
SATISFIED?
RING RING
DON'T ANSWER THAT.
I HAVE TO, THAT'S THE DEDICATED JEAN GREY SCHOOL LINE...
I, UH, PROMISED WOLVERINE I'D HELP OUT IF HE HAD ANY TROUBLE AT HIS SCHOOL. OR IF HE NEEDED A FRENCH TEACHER.
OH. GREAT. THANKS FOR WAITING TO MENTION THAT UNTIL NOW.
WHAT THE HELL DO YOU WANT, WOLVERINE?

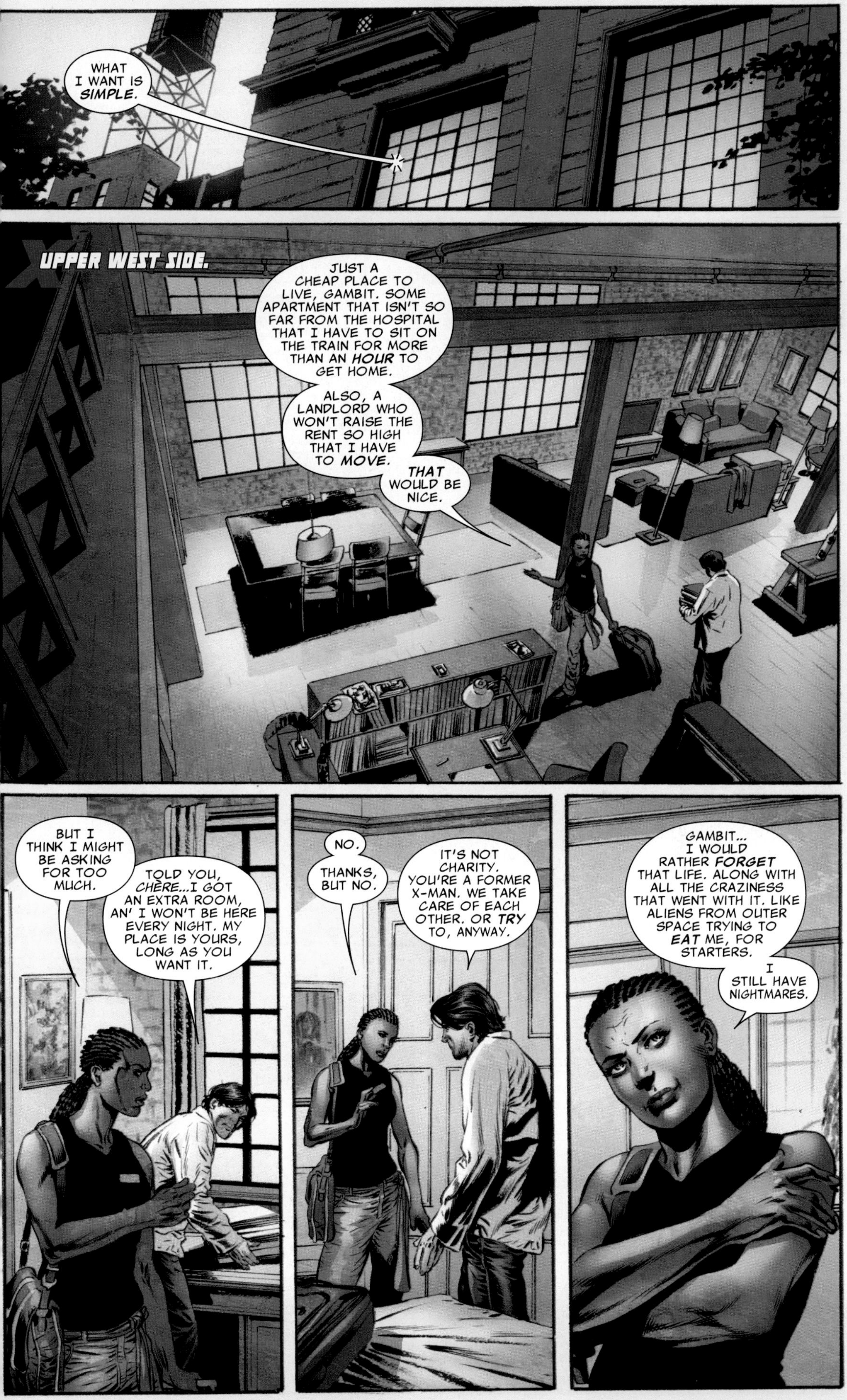
WHAT I WANT IS SIMPLE.
UPPER WEST SIDE.
JUST A CHEAP PLACE TO LIVE, GAMBIT. SOME APARTMENT THAT ISN'T SO FAR FROM THE HOSPITAL THAT I HAVE TO SIT ON THE TRAIN FOR MORE THAN AN HOUR TO GET HOME.
ALSO, A LANDLORD WHO WON'T RAISE THE RENT SO HIGH THAT I HAVE TO MOVE.
THAT WOULD BE NICE.
BUT I THINK I MIGHT BE ASKING FOR TOO MUCH.
TOLD YOU, CHÈRE...I GOT AN EXTRA ROOM, AN' I WON'T BE HERE EVERY NIGHT. MY PLACE IS YOURS, LONG AS YOU WANT IT.
NO.
THANKS, BUT NO.
IT'S NOT CHARITY. YOU'RE A FORMER X-MAN. WE TAKE CARE OF EACH OTHER. OR TRY TO, ANYWAY.
GAMBIT... I WOULD RATHER FORGET THAT LIFE. ALONG WITH ALL THE CRAZINESS THAT WENT WITH IT. LIKE ALIENS FROM OUTER SPACE TRYING TO EAT ME, FOR STARTERS.
I STILL HAVE NIGHTMARES.

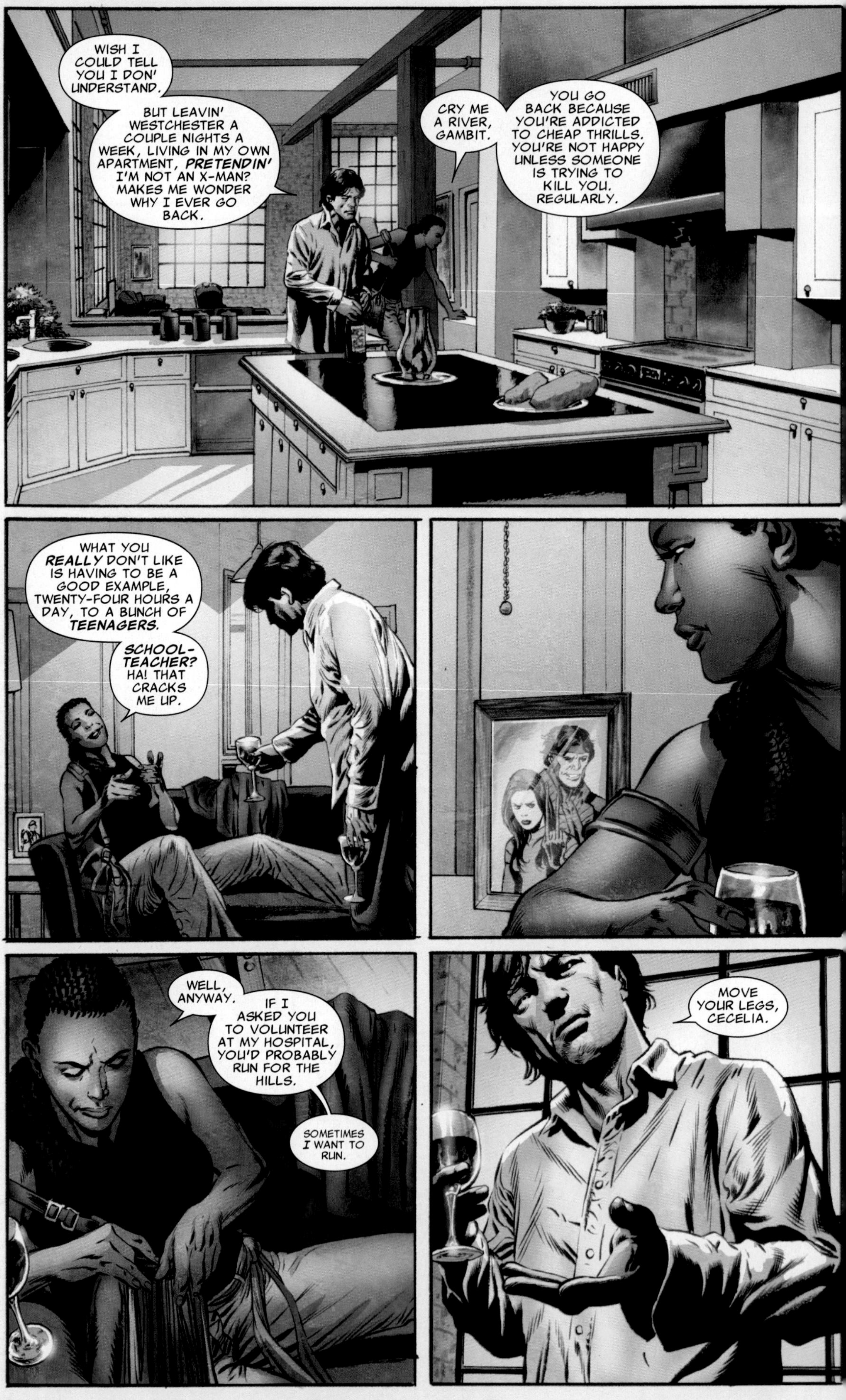

WISH I COULD TELL YOU I DON' UNDERSTAND.
BUT LEAVIN' WESTCHESTER A COUPLE NIGHTS A WEEK, LIVING IN MY OWN APARTMENT, PRETENDIN' I'M NOT AN X-MAN? MAKES ME WONDER WHY I EVER GO BACK.
CRY ME A RIVER, GAMBIT.
YOU GO BACK BECAUSE YOU'RE ADDICTED TO CHEAP THRILLS. YOU'RE NOT HAPPY UNLESS SOMEONE IS TRYING TO KILL YOU. REGULARLY.
WHAT YOU REALLY DON'T LIKE IS HAVING TO BE A GOOD EXAMPLE, TWENTY-FOUR HOURS A DAY, TO A BUNCH OF TEENAGERS.
SCHOOL-TEACHER? HA! THAT CRACKS ME UP.
WELL, ANYWAY.
IF I ASKED YOU TO VOLUNTEER AT MY HOSPITAL, YOU'D PROBABLY RUN FOR THE HILLS.
SOMETIMES I WANT TO RUN.
MOVE YOUR LEGS, CECELIA.

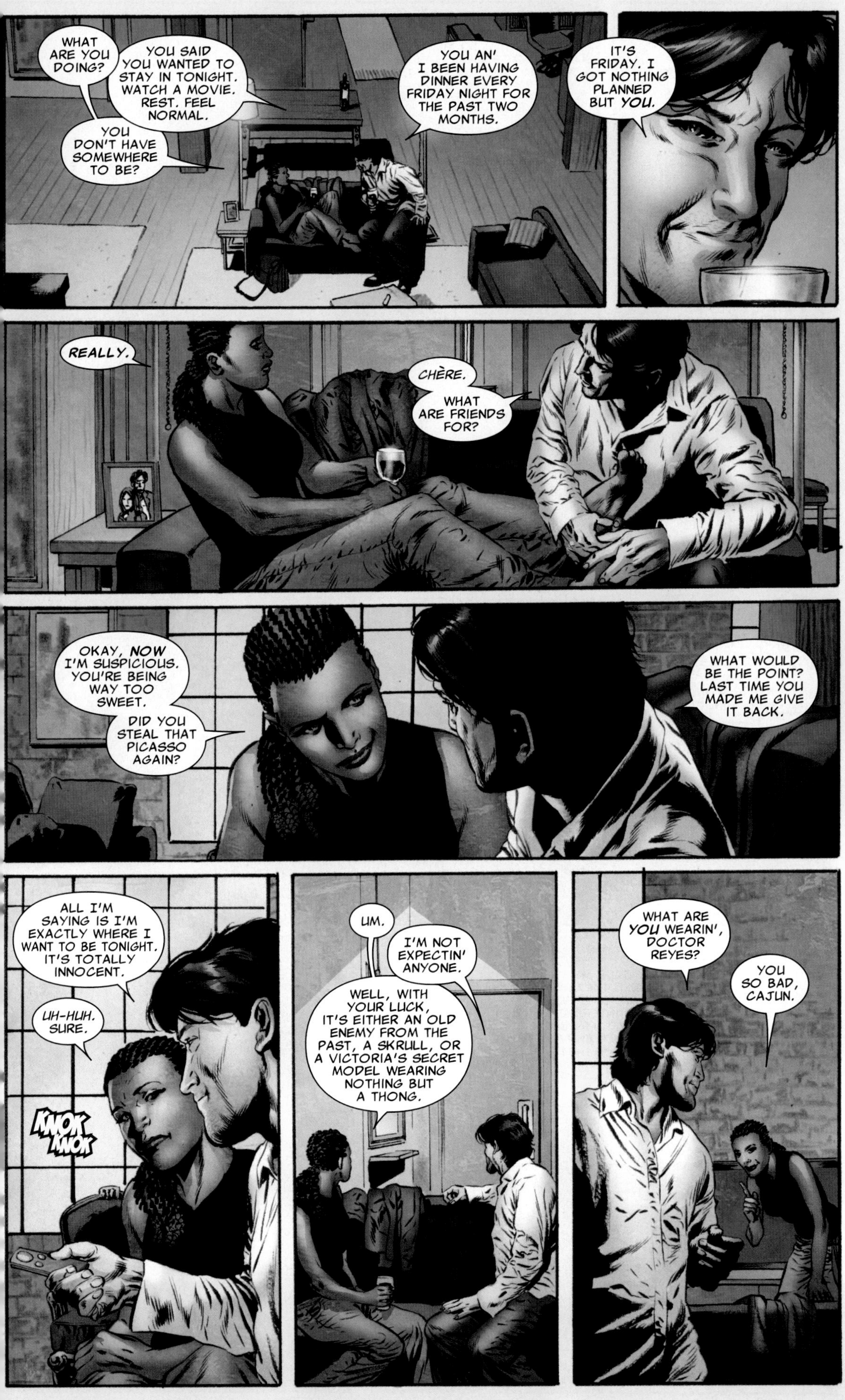

WHAT ARE YOU DOING?
YOU SAID YOU WANTED TO STAY IN TONIGHT. WATCH A MOVIE. REST. FEEL NORMAL.
YOU DON'T HAVE SOMEWHERE TO BE?
YOU AN' I BEEN HAVING DINNER EVERY FRIDAY NIGHT FOR THE PAST TWO MONTHS.
IT'S FRIDAY. I GOT NOTHING PLANNED BUT YOU.
REALLY.
CHÈRE.
WHAT ARE FRIENDS FOR?
OKAY, NOW I'M SUSPICIOUS. YOU'RE BEING WAY TOO SWEET.
DID YOU STEAL THAT PICASSO AGAIN?
WHAT WOULD BE THE POINT? LAST TIME YOU MADE ME GIVE IT BACK.
ALL I'M SAYING IS I'M EXACTLY WHERE I WANT TO BE TONIGHT. IT'S TOTALLY INNOCENT.
UH-HUH. SURE.
KNOK KNOK
UM.
I'M NOT EXPECTIN' ANYONE.
WELL, WITH YOUR LUCK, IT'S EITHER AN OLD ENEMY FROM THE PAST, A SKRULL, OR A VICTORIA'S SECRET MODEL WEARING NOTHING BUT A THONG.
WHAT ARE YOU WEARIN', DOCTOR REYES?
YOU SO BAD, CAJUN.

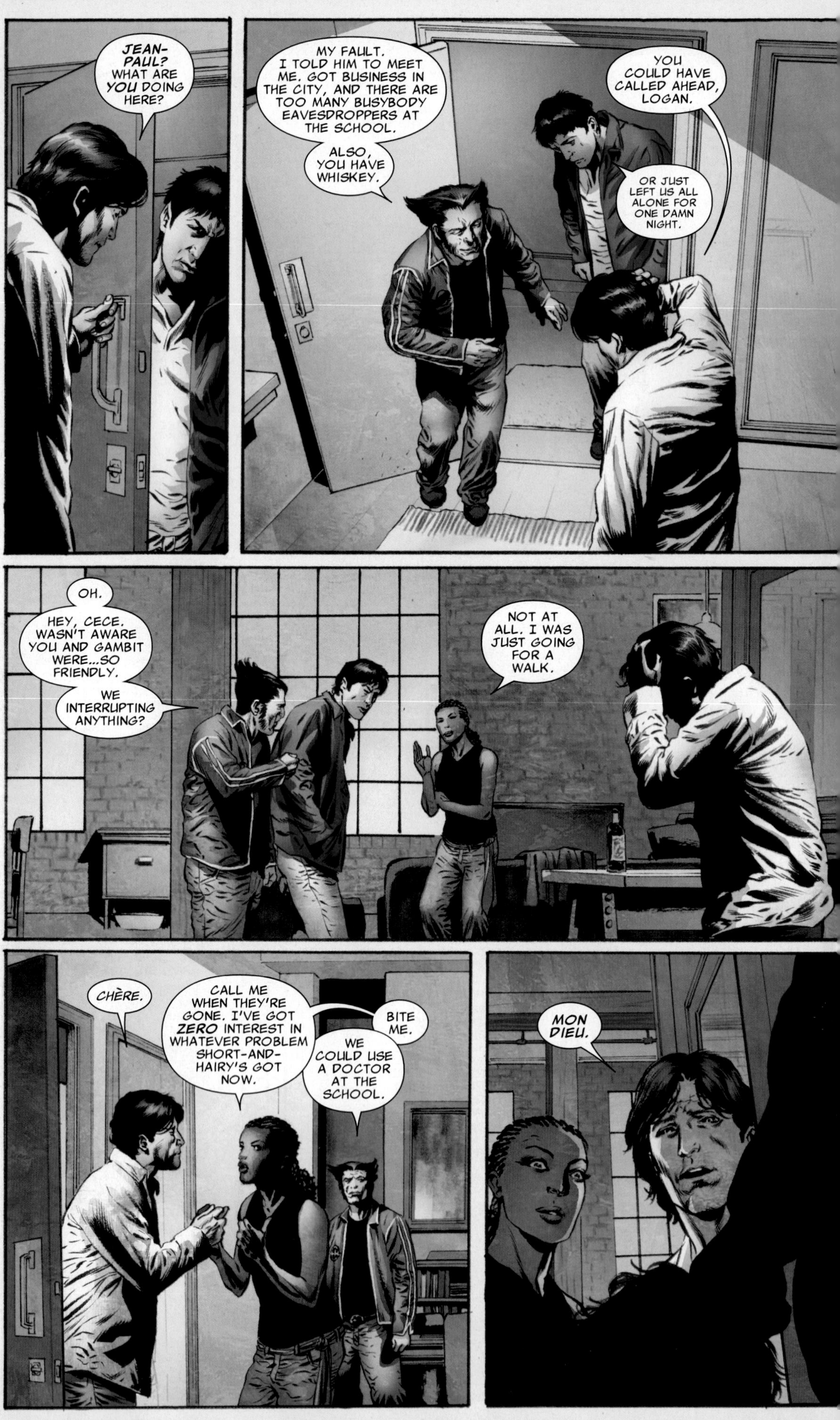
JEAN-PAUL? WHAT ARE YOU DOING HERE?
MY FAULT. I TOLD HIM TO MEET ME. GOT BUSINESS IN THE CITY, AND THERE ARE TOO MANY BUSYBODY EAVESDROPPERS AT THE SCHOOL.
ALSO, YOU HAVE WHISKEY.
YOU COULD HAVE CALLED AHEAD, LOGAN.
OR JUST LEFT US ALL ALONE FOR ONE DAMN NIGHT.
OH.
HEY, CECE. WASN'T AWARE YOU AND GAMBIT WERE...SO FRIENDLY.
WE INTERRUPTING ANYTHING?
NOT AT ALL. I WAS JUST GOING FOR A WALK.
CHÈRE.
CALL ME WHEN THEY'RE GONE. I'VE GOT ZERO INTEREST IN WHATEVER PROBLEM SHORT-AND-HAIRY'S GOT NOW.
BITE ME.
WE COULD USE A DOCTOR AT THE SCHOOL.
MON DIEU.

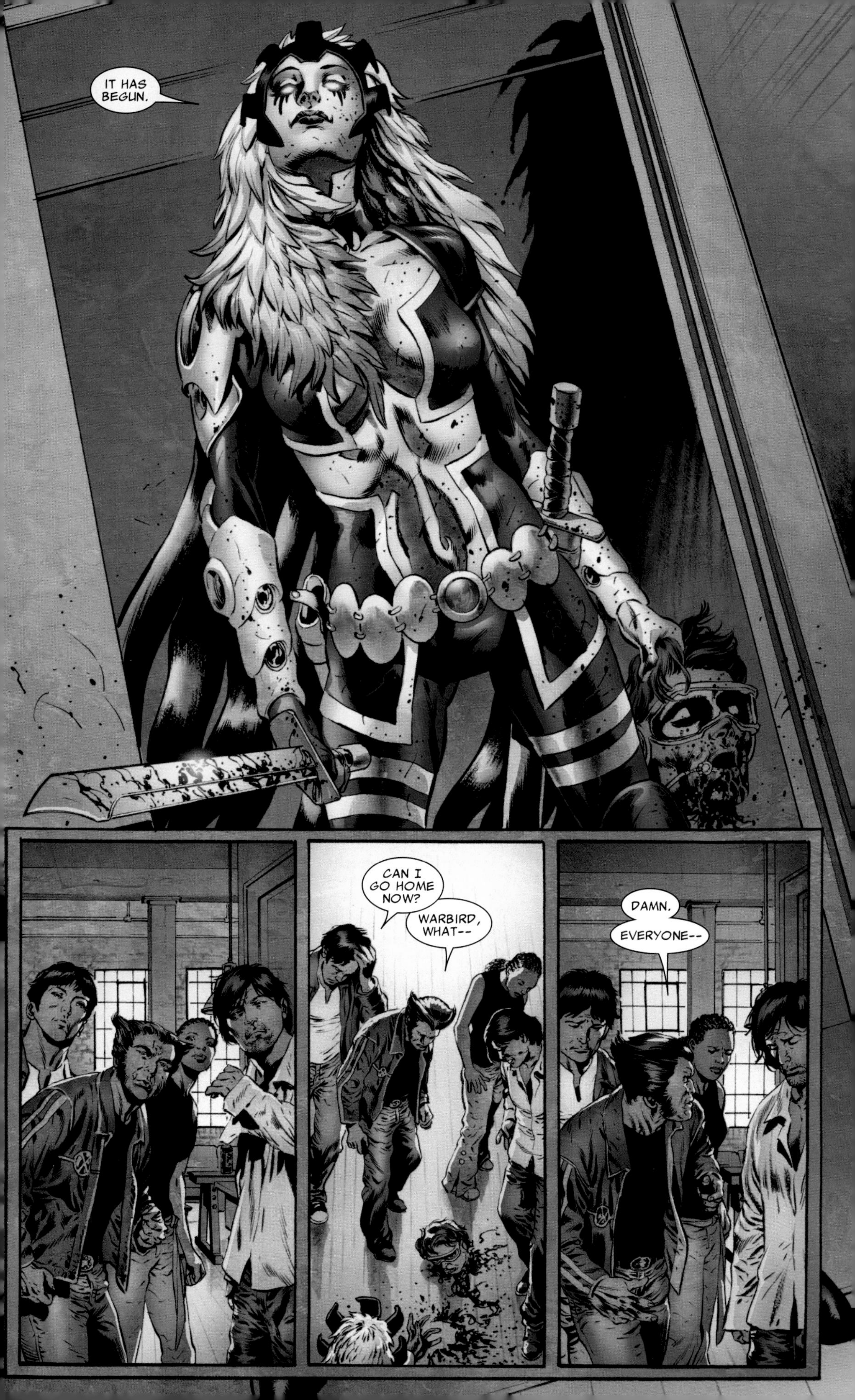
IT HAS BEGUN.
CAN I GO HOME NOW?
WARBIRD, WHAT--
DAMN.
EVERYONE--

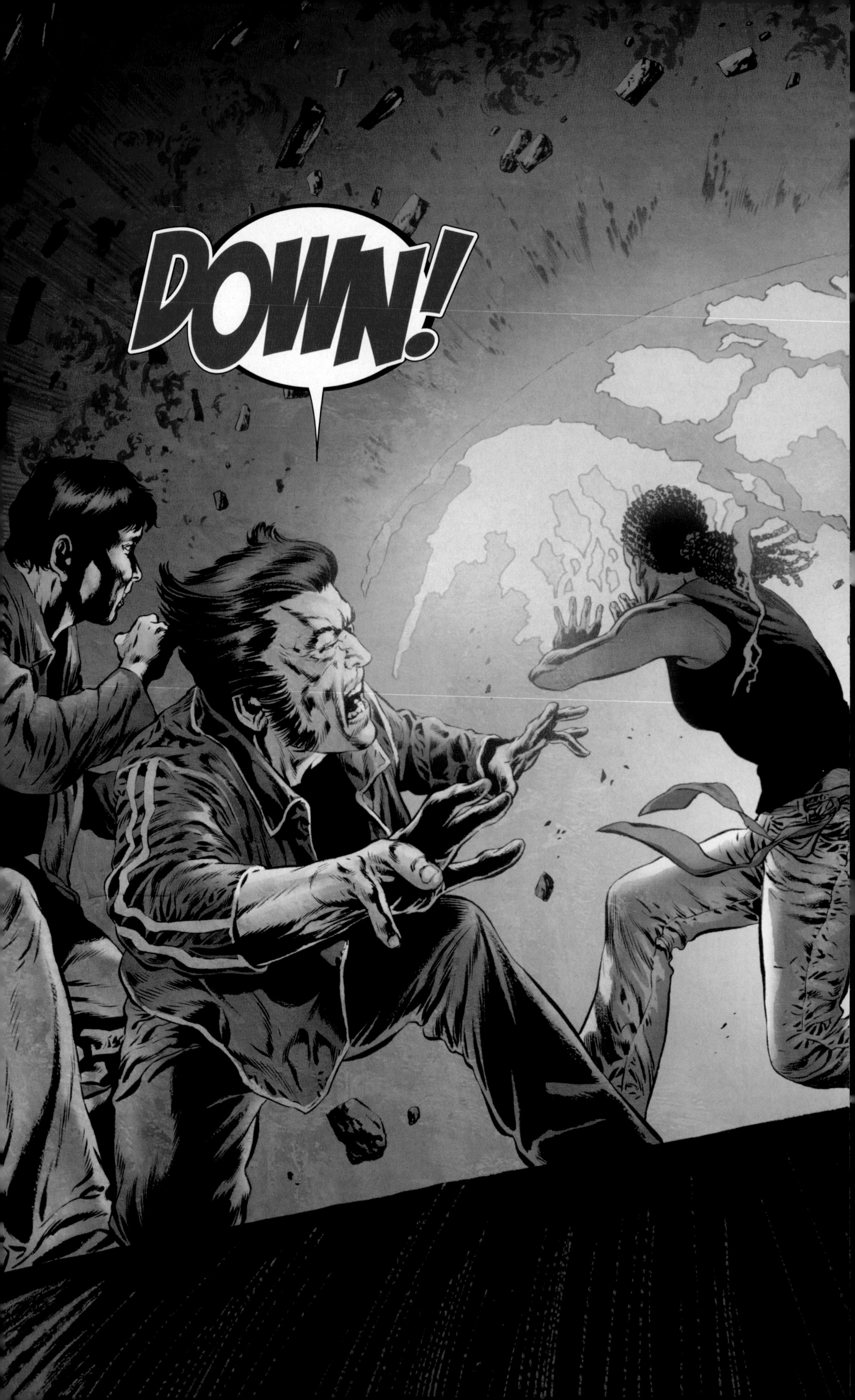
DOWN!

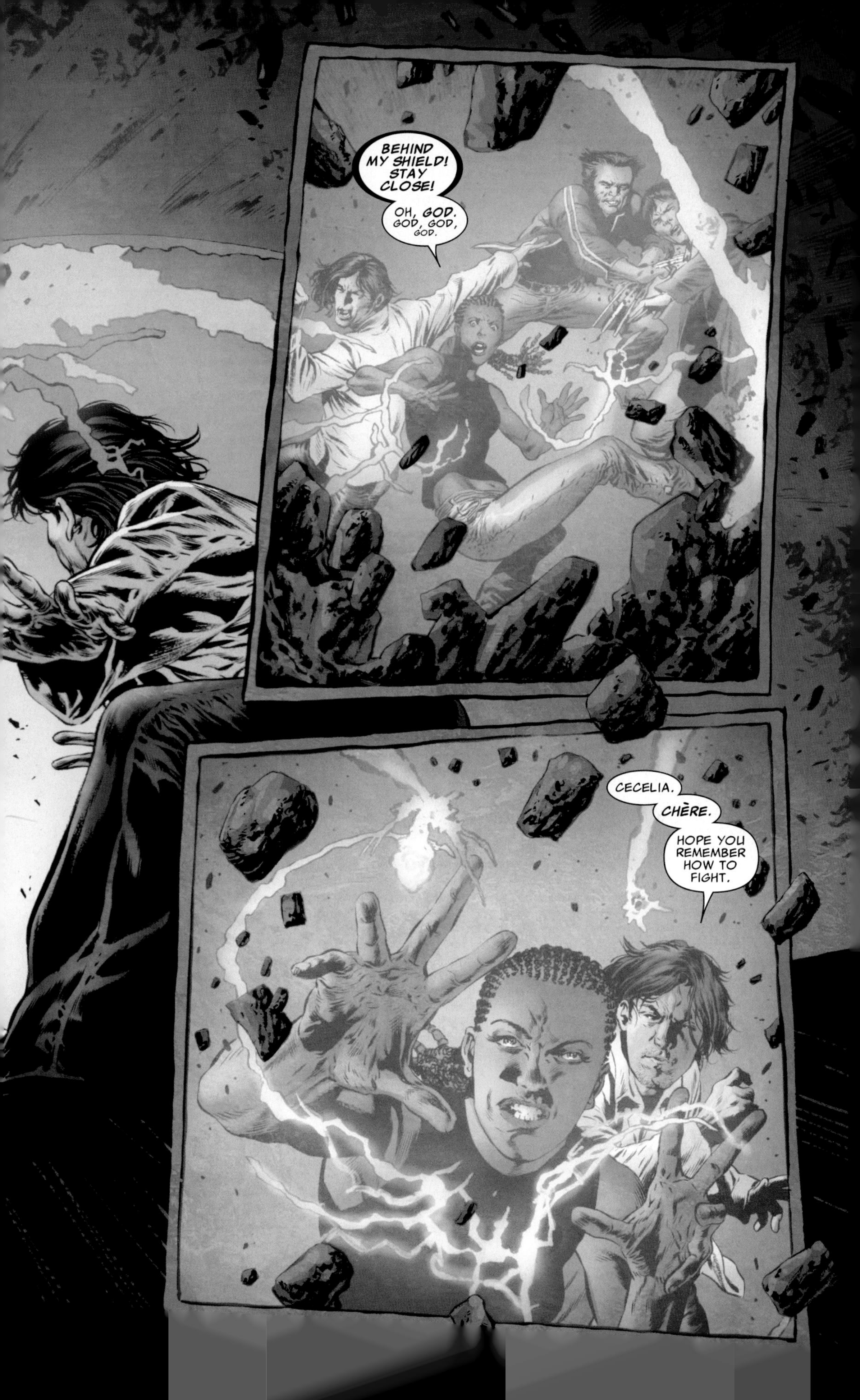

BEHIND MY SHIELD! STAY CLOSE!
OH, GOD. GOD, GOD, GOD.
CECELIA.
CHÈRE.
HOPE YOU REMEMBER HOW TO FIGHT.

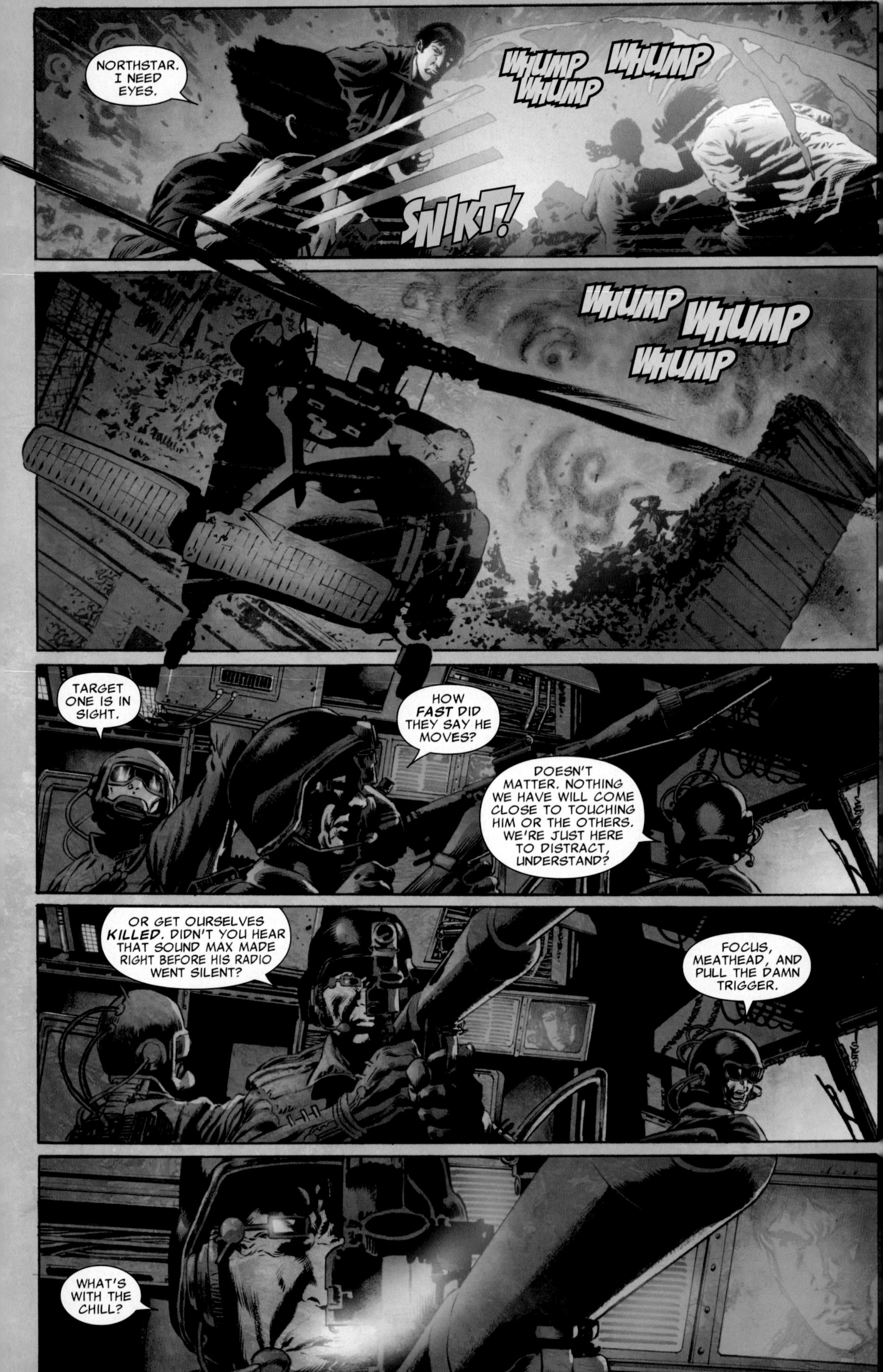
NORTHSTAR. I NEED EYES.
WHUMP WHUMP WHUMP
SNIKT!
WHUMP WHUMP WHUMP
TARGET ONE IS IN SIGHT.
HOW FAST DID THEY SAY HE MOVES?
DOESN'T MATTER. NOTHING WE HAVE WILL COME CLOSE TO TOUCHING HIM OR THE OTHERS. WE'RE JUST HERE TO DISTRACT, UNDERSTAND?
OR GET OURSELVES KILLED. DIDN'T YOU HEAR THAT SOUND MAX MADE RIGHT BEFORE HIS RADIO WENT SILENT?
FOCUS, MEATHEAD, AND PULL THE DAMN TRIGGER.
WHAT'S WITH THE CHILL?

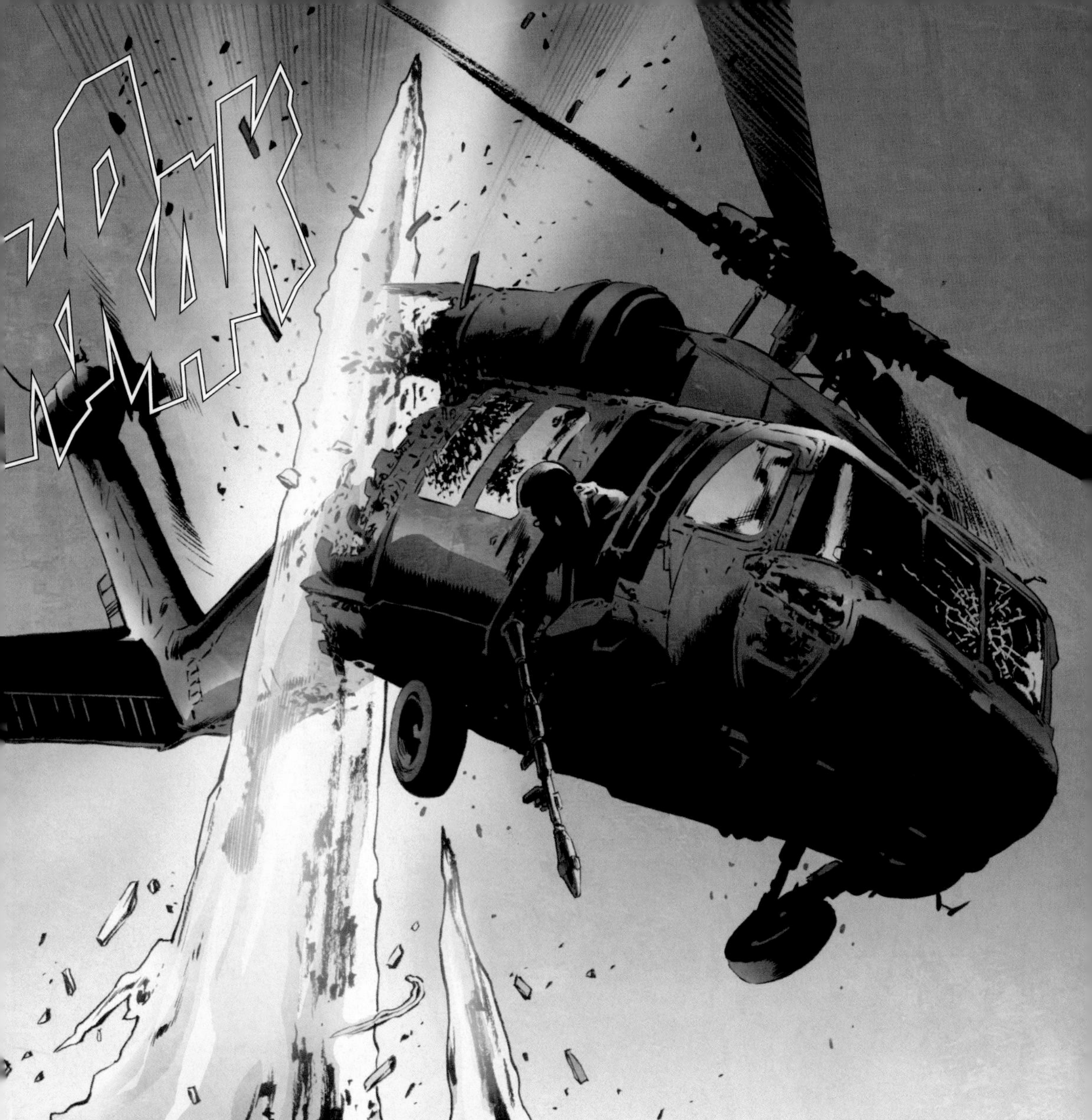

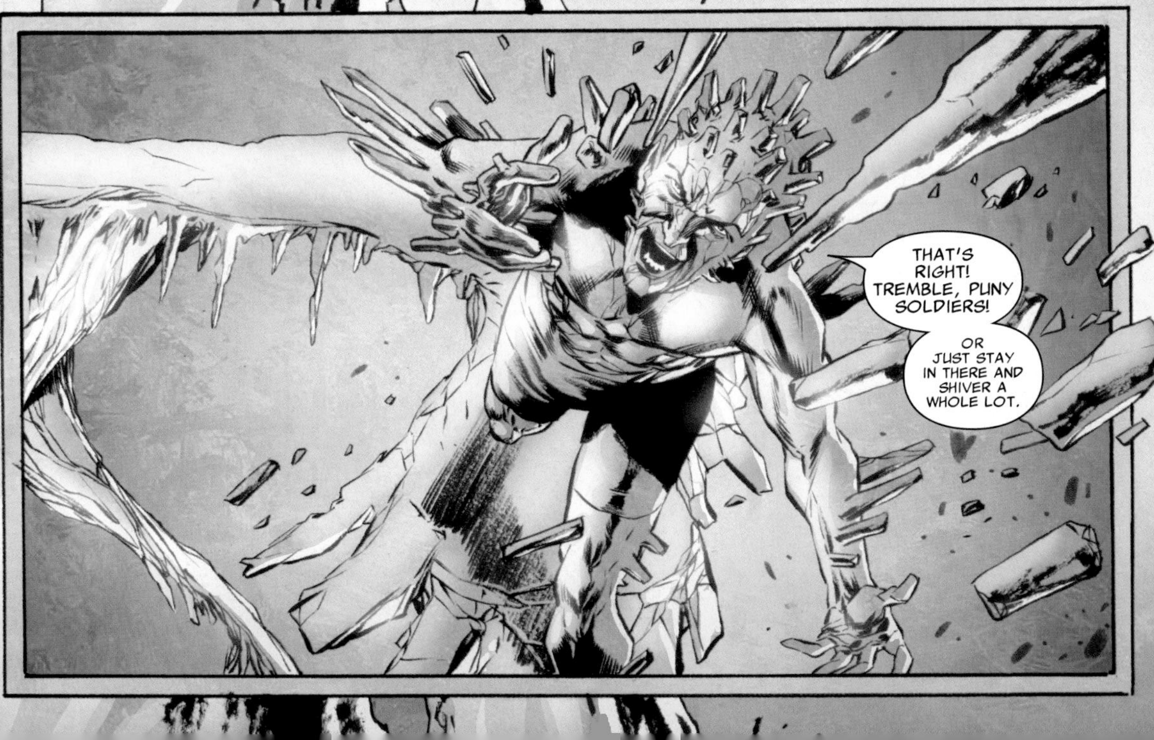
THAT'S RIGHT! TREMBLE, PUNY SOLDIERS!
OR JUST STAY IN THERE AND SHIVER A WHOLE LOT.

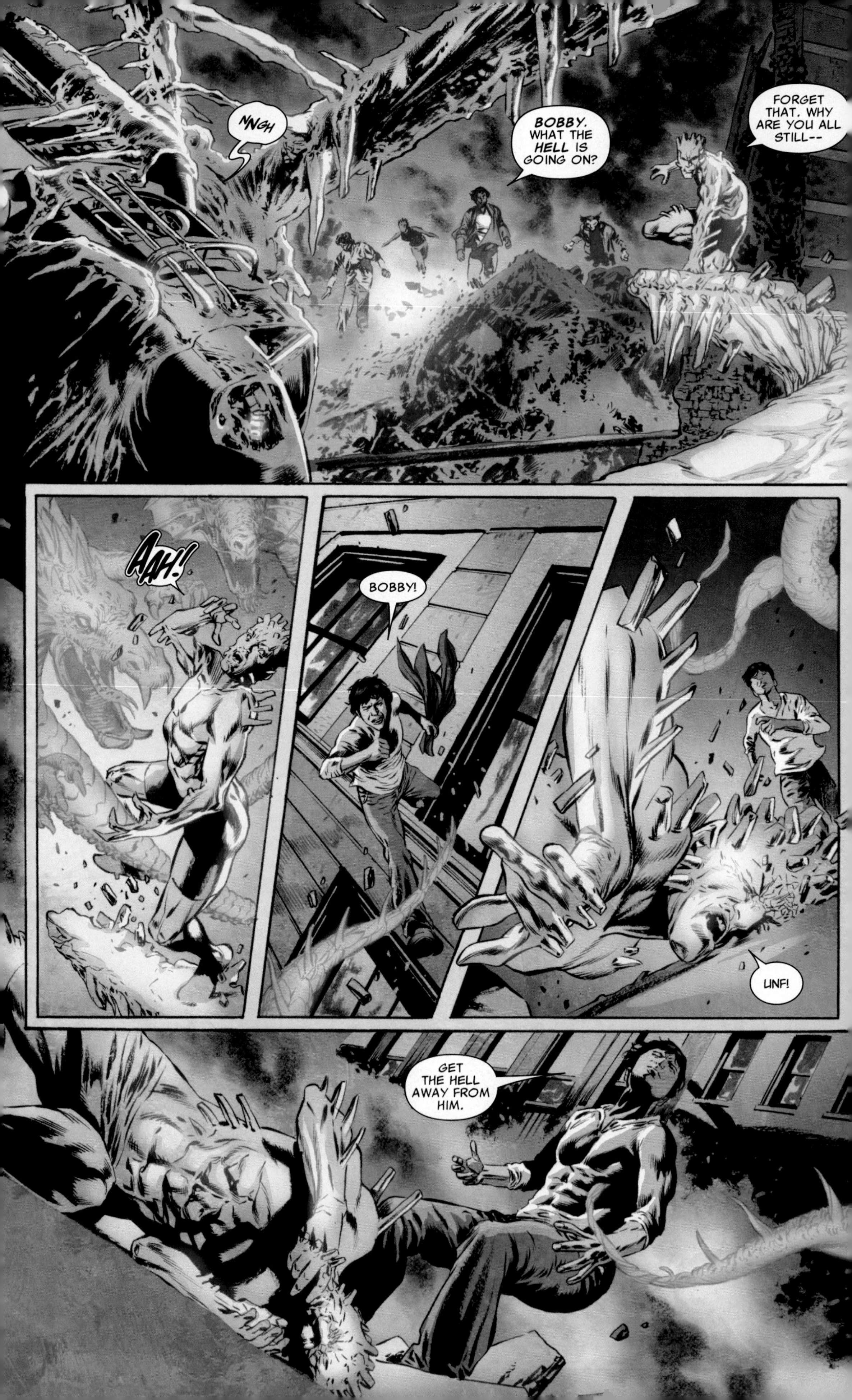
NNGH
BOBBY. WHAT THE HELL IS GOING ON?
FORGET THAT. WHY ARE YOU ALL STILL--
AAH!
BOBBY!
UNF!
GET THE HELL AWAY FROM HIM.

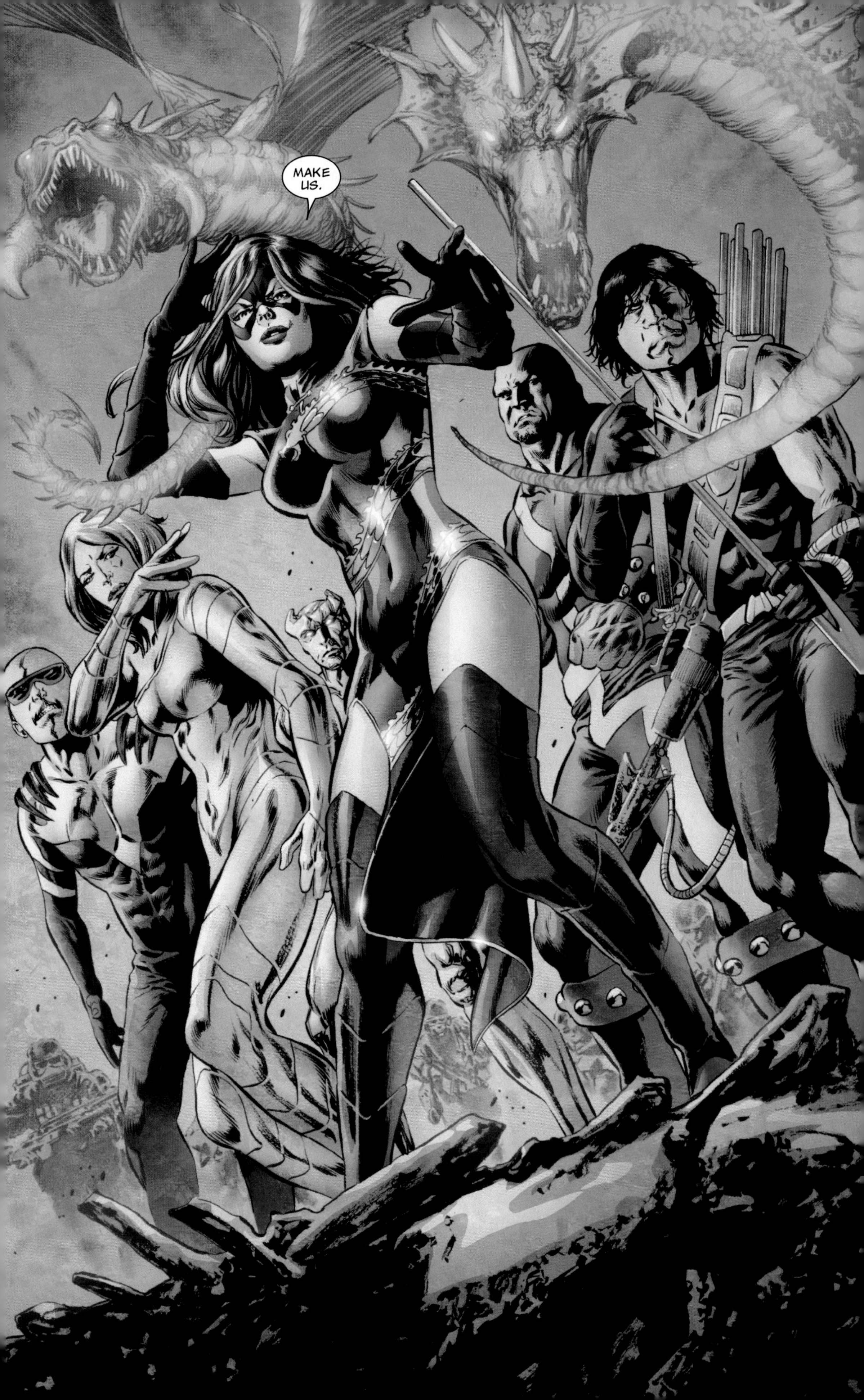
MAKE US.

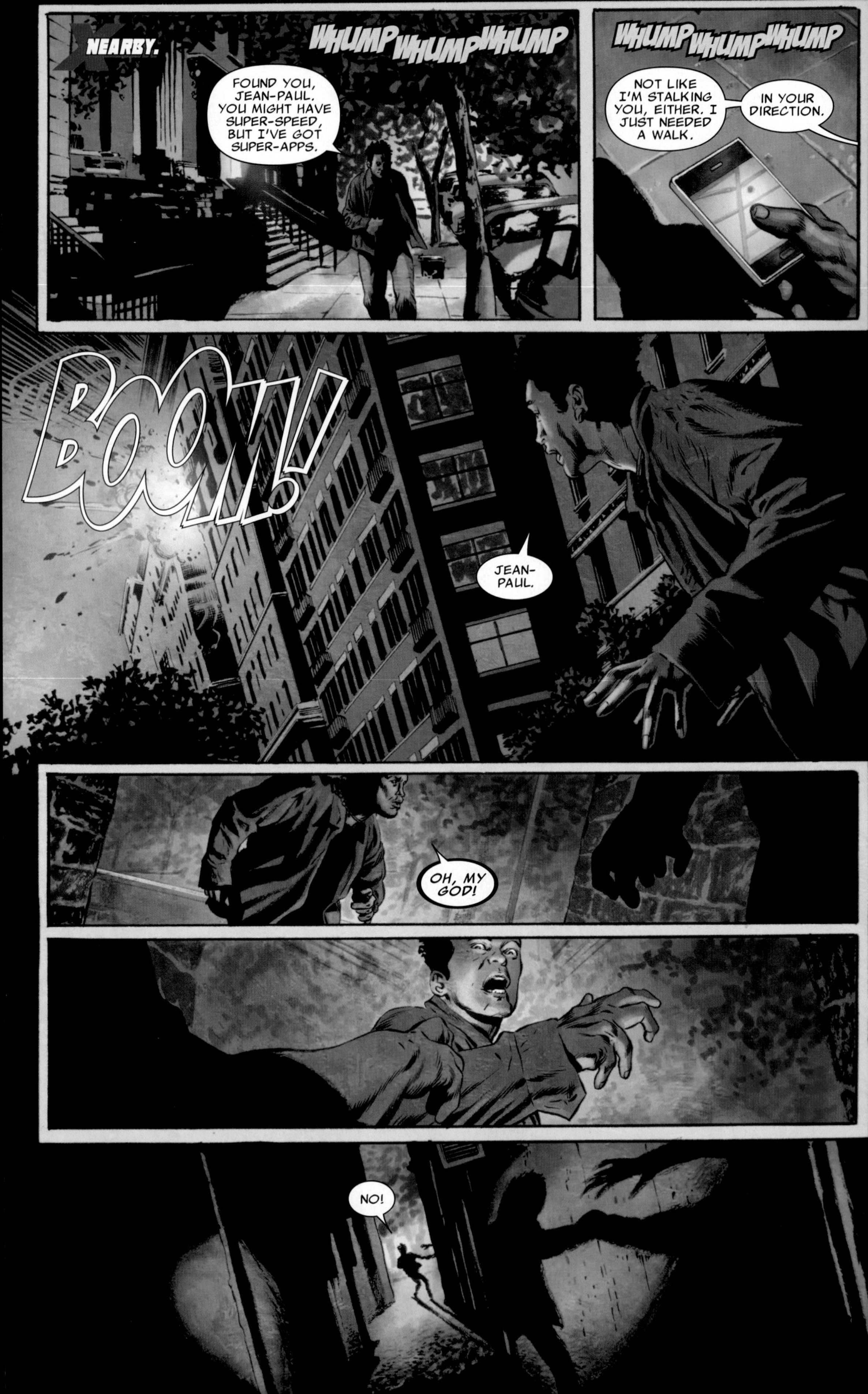
NEARBY.
WHUMP WHUMP WHUMP
FOUND YOU, JEAN-PAUL. YOU MIGHT HAVE SUPER-SPEED, BUT I'VE GOT SUPER-APPS.
WHUMP WHUMP WHUMP
NOT LIKE I'M STALKING YOU, EITHER. I JUST NEEDED A WALK.
IN YOUR DIRECTION.
BOOM!
JEAN-PAUL.
OH, MY GOD!
NO!

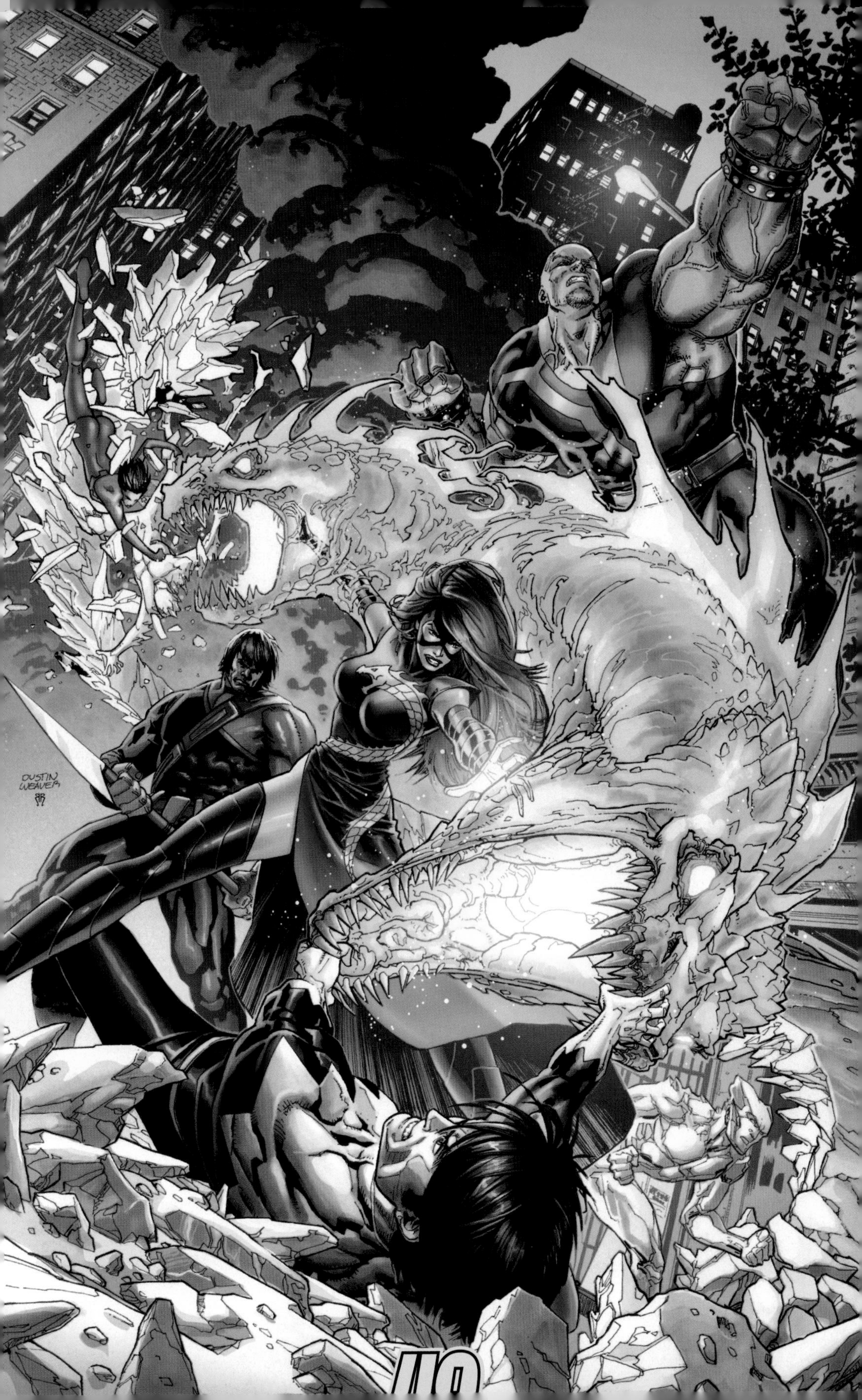
DUSTIN
WEAVER

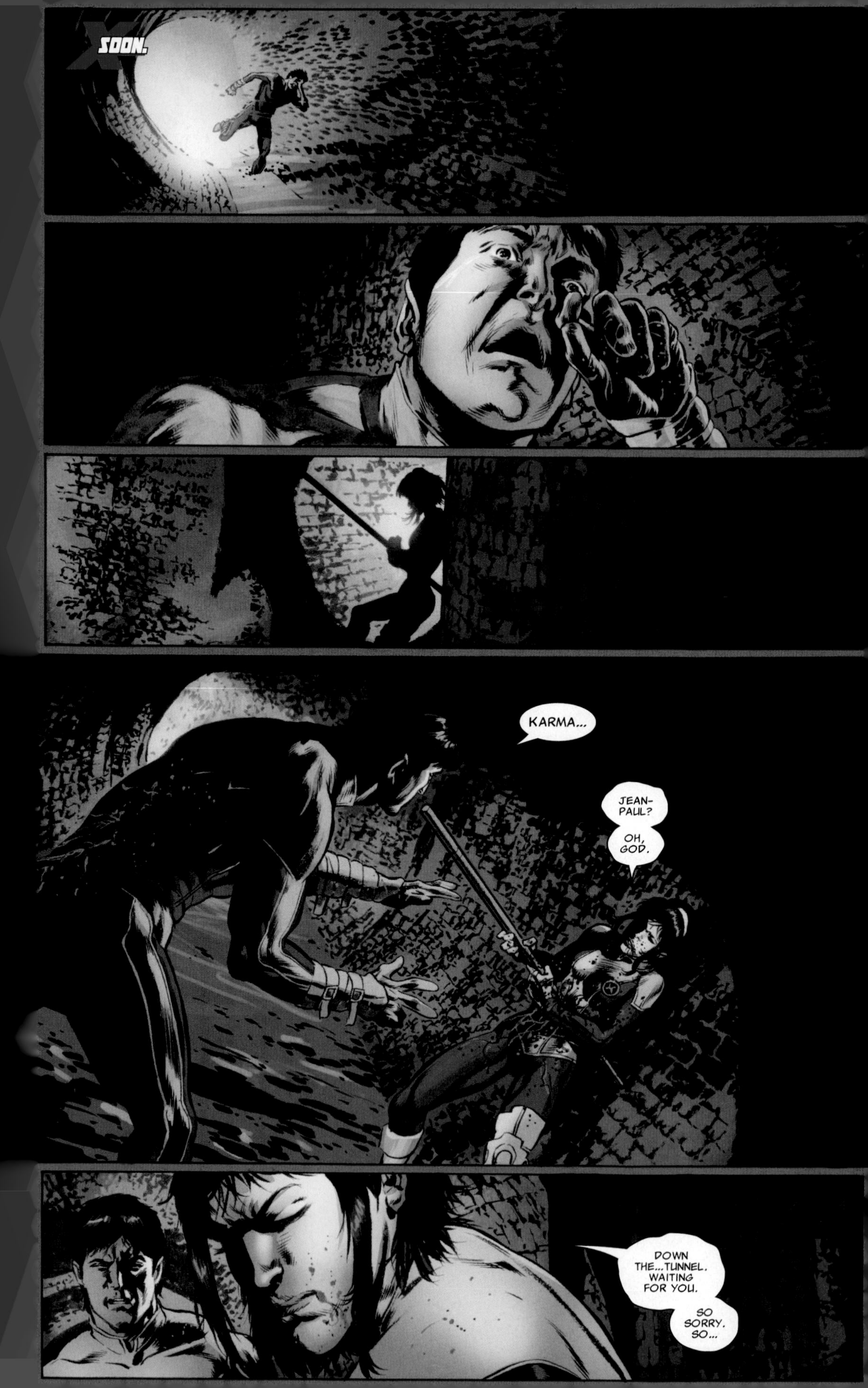
SOON.
KARMA...
JEAN-PAUL?
OH, GOD.
DOWN THE...TUNNEL. WAITING FOR YOU.
SO SORRY. SO...

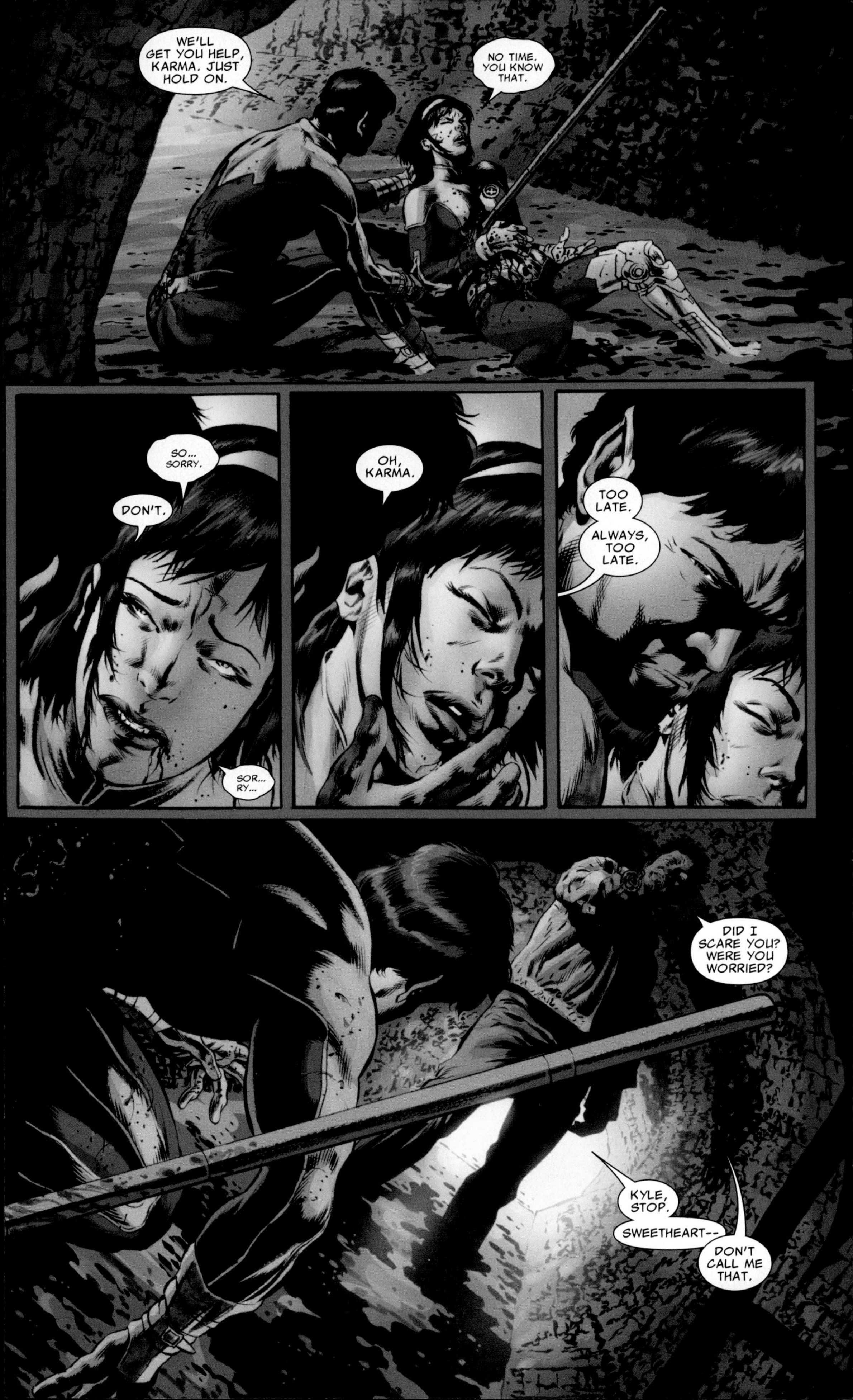
WE'LL GET YOU HELP, KARMA. JUST HOLD ON.
NO TIME. YOU KNOW THAT.
SO... SORRY.
DON'T.
SOR... RY...
OH, KARMA.
TOO LATE.
ALWAYS, TOO LATE.
DID I SCARE YOU? WERE YOU WORRIED?
KYLE, STOP.
SWEETHEART--
DON'T CALL ME THAT.

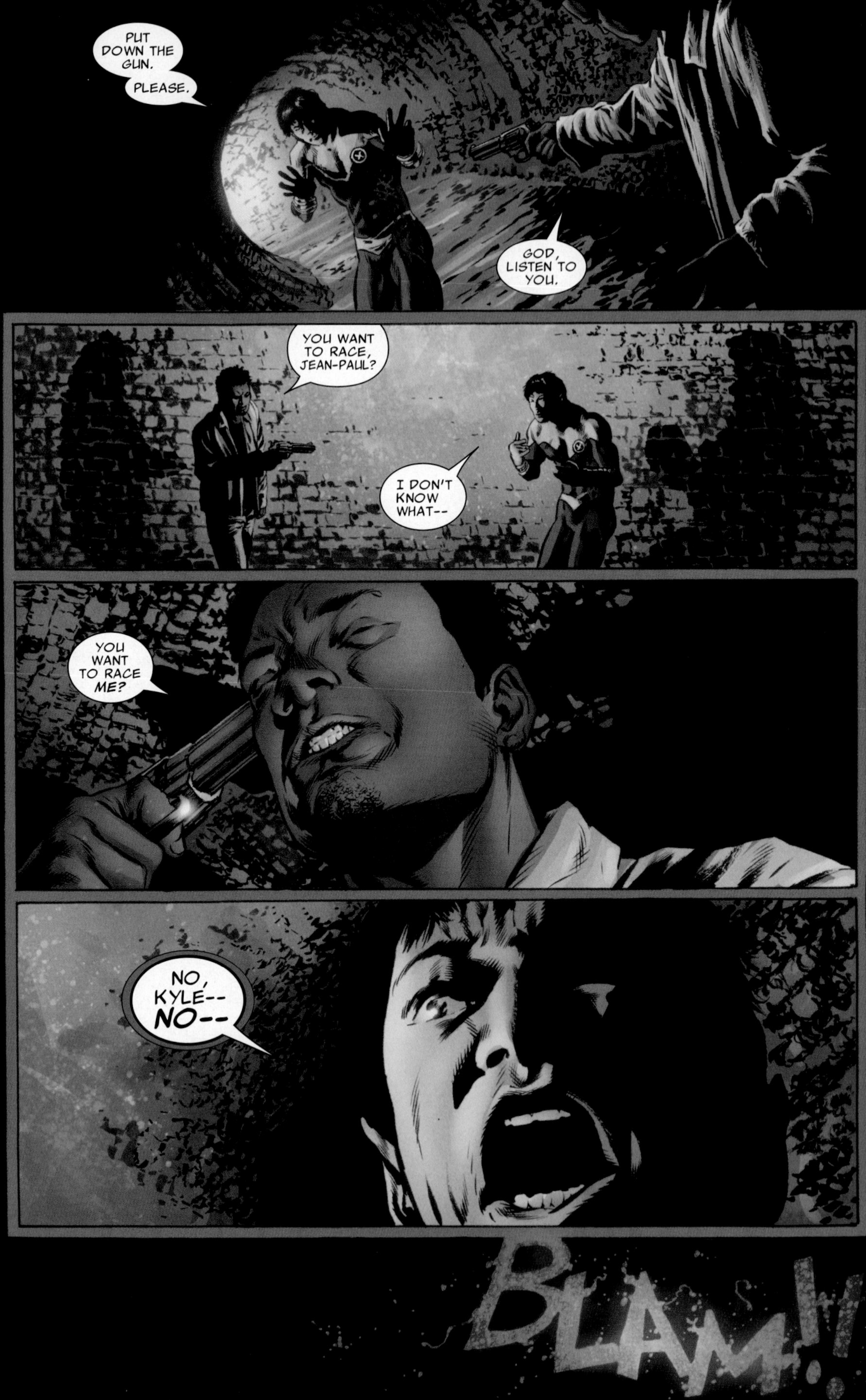
PUT DOWN THE GUN.
PLEASE.
GOD, LISTEN TO YOU.
YOU WANT TO RACE, JEAN-PAUL?
I DON'T KNOW WHAT--
YOU WANT TO RACE *ME?*
NO, KYLE-- **NO--**
BLAM!!

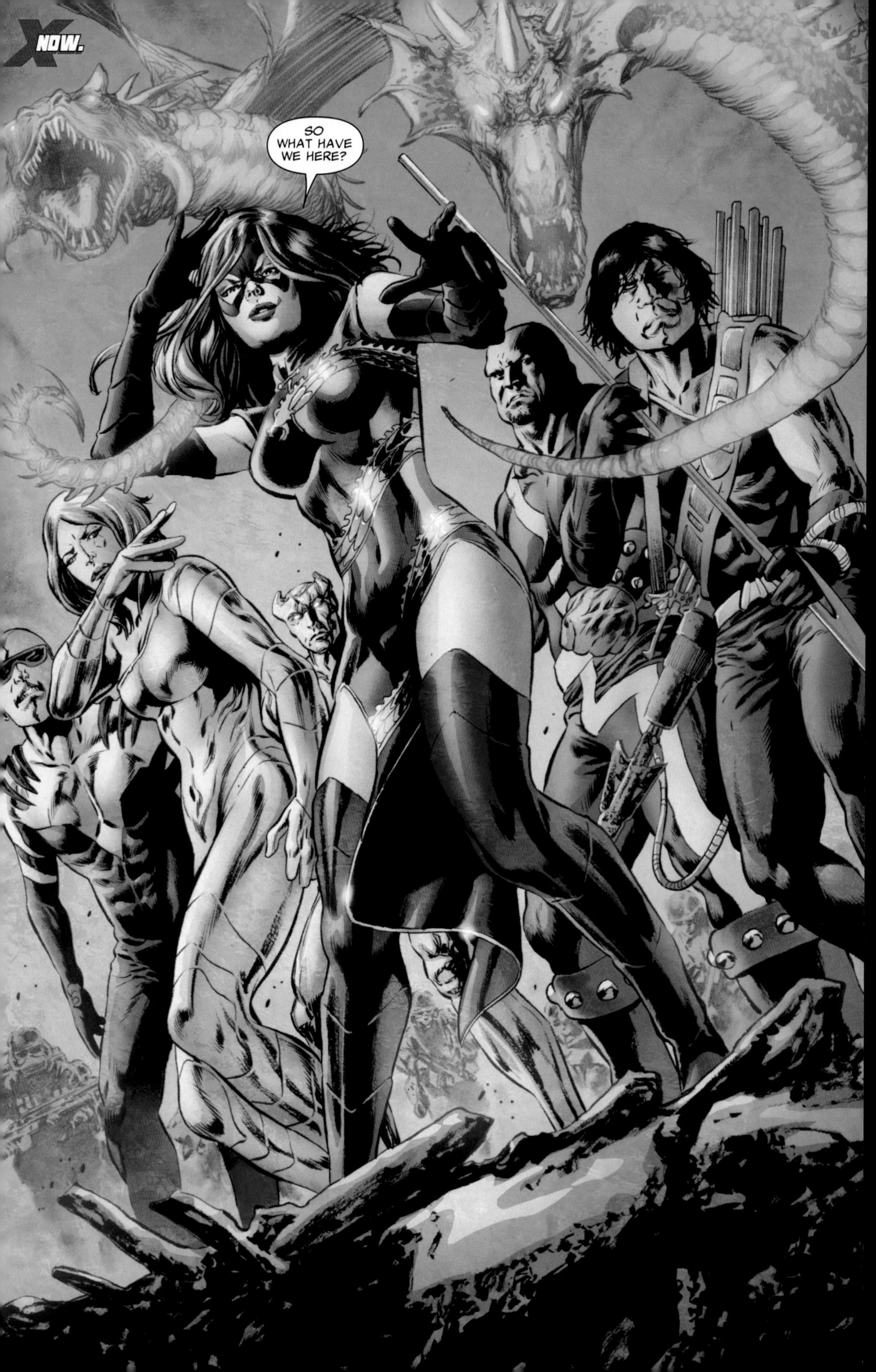
X NOW.
SO WHAT HAVE WE HERE?

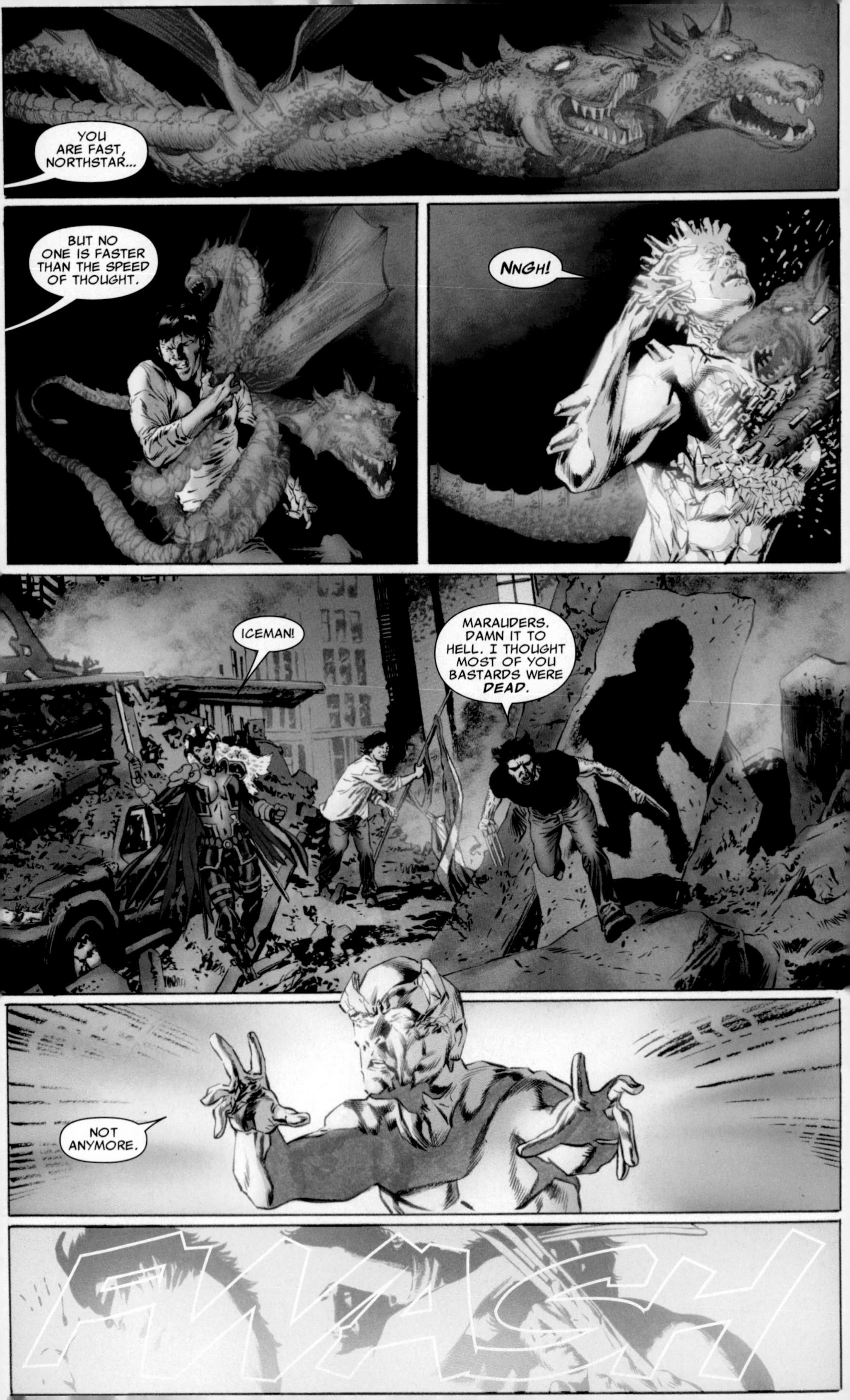
YOU ARE FAST, NORTHSTAR...
BUT NO ONE IS FASTER THAN THE SPEED OF THOUGHT.
NNGH!
ICEMAN!
MARAUDERS. DAMN IT TO HELL. I THOUGHT MOST OF YOU BASTARDS WERE DEAD.
NOT ANYMORE.
FWACH

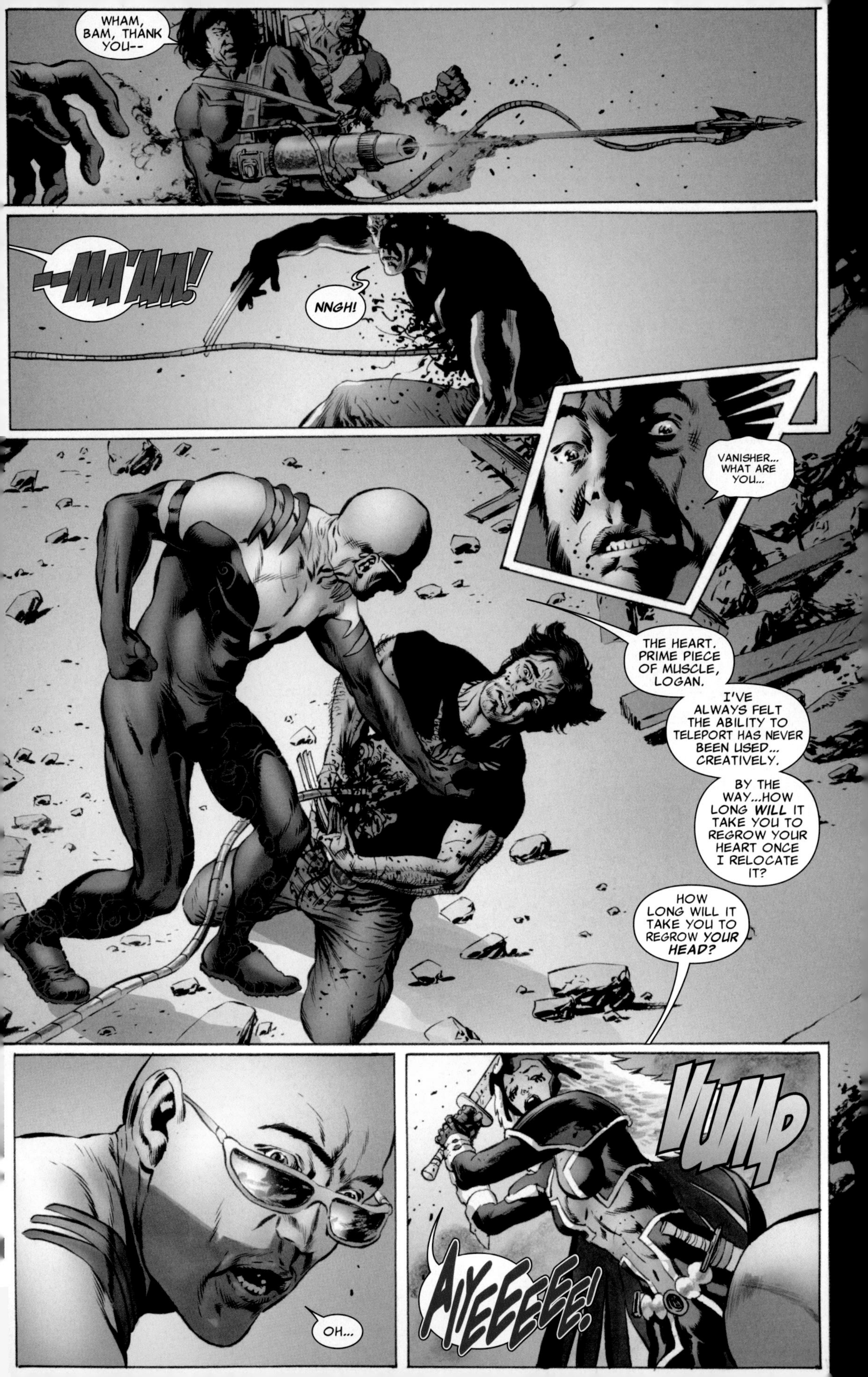
WHAM, BAM, THANK YOU--
--MA'AM!
NNGH!
VANISHER... WHAT ARE YOU...
THE HEART. PRIME PIECE OF MUSCLE, LOGAN.
I'VE ALWAYS FELT THE ABILITY TO TELEPORT HAS NEVER BEEN USED... CREATIVELY.
BY THE WAY...HOW LONG WILL IT TAKE YOU TO REGROW YOUR HEART ONCE I RELOCATE IT?
HOW LONG WILL IT TAKE YOU TO REGROW YOUR HEAD?
OH...
VUMP
AIYEEEEE!

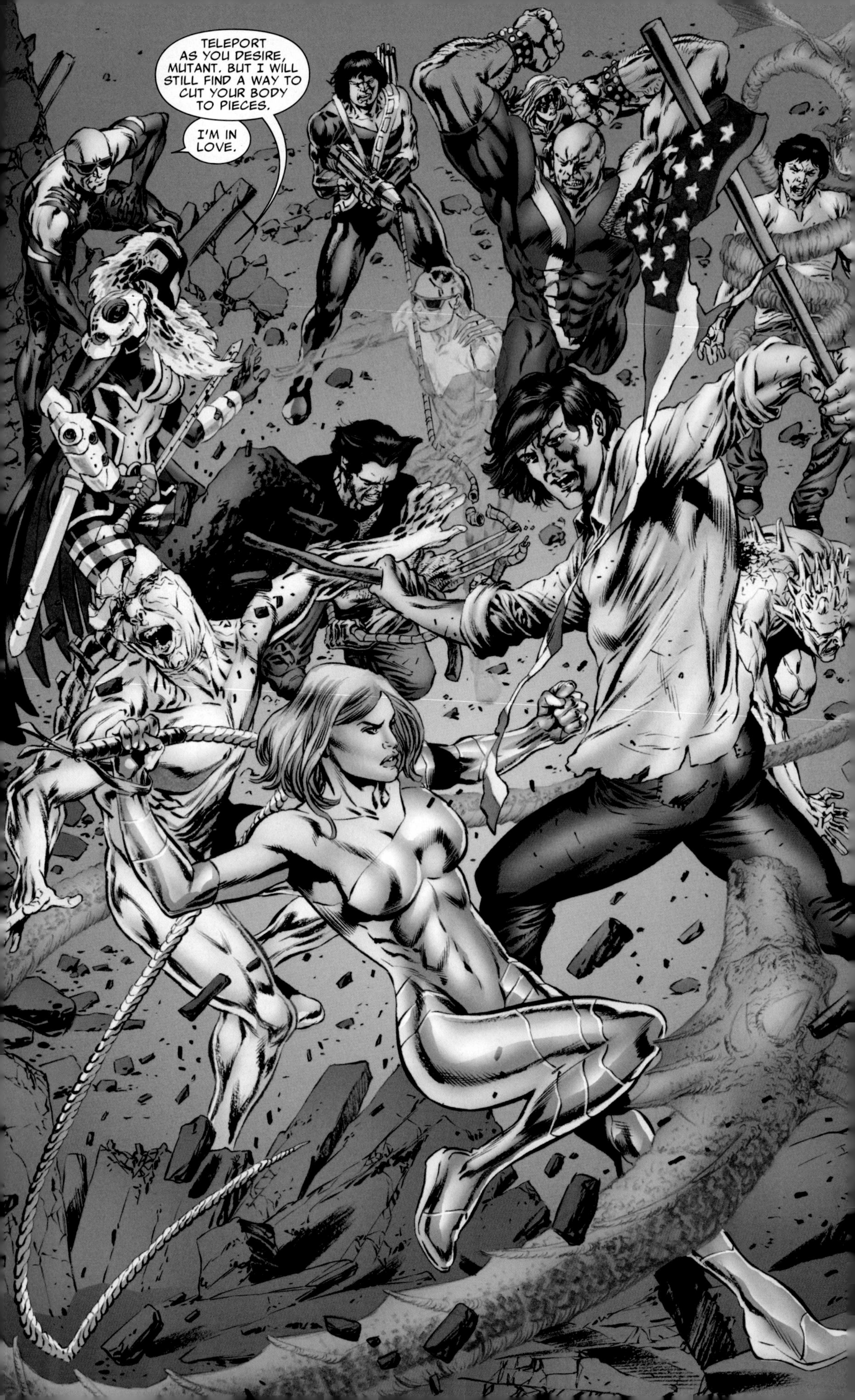
TELEPORT AS YOU DESIRE, MUTANT. BUT I WILL STILL FIND A WAY TO CUT YOUR BODY TO PIECES.
I'M IN LOVE.

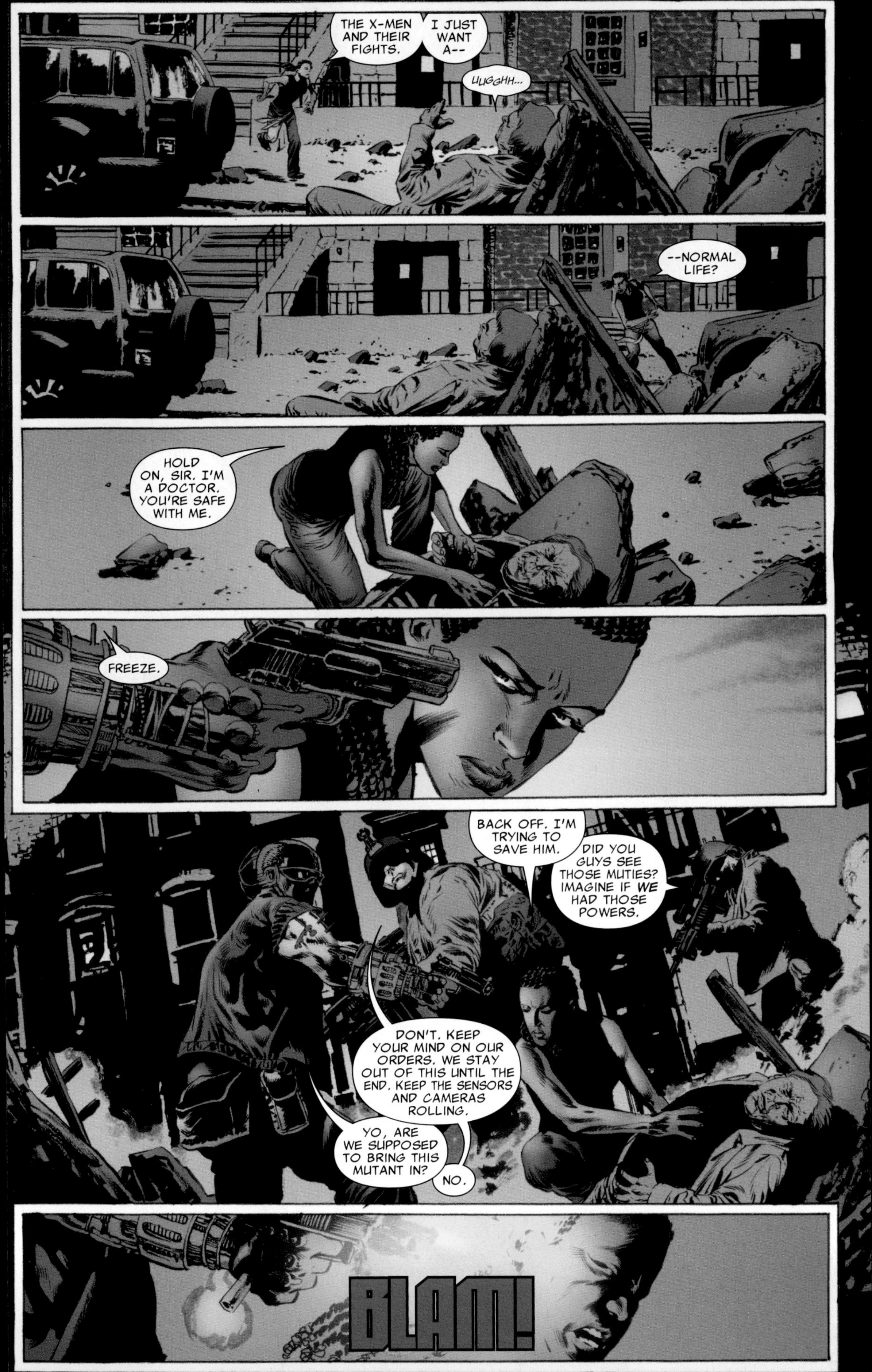
THE X-MEN AND THEIR FIGHTS.
I JUST WANT A--
UUGGHH...
--NORMAL LIFE?
HOLD ON, SIR. I'M A DOCTOR. YOU'RE SAFE WITH ME.
FREEZE.
BACK OFF. I'M TRYING TO SAVE HIM.
DID YOU GUYS SEE THOSE MUTIES? IMAGINE IF WE HAD THOSE POWERS.
DON'T. KEEP YOUR MIND ON OUR ORDERS. WE STAY OUT OF THIS UNTIL THE END. KEEP THE SENSORS AND CAMERAS ROLLING.
YO, ARE WE SUPPOSED TO BRING THIS MUTANT IN?
NO.
BLAM!

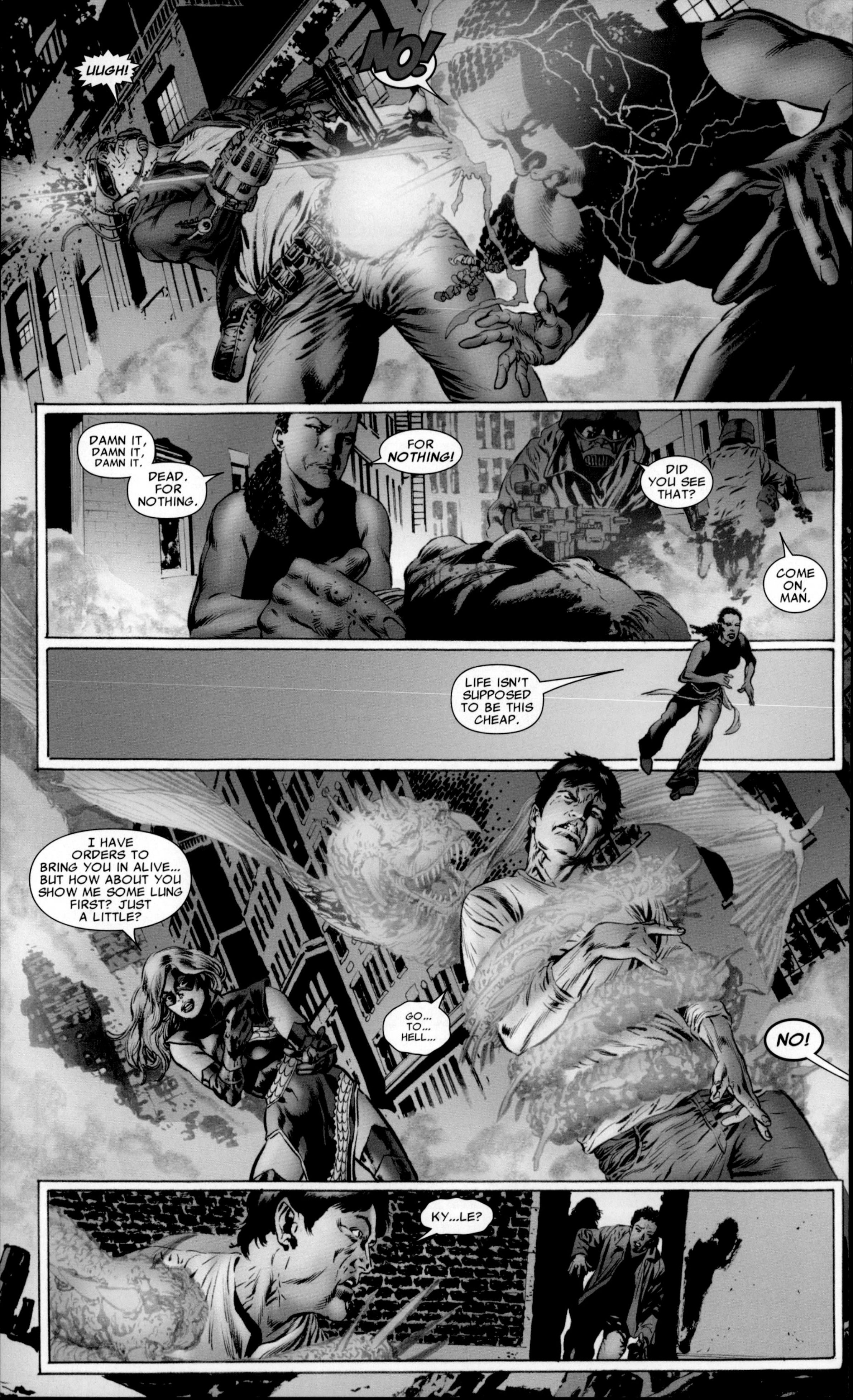
UUGH!
NO!
DAMN IT, DAMN IT, DAMN IT.
DEAD. FOR NOTHING.
FOR NOTHING!
DID YOU SEE THAT?
COME ON, MAN.
LIFE ISN'T SUPPOSED TO BE THIS CHEAP.
I HAVE ORDERS TO BRING YOU IN ALIVE... BUT HOW ABOUT YOU SHOW ME SOME LUNG FIRST? JUST A LITTLE?
GO... TO... HELL...
NO!
KY...LE?

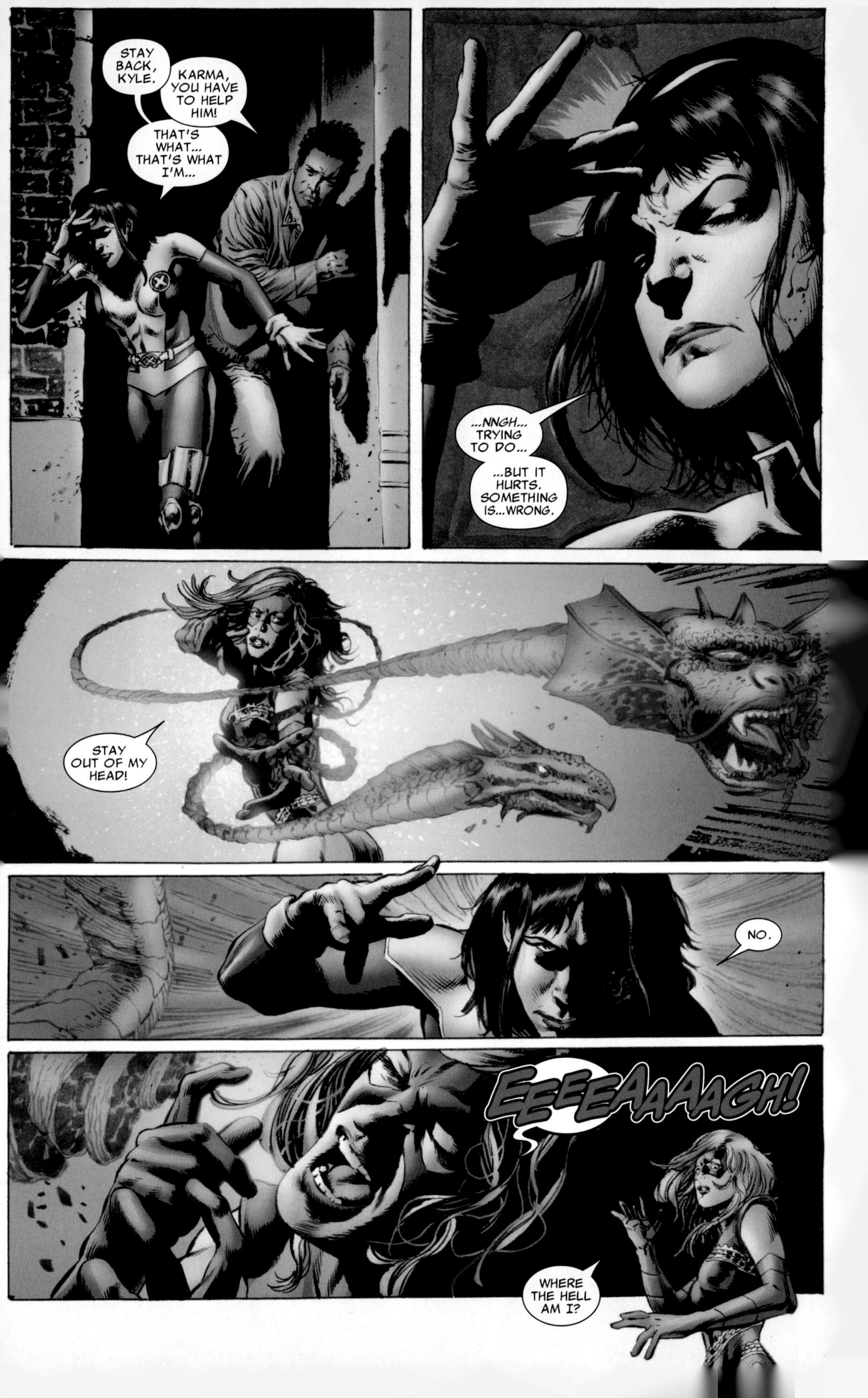
STAY BACK, KYLE.
KARMA, YOU HAVE TO HELP HIM!
THAT'S WHAT... THAT'S WHAT I'M...
...NNGH... TRYING TO DO...
...BUT IT HURTS. SOMETHING IS...WRONG.
STAY OUT OF MY HEAD!
NO.
EEEEAAAAAGH!
WHERE THE HELL AM I?

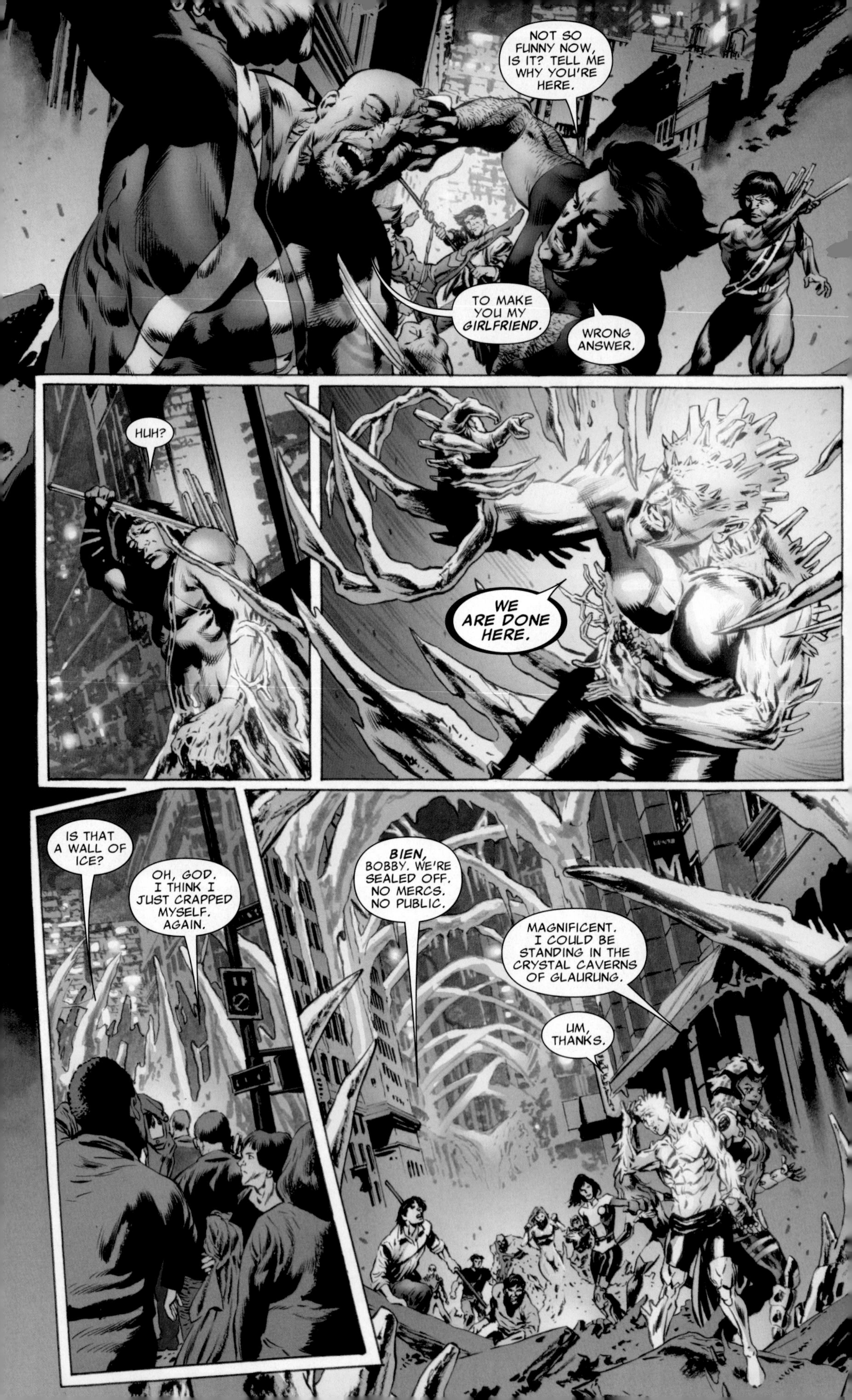
NOT SO FUNNY NOW, IS IT? TELL ME WHY YOU'RE HERE.
TO MAKE YOU MY GIRLFRIEND.
WRONG ANSWER.
HUH?
WE ARE DONE HERE.
IS THAT A WALL OF ICE?
OH, GOD. I THINK I JUST CRAPPED MYSELF. AGAIN.
BIEN, BOBBY. WE'RE SEALED OFF. NO MERCS. NO PUBLIC.
MAGNIFICENT. I COULD BE STANDING IN THE CRYSTAL CAVERNS OF GLAURUNG.
UM, THANKS.

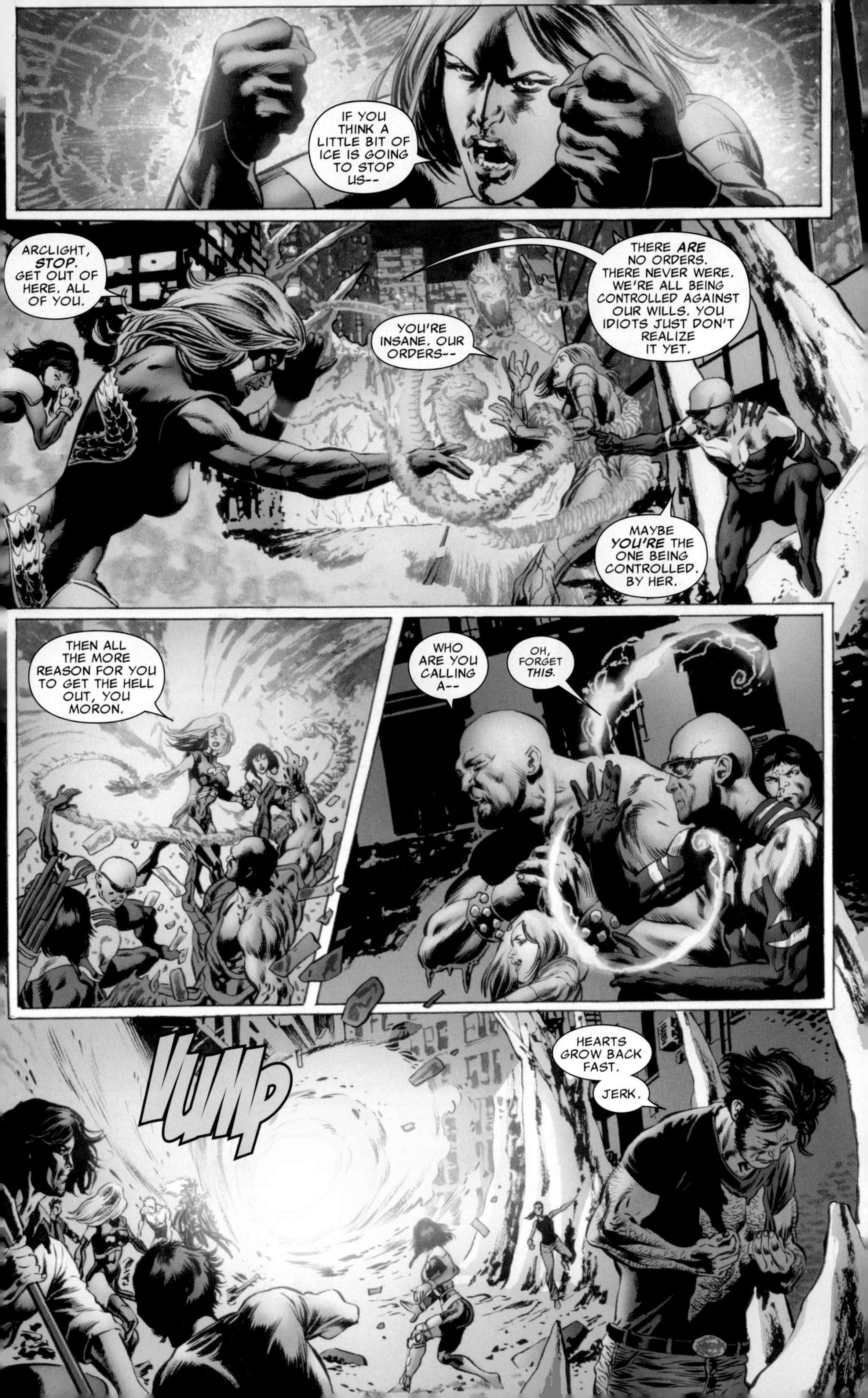
IF YOU THINK A LITTLE BIT OF ICE IS GOING TO STOP US--
ARCLIGHT, STOP. GET OUT OF HERE. ALL OF YOU.
YOU'RE INSANE. OUR ORDERS--
THERE ARE NO ORDERS. THERE NEVER WERE. WE'RE ALL BEING CONTROLLED AGAINST OUR WILLS. YOU IDIOTS JUST DON'T REALIZE IT YET.
MAYBE YOU'RE THE ONE BEING CONTROLLED. BY HER.
THEN ALL THE MORE REASON FOR YOU TO GET THE HELL OUT, YOU MORON.
WHO ARE YOU CALLING A--
OH, FORGET THIS.
VUMP
HEARTS GROW BACK FAST.
JERK.

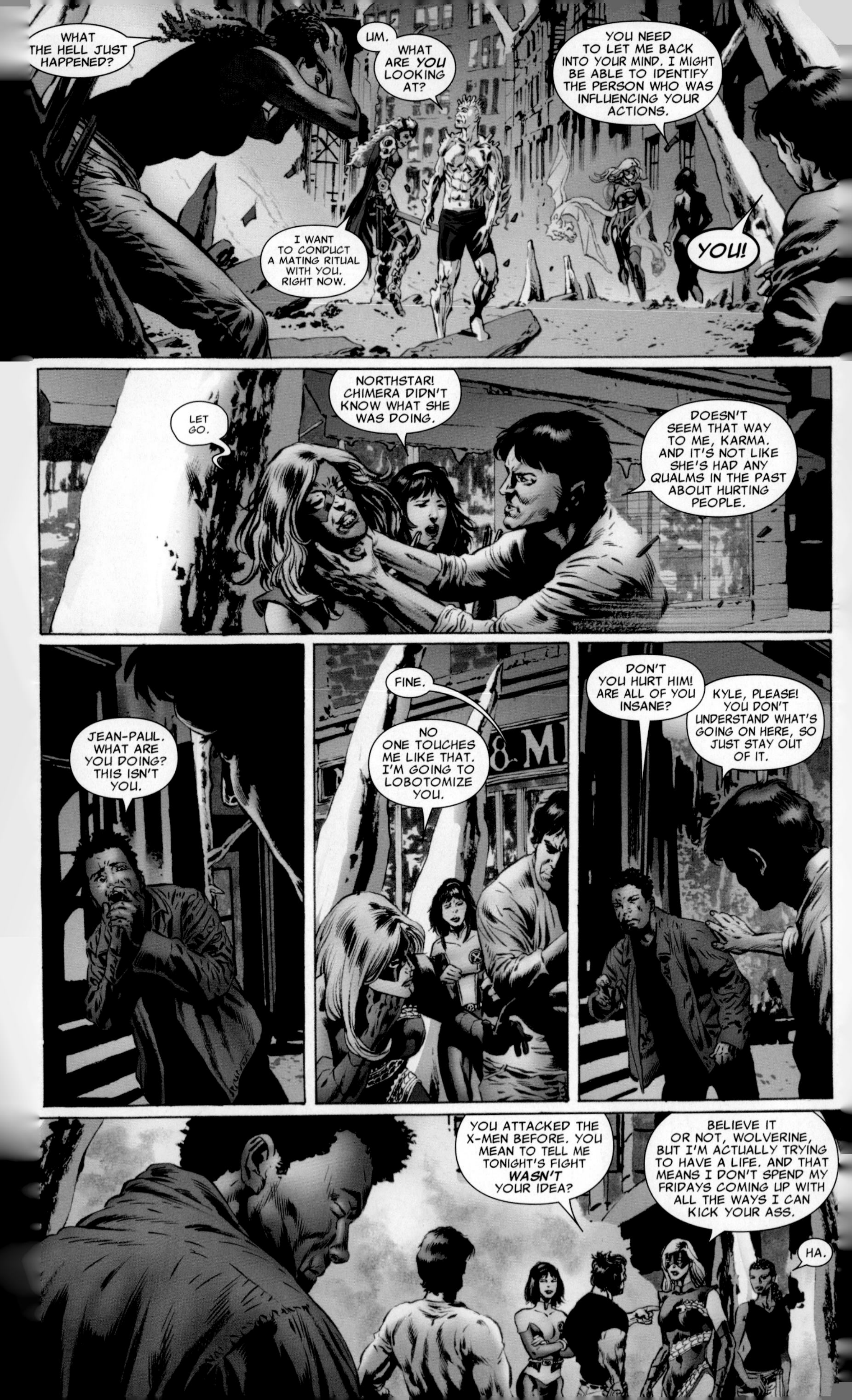
WHAT THE HELL JUST HAPPENED?
UM. WHAT ARE YOU LOOKING AT?
YOU NEED TO LET ME BACK INTO YOUR MIND. I MIGHT BE ABLE TO IDENTIFY THE PERSON WHO WAS INFLUENCING YOUR ACTIONS.
I WANT TO CONDUCT A MATING RITUAL WITH YOU. RIGHT NOW.
YOU!
LET GO.
NORTHSTAR! CHIMERA DIDN'T KNOW WHAT SHE WAS DOING.
DOESN'T SEEM THAT WAY TO ME, KARMA. AND IT'S NOT LIKE SHE'S HAD ANY QUALMS IN THE PAST ABOUT HURTING PEOPLE.
JEAN-PAUL. WHAT ARE YOU DOING? THIS ISN'T YOU.
FINE.
NO ONE TOUCHES ME LIKE THAT. I'M GOING TO LOBOTOMIZE YOU.
DON'T YOU HURT HIM! ARE ALL OF YOU INSANE?
KYLE, PLEASE! YOU DON'T UNDERSTAND WHAT'S GOING ON HERE, SO JUST STAY OUT OF IT.
YOU ATTACKED THE X-MEN BEFORE. YOU MEAN TO TELL ME TONIGHT'S FIGHT WASN'T YOUR IDEA?
BELIEVE IT OR NOT, WOLVERINE, BUT I'M ACTUALLY TRYING TO HAVE A LIFE. AND THAT MEANS I DON'T SPEND MY FRIDAYS COMING UP WITH ALL THE WAYS I CAN KICK YOUR ASS.
HA.

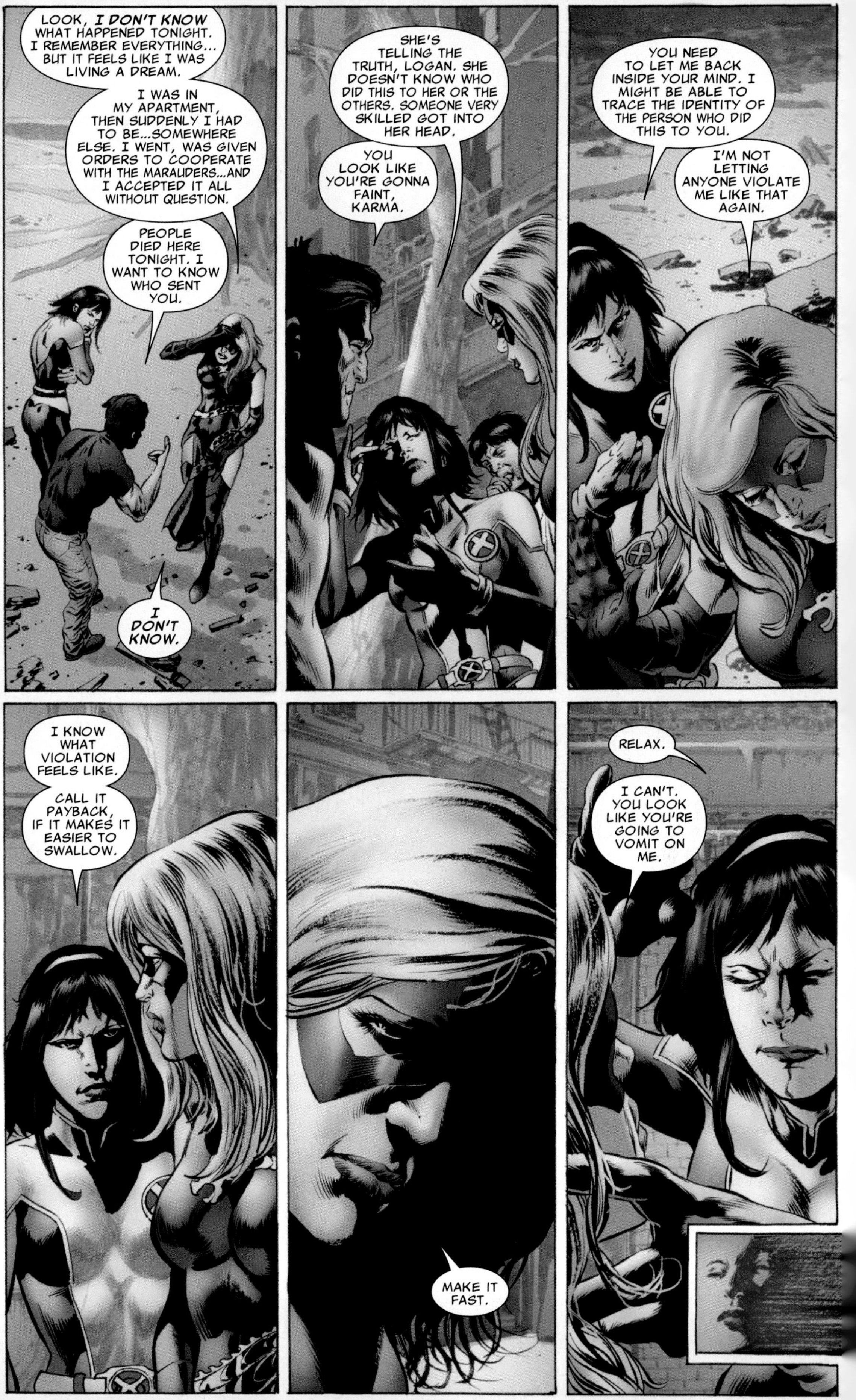
LOOK, I DON'T KNOW WHAT HAPPENED TONIGHT. I REMEMBER EVERYTHING... BUT IT FEELS LIKE I WAS LIVING A DREAM.
I WAS IN MY APARTMENT, THEN SUDDENLY I HAD TO BE...SOMEWHERE ELSE. I WENT, WAS GIVEN ORDERS TO COOPERATE WITH THE MARAUDERS...AND I ACCEPTED IT ALL WITHOUT QUESTION.
PEOPLE DIED HERE TONIGHT. I WANT TO KNOW WHO SENT YOU.
I DON'T KNOW.
SHE'S TELLING THE TRUTH, LOGAN. SHE DOESN'T KNOW WHO DID THIS TO HER OR THE OTHERS. SOMEONE VERY SKILLED GOT INTO HER HEAD.
YOU LOOK LIKE YOU'RE GONNA FAINT, KARMA.
YOU NEED TO LET ME BACK INSIDE YOUR MIND. I MIGHT BE ABLE TO TRACE THE IDENTITY OF THE PERSON WHO DID THIS TO YOU.
I'M NOT LETTING ANYONE VIOLATE ME LIKE THAT AGAIN.
I KNOW WHAT VIOLATION FEELS LIKE.
CALL IT PAYBACK, IF IT MAKES IT EASIER TO SWALLOW.
MAKE IT FAST.
RELAX.
I CAN'T. YOU LOOK LIKE YOU'RE GOING TO VOMIT ON ME.

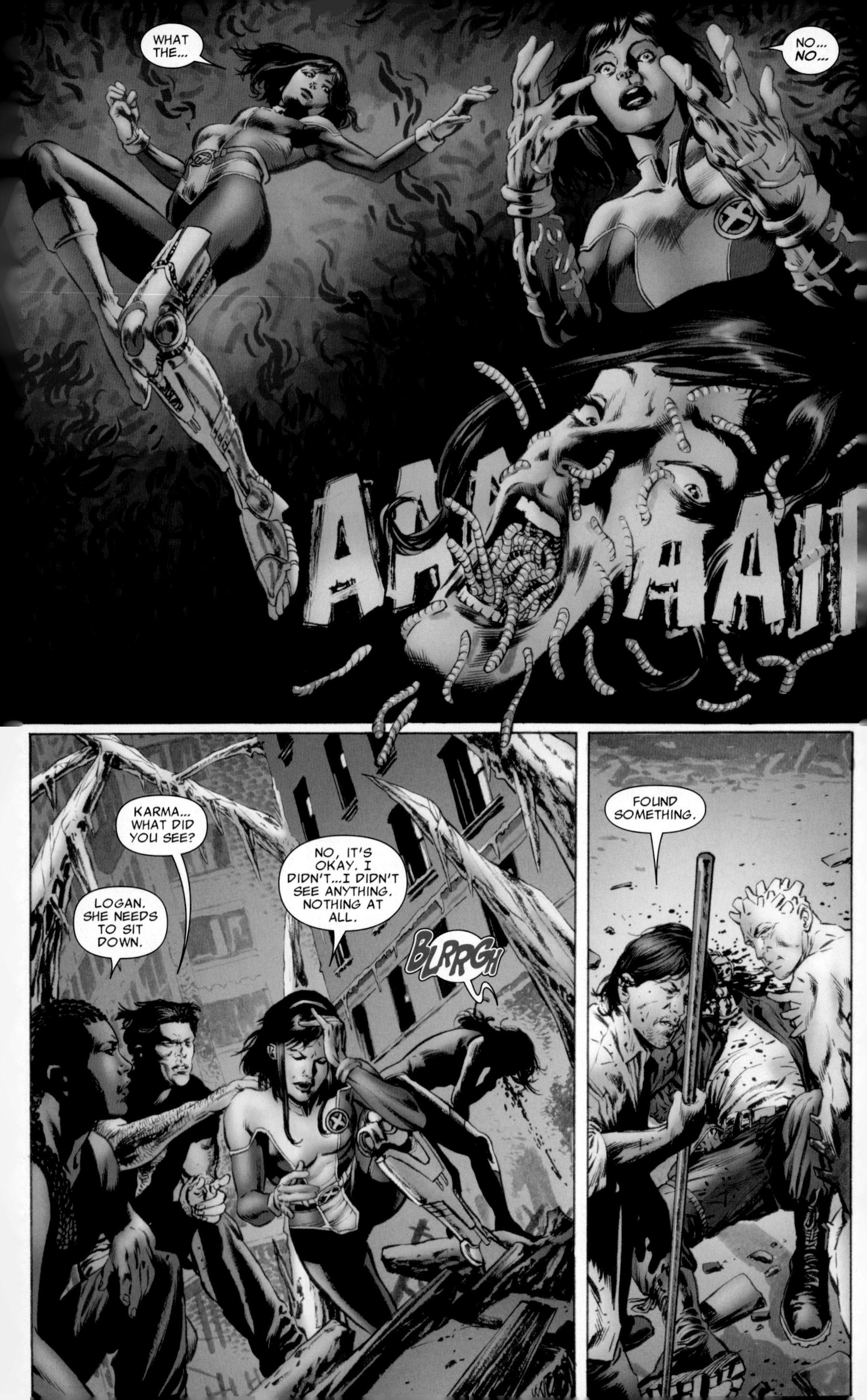
WHAT THE...
NO... NO...
AAAAAH
KARMA... WHAT DID YOU SEE?
LOGAN. SHE NEEDS TO SIT DOWN.
NO, IT'S OKAY. I DIDN'T...I DIDN'T SEE ANYTHING. NOTHING AT ALL.
BLRRGH
FOUND SOMETHING.

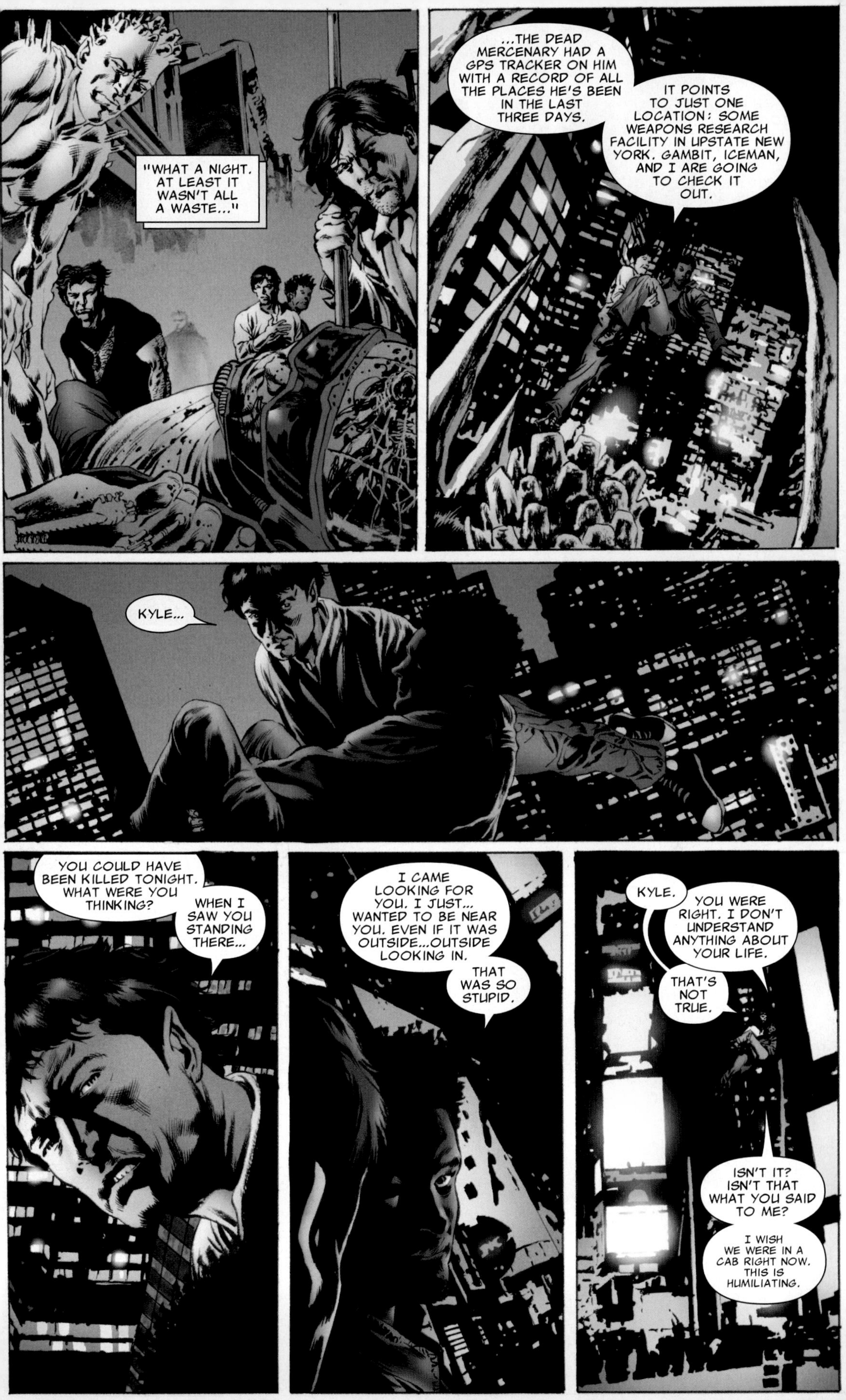
"WHAT A NIGHT. AT LEAST IT WASN'T ALL A WASTE..."
...THE DEAD MERCENARY HAD A GPS TRACKER ON HIM WITH A RECORD OF ALL THE PLACES HE'S BEEN IN THE LAST THREE DAYS.
IT POINTS TO JUST ONE LOCATION: SOME WEAPONS RESEARCH FACILITY IN UPSTATE NEW YORK. GAMBIT, ICEMAN, AND I ARE GOING TO CHECK IT OUT.
KYLE...
YOU COULD HAVE BEEN KILLED TONIGHT. WHAT WERE YOU THINKING?
WHEN I SAW YOU STANDING THERE...
I CAME LOOKING FOR YOU. I JUST... WANTED TO BE NEAR YOU. EVEN IF IT WAS OUTSIDE...OUTSIDE LOOKING IN.
THAT WAS SO STUPID.
KYLE.
YOU WERE RIGHT. I DON'T UNDERSTAND ANYTHING ABOUT YOUR LIFE.
THAT'S NOT TRUE.
ISN'T IT? ISN'T THAT WHAT YOU SAID TO ME?
I WISH WE WERE IN A CAB RIGHT NOW. THIS IS HUMILIATING.

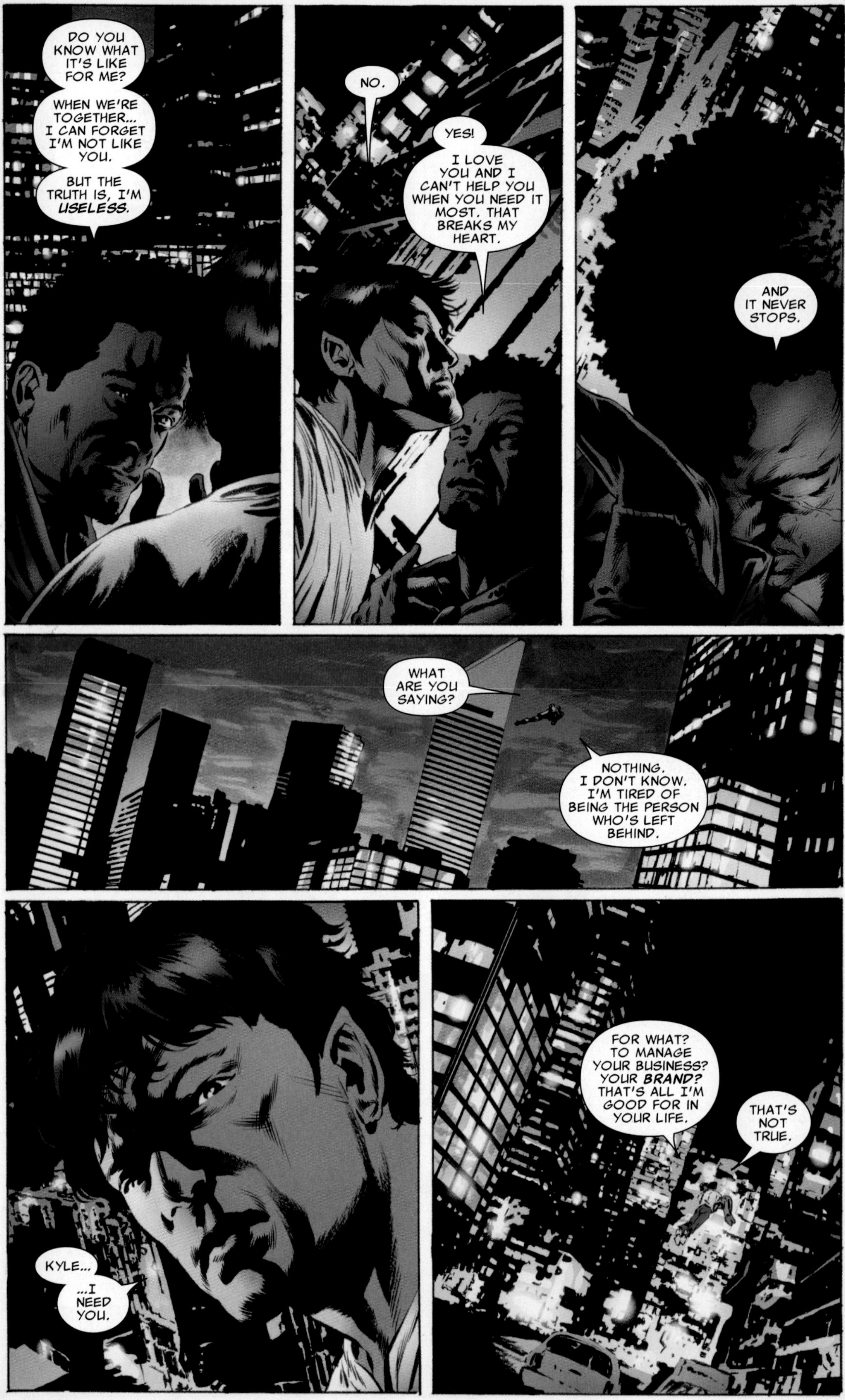
DO YOU KNOW WHAT IT'S LIKE FOR ME?
WHEN WE'RE TOGETHER... I CAN FORGET I'M NOT LIKE YOU.
BUT THE TRUTH IS, I'M *USELESS.*
NO.
YES!
I LOVE YOU AND I CAN'T HELP YOU WHEN YOU NEED IT MOST. THAT BREAKS MY HEART.
AND IT NEVER STOPS.
WHAT ARE YOU SAYING?
NOTHING. I DON'T KNOW. I'M TIRED OF BEING THE PERSON WHO'S LEFT BEHIND.
KYLE...
...I NEED YOU.
FOR WHAT? TO MANAGE YOUR BUSINESS? YOUR *BRAND?* THAT'S ALL I'M GOOD FOR IN YOUR LIFE.
THAT'S NOT TRUE.

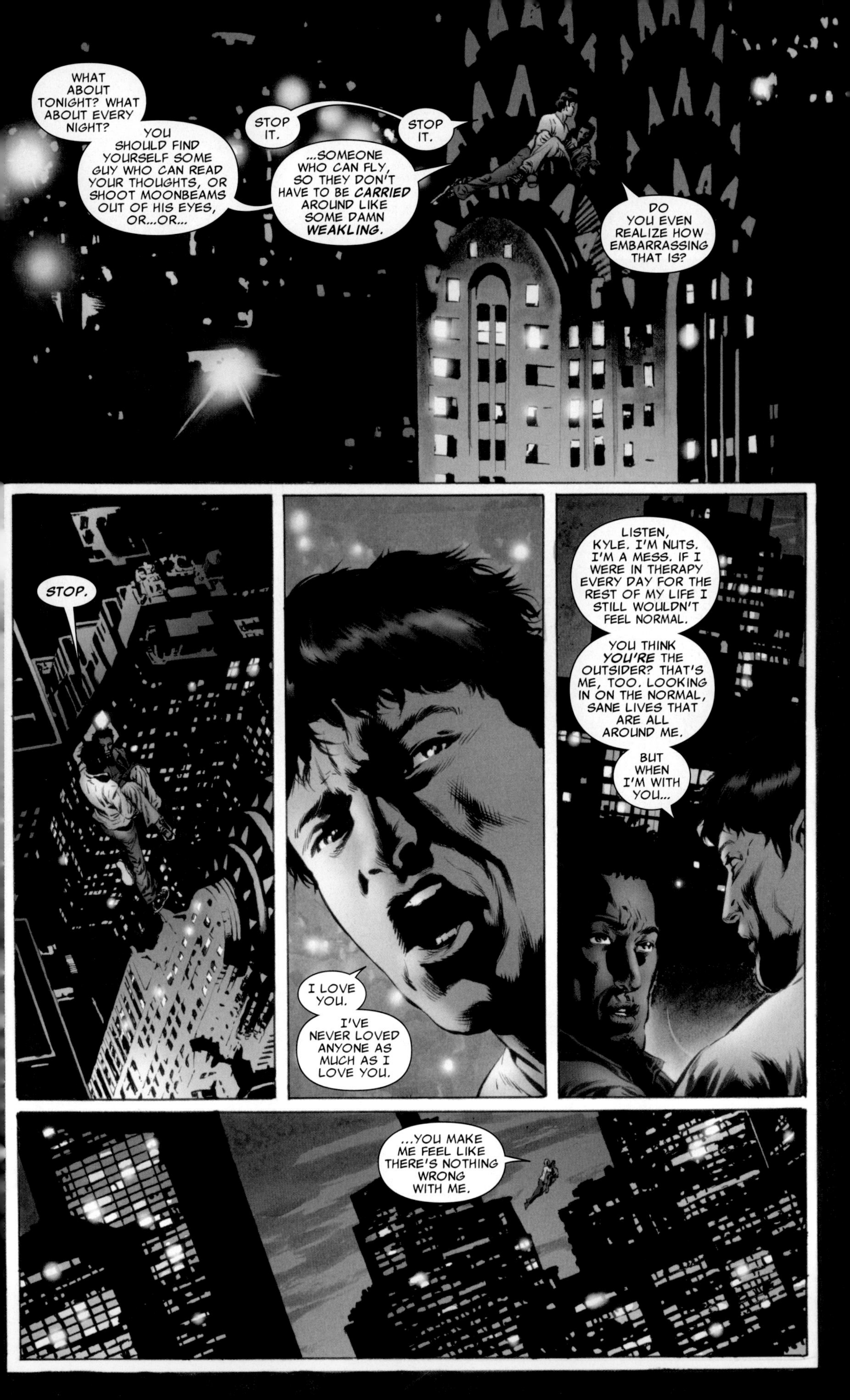
WHAT ABOUT TONIGHT? WHAT ABOUT EVERY NIGHT?
YOU SHOULD FIND YOURSELF SOME GUY WHO CAN READ YOUR THOUGHTS, OR SHOOT MOONBEAMS OUT OF HIS EYES, OR...OR...
STOP IT.
STOP IT.
...SOMEONE WHO CAN FLY, SO THEY DON'T HAVE TO BE CARRIED AROUND LIKE SOME DAMN WEAKLING.
DO YOU EVEN REALIZE HOW EMBARRASSING THAT IS?
STOP.
I LOVE YOU.
I'VE NEVER LOVED ANYONE AS MUCH AS I LOVE YOU.
LISTEN, KYLE. I'M NUTS. I'M A MESS. IF I WERE IN THERAPY EVERY DAY FOR THE REST OF MY LIFE I STILL WOULDN'T FEEL NORMAL.
YOU THINK YOU'RE THE OUTSIDER? THAT'S ME, TOO. LOOKING IN ON THE NORMAL, SANE LIVES THAT ARE ALL AROUND ME.
BUT WHEN I'M WITH YOU...
...YOU MAKE ME FEEL LIKE THERE'S NOTHING WRONG WITH ME.

I KNOW THIS IS NO LIFE FOR YOU. IT'S HARD AND IMPOSSIBLE...AND IF I WERE A BETTER MAN, I'D LET YOU GO.

BUT I'M SELFISH. I'M HORRIBLE. WHICH IS WHY I'LL DO ANYTHING TO KEEP YOU WITH ME. ANYTHING, KYLE, TO MAKE YOU HAPPY.

I CAN'T MAKE THIS A PERFECT LIFE FOR US, BUT I'LL TRY TO MAKE UP FOR WHAT ISN'T RIGHT. I'LL TRY.

BECAUSE YOU LOVE ME.

BECAUSE I LOVE YOU.

THAT'S ALL I NEED, JEAN-PAUL. IF YOU LOVE ME, THAT'S ALL I NEED.

ALSO, FOR YOU TO DO THE LAUNDRY AND ALL THE CLEANING.

BUT MOSTLY JUST YOUR LOVE.

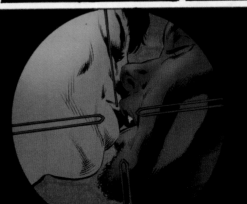

"IT WENT WELL, YOU THINK?"

"TOO SOON TO TELL. MUCH TOO SOON."

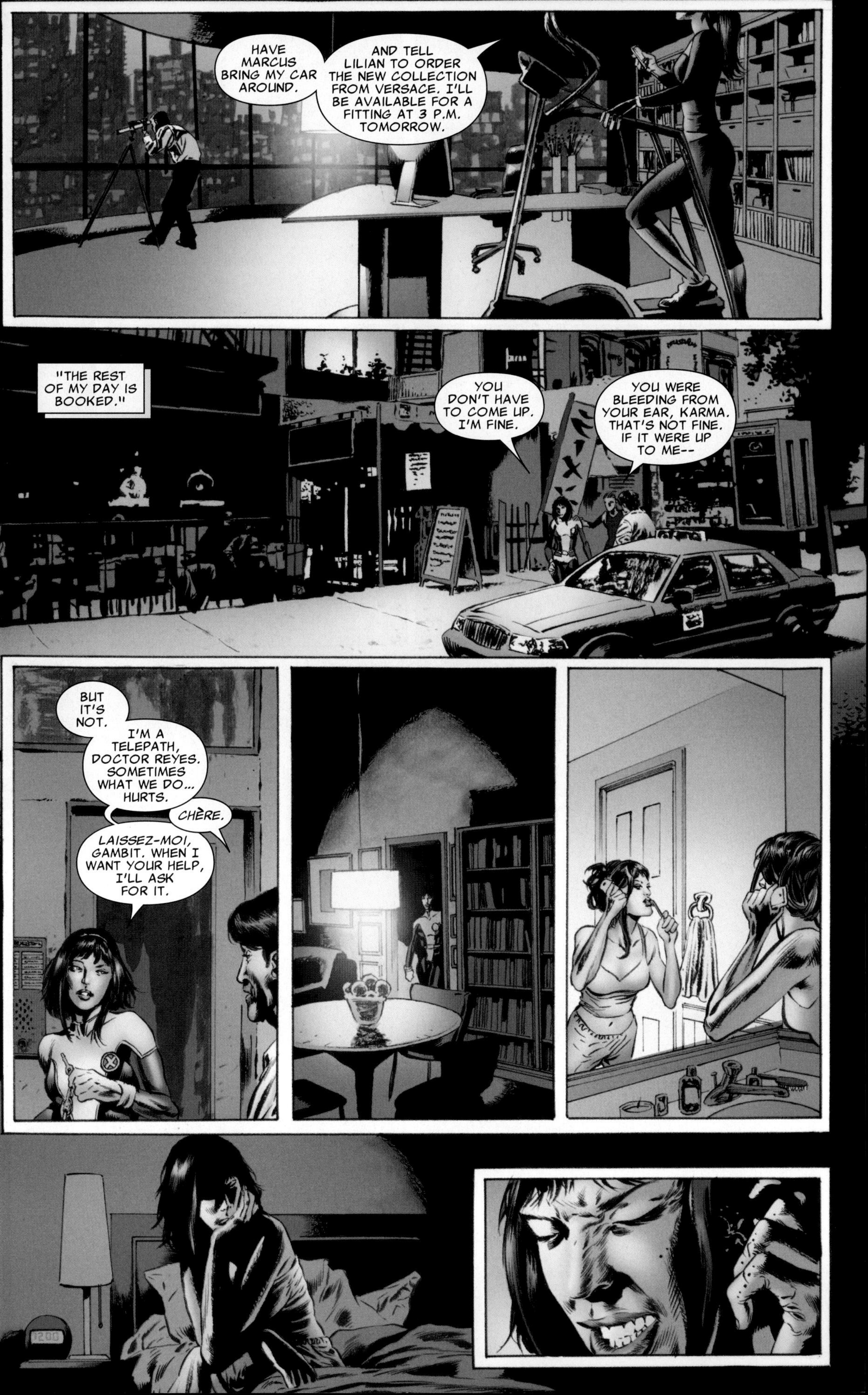
HAVE MARCUS BRING MY CAR AROUND.
AND TELL LILIAN TO ORDER THE NEW COLLECTION FROM VERSACE. I'LL BE AVAILABLE FOR A FITTING AT 3 P.M. TOMORROW.
"THE REST OF MY DAY IS BOOKED."
YOU DON'T HAVE TO COME UP. I'M FINE.
YOU WERE BLEEDING FROM YOUR EAR, KARMA. THAT'S NOT FINE. IF IT WERE UP TO ME--
BUT IT'S NOT.
I'M A TELEPATH, DOCTOR REYES. SOMETIMES WHAT WE DO... HURTS.
CHÈRE.
LAISSEZ-MOI, GAMBIT. WHEN I WANT YOUR HELP, I'LL ASK FOR IT.

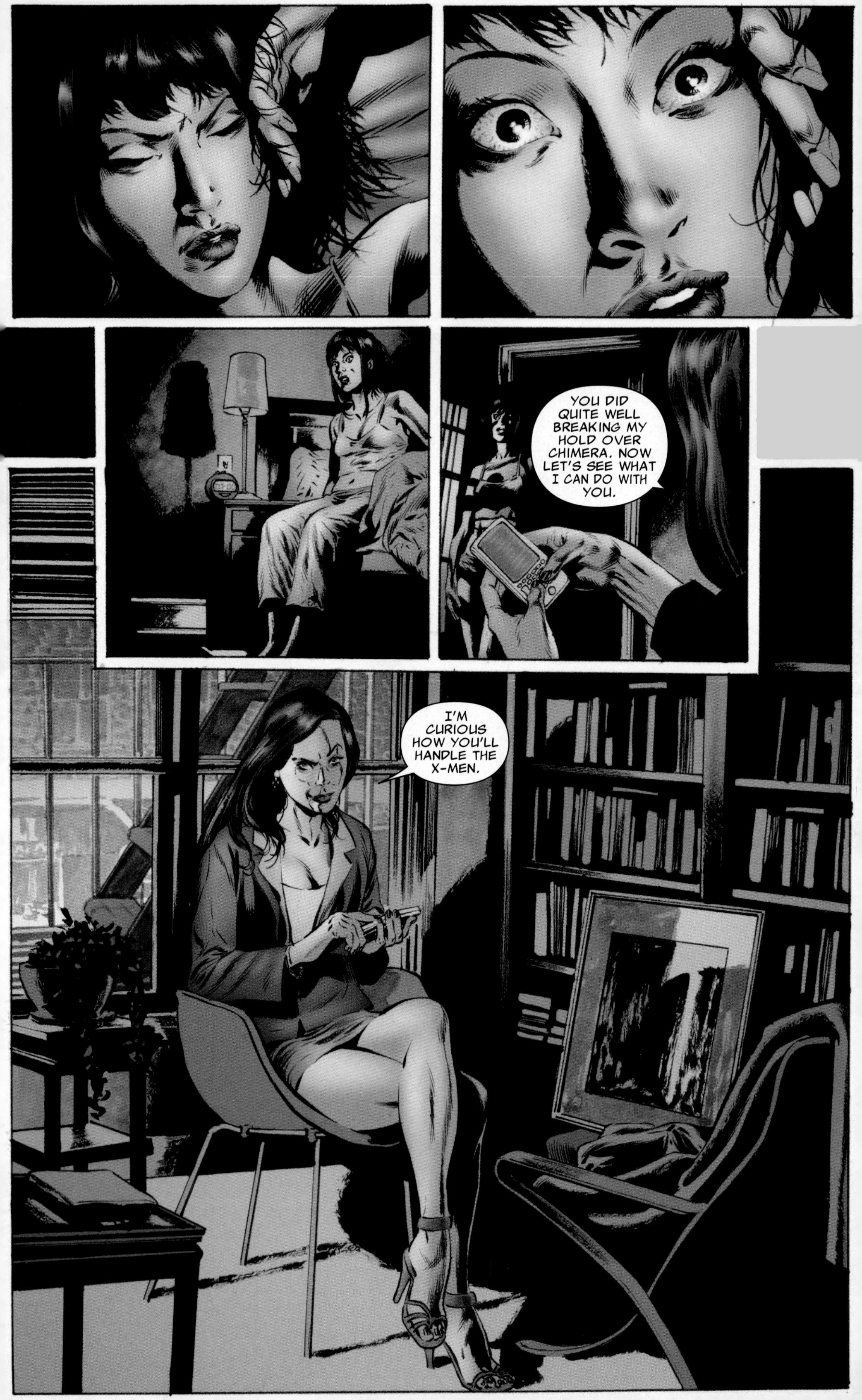
YOU DID QUITE WELL BREAKING MY HOLD OVER CHIMERA. NOW LET'S SEE WHAT I CAN DO WITH YOU.
I'M CURIOUS HOW YOU'LL HANDLE THE X-MEN.

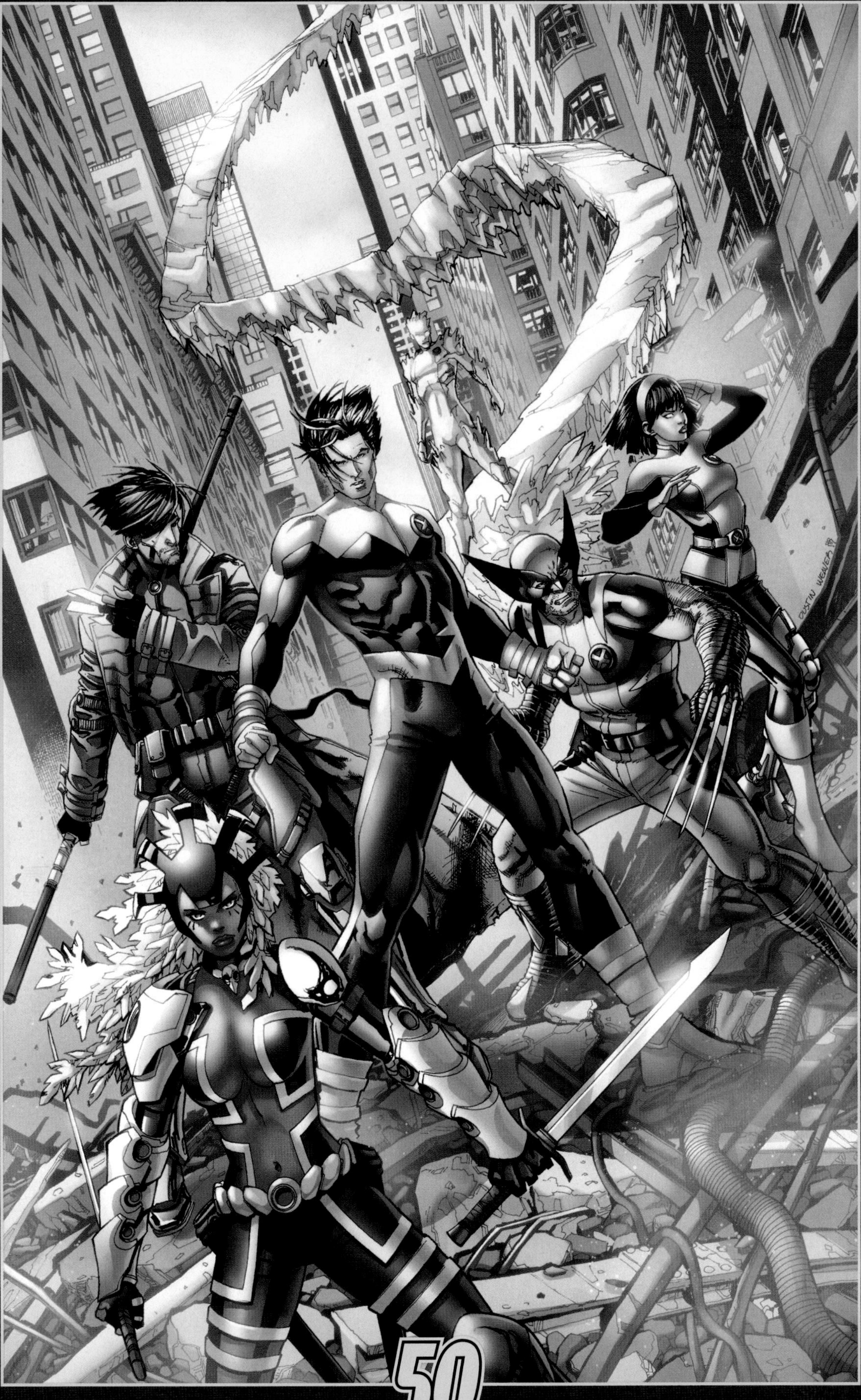

50

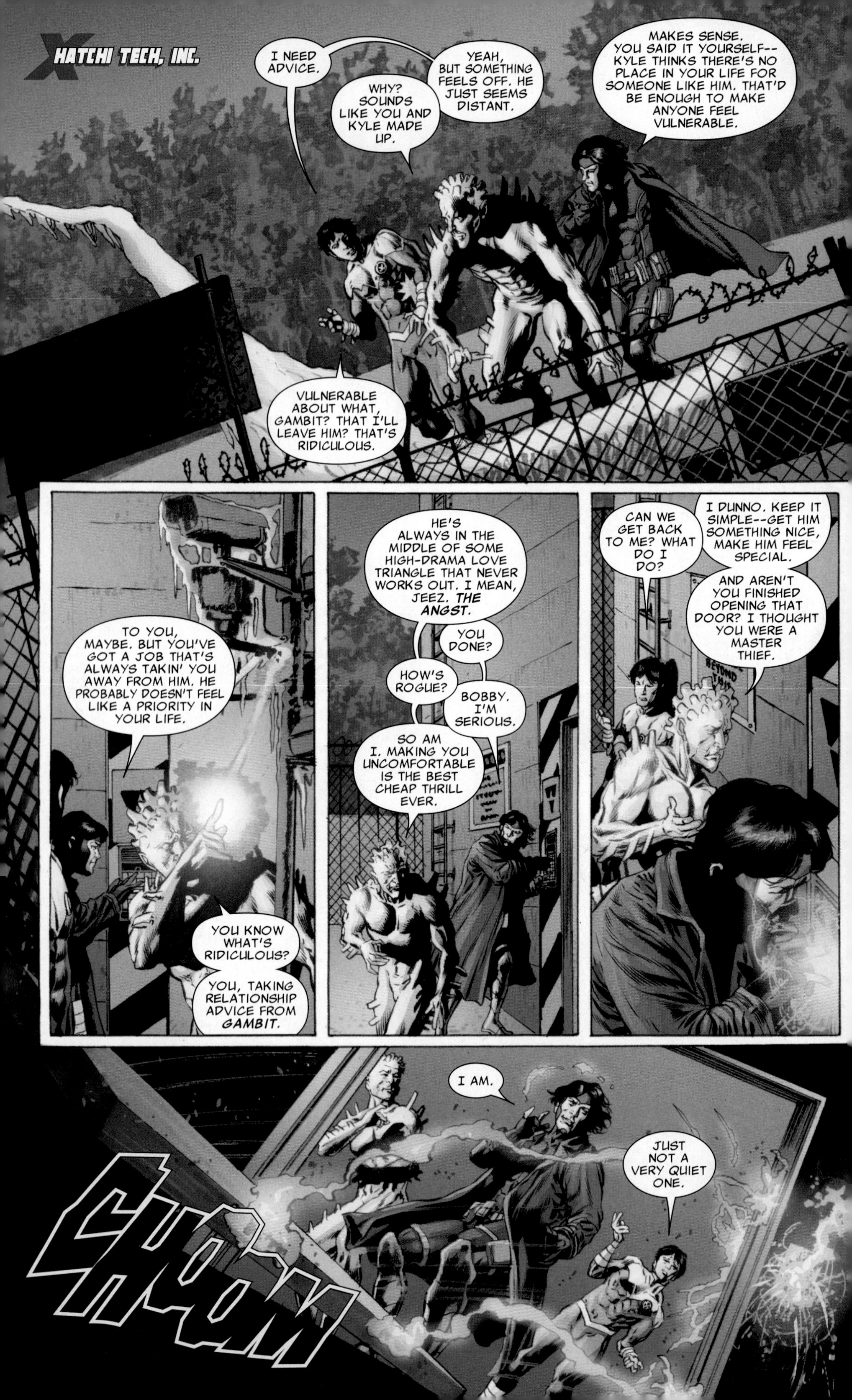
HATCHI TECH, INC.
I NEED ADVICE.
WHY? SOUNDS LIKE YOU AND KYLE MADE UP.
YEAH, BUT SOMETHING FEELS OFF. HE JUST SEEMS DISTANT.
MAKES SENSE. YOU SAID IT YOURSELF--KYLE THINKS THERE'S NO PLACE IN YOUR LIFE FOR SOMEONE LIKE HIM. THAT'D BE ENOUGH TO MAKE ANYONE FEEL VULNERABLE.
VULNERABLE ABOUT WHAT, GAMBIT? THAT I'LL LEAVE HIM? THAT'S RIDICULOUS.
TO YOU, MAYBE. BUT YOU'VE GOT A JOB THAT'S ALWAYS TAKIN' YOU AWAY FROM HIM. HE PROBABLY DOESN'T FEEL LIKE A PRIORITY IN YOUR LIFE.
YOU KNOW WHAT'S RIDICULOUS?
YOU, TAKING RELATIONSHIP ADVICE FROM *GAMBIT*.
HE'S ALWAYS IN THE MIDDLE OF SOME HIGH-DRAMA LOVE TRIANGLE THAT NEVER WORKS OUT. I MEAN, JEEZ. ***THE ANGST.***
YOU DONE?
HOW'S ROGUE?
BOBBY. I'M SERIOUS.
SO AM I. MAKING YOU UNCOMFORTABLE IS THE BEST CHEAP THRILL EVER.
CAN WE GET BACK TO ME? WHAT DO I DO?
I DUNNO. KEEP IT SIMPLE--GET HIM SOMETHING NICE, MAKE HIM FEEL SPECIAL.
AND AREN'T YOU FINISHED OPENING THAT DOOR? I THOUGHT YOU WERE A MASTER THIEF.
I AM.
JUST NOT A VERY QUIET ONE.

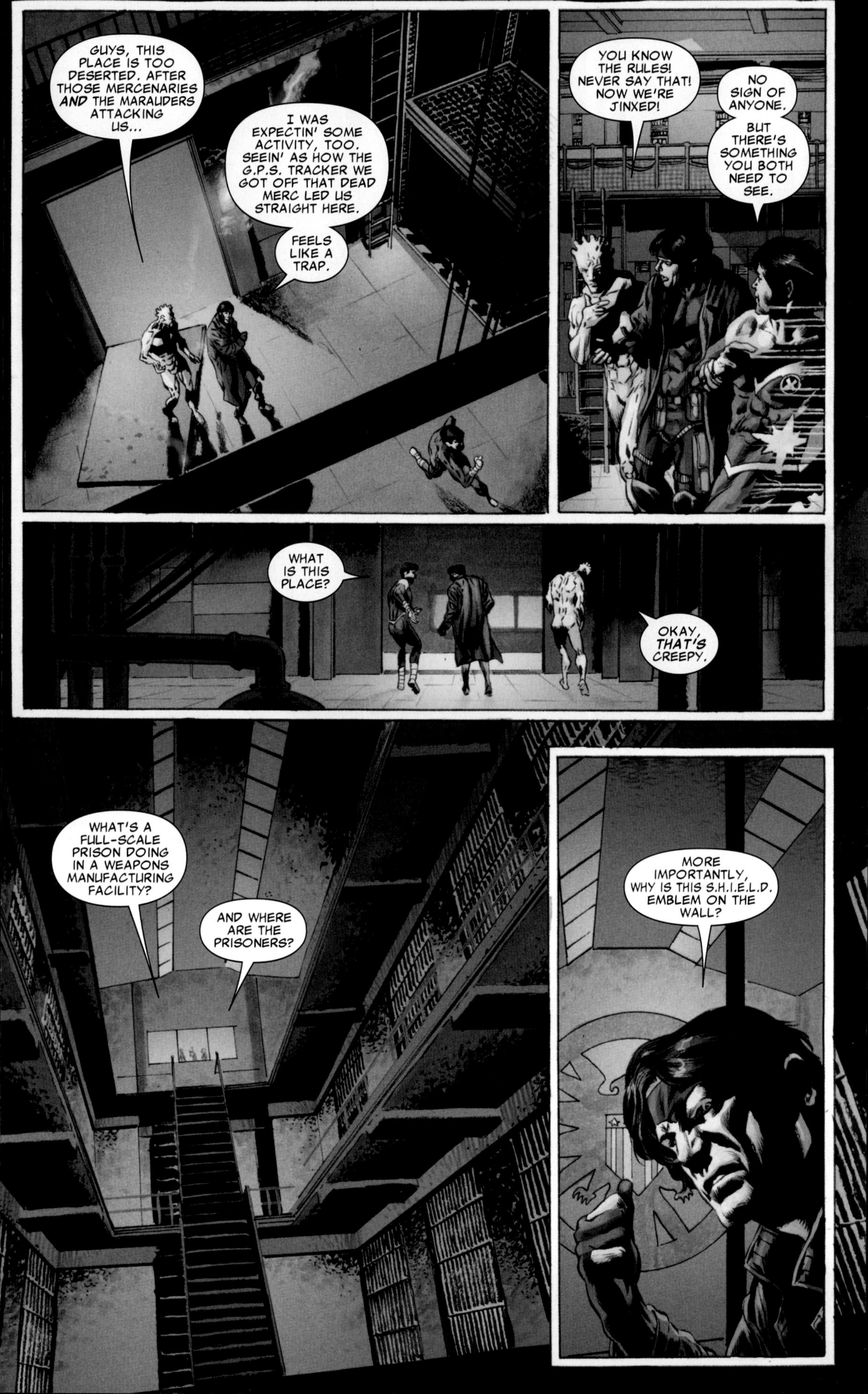
GUYS, THIS PLACE IS TOO DESERTED. AFTER THOSE MERCENARIES *AND* THE MARAUDERS ATTACKING US...
I WAS EXPECTIN' SOME ACTIVITY, TOO. SEEIN' AS HOW THE G.P.S. TRACKER WE GOT OFF THAT DEAD MERC LED US STRAIGHT HERE.
FEELS LIKE A TRAP.
YOU KNOW THE RULES! NEVER SAY THAT! NOW WE'RE JINXED!
NO SIGN OF ANYONE.
BUT THERE'S SOMETHING YOU BOTH NEED TO SEE.
WHAT IS THIS PLACE?
OKAY, *THAT'S* CREEPY.
WHAT'S A FULL-SCALE PRISON DOING IN A WEAPONS MANUFACTURING FACILITY?
AND WHERE ARE THE PRISONERS?
MORE IMPORTANTLY, WHY IS THIS S.H.I.E.L.D. EMBLEM ON THE WALL?

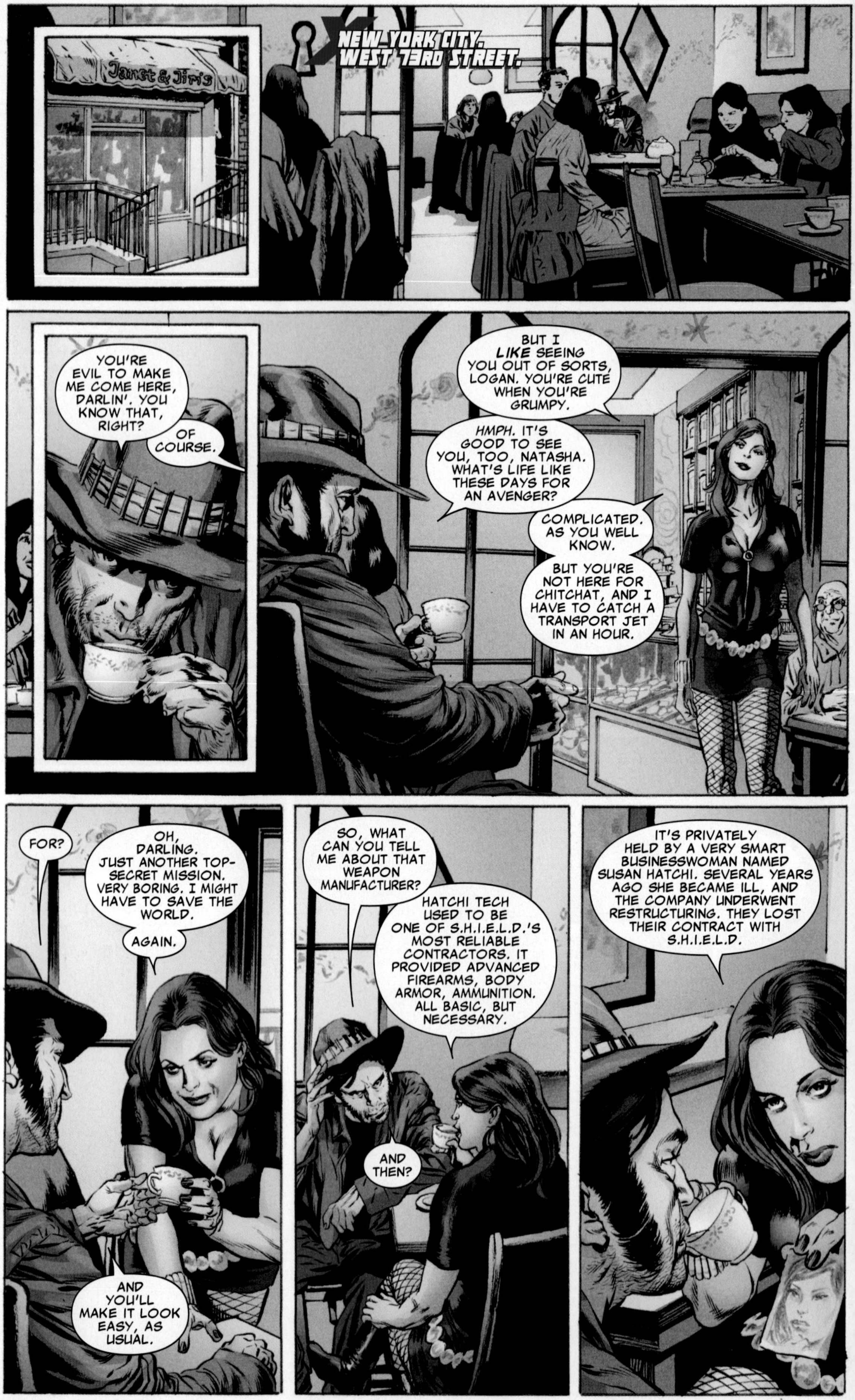
NEW YORK CITY.
WEST 73RD STREET.
Janet & Jiri's
YOU'RE EVIL TO MAKE ME COME HERE, DARLIN'. YOU KNOW THAT, RIGHT?
OF COURSE.
BUT I *LIKE* SEEING YOU OUT OF SORTS, LOGAN. YOU'RE CUTE WHEN YOU'RE GRUMPY.
HMPH. IT'S GOOD TO SEE YOU, TOO, NATASHA. WHAT'S LIFE LIKE THESE DAYS FOR AN AVENGER?
COMPLICATED. AS YOU WELL KNOW.
BUT YOU'RE NOT HERE FOR CHITCHAT, AND I HAVE TO CATCH A TRANSPORT JET IN AN HOUR.
FOR?
OH, DARLING. JUST ANOTHER TOP-SECRET MISSION. VERY BORING. I MIGHT HAVE TO SAVE THE WORLD.
AGAIN.
AND YOU'LL MAKE IT LOOK EASY, AS USUAL.
SO, WHAT CAN YOU TELL ME ABOUT THAT WEAPON MANUFACTURER?
HATCHI TECH USED TO BE ONE OF S.H.I.E.L.D.'S MOST RELIABLE CONTRACTORS. IT PROVIDED ADVANCED FIREARMS, BODY ARMOR, AMMUNITION. ALL BASIC, BUT NECESSARY.
AND THEN?
IT'S PRIVATELY HELD BY A VERY SMART BUSINESSWOMAN NAMED SUSAN HATCHI. SEVERAL YEARS AGO SHE BECAME ILL, AND THE COMPANY UNDERWENT RESTRUCTURING. THEY LOST THEIR CONTRACT WITH S.H.I.E.L.D.

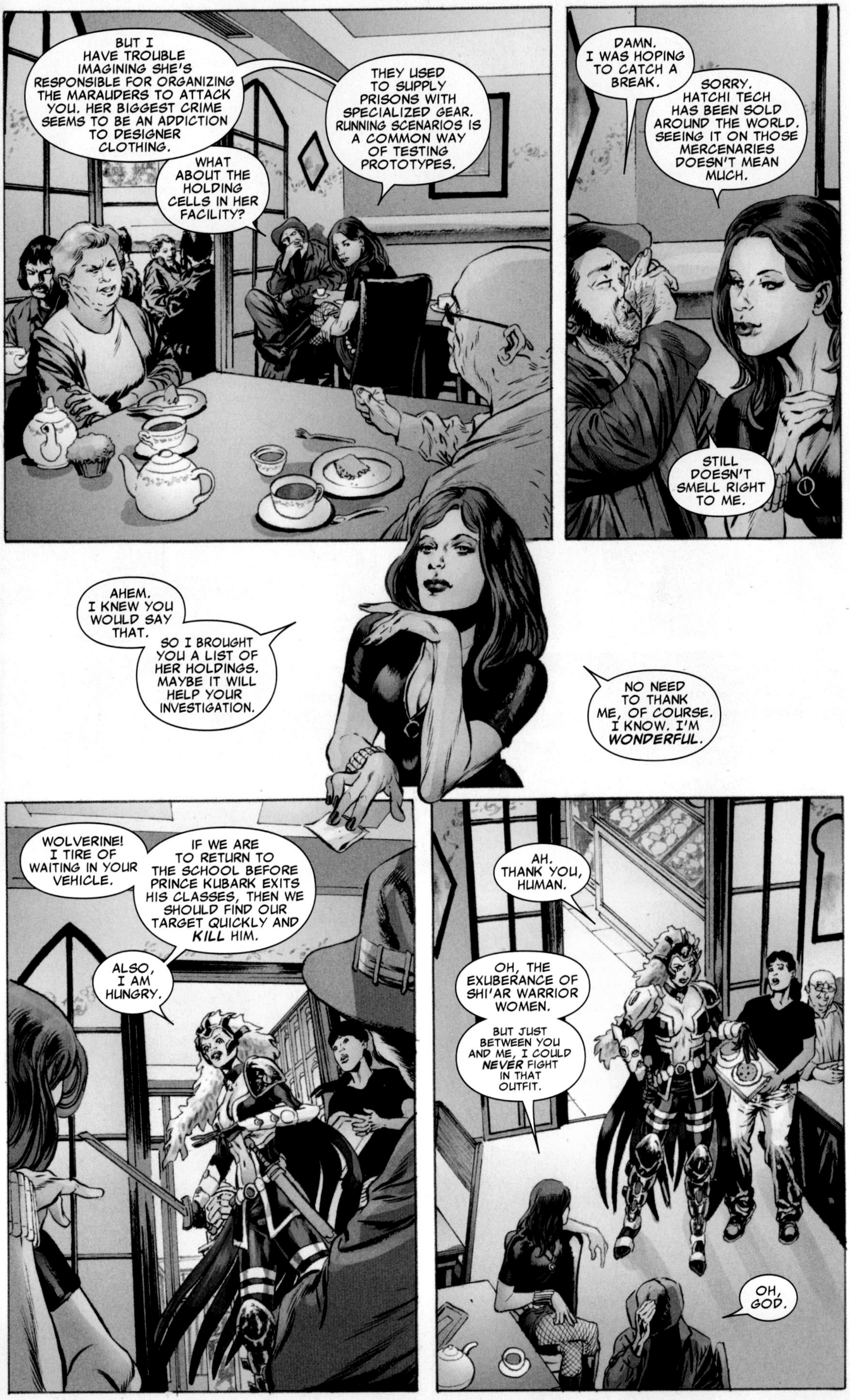

BUT I HAVE TROUBLE IMAGINING SHE'S RESPONSIBLE FOR ORGANIZING THE MARAUDERS TO ATTACK YOU. HER BIGGEST CRIME SEEMS TO BE AN ADDICTION TO DESIGNER CLOTHING.
WHAT ABOUT THE HOLDING CELLS IN HER FACILITY?
THEY USED TO SUPPLY PRISONS WITH SPECIALIZED GEAR. RUNNING SCENARIOS IS A COMMON WAY OF TESTING PROTOTYPES.
DAMN. I WAS HOPING TO CATCH A BREAK.
SORRY. HATCHI TECH HAS BEEN SOLD AROUND THE WORLD. SEEING IT ON THOSE MERCENARIES DOESN'T MEAN MUCH.
STILL DOESN'T SMELL RIGHT TO ME.
AHEM. I KNEW YOU WOULD SAY THAT.
SO I BROUGHT YOU A LIST OF HER HOLDINGS. MAYBE IT WILL HELP YOUR INVESTIGATION.
NO NEED TO THANK ME, OF COURSE. I KNOW. I'M ***WONDERFUL***.
WOLVERINE! I TIRE OF WAITING IN YOUR VEHICLE.
IF WE ARE TO RETURN TO THE SCHOOL BEFORE PRINCE KUBARK EXITS HIS CLASSES, THEN WE SHOULD FIND OUR TARGET QUICKLY AND ***KILL*** HIM.
ALSO, I AM HUNGRY.
AH. THANK YOU, HUMAN.
OH, THE EXUBERANCE OF SHI'AR WARRIOR WOMEN.
BUT JUST BETWEEN YOU AND ME, I COULD ***NEVER*** FIGHT IN THAT OUTFIT.
OH, GOD.

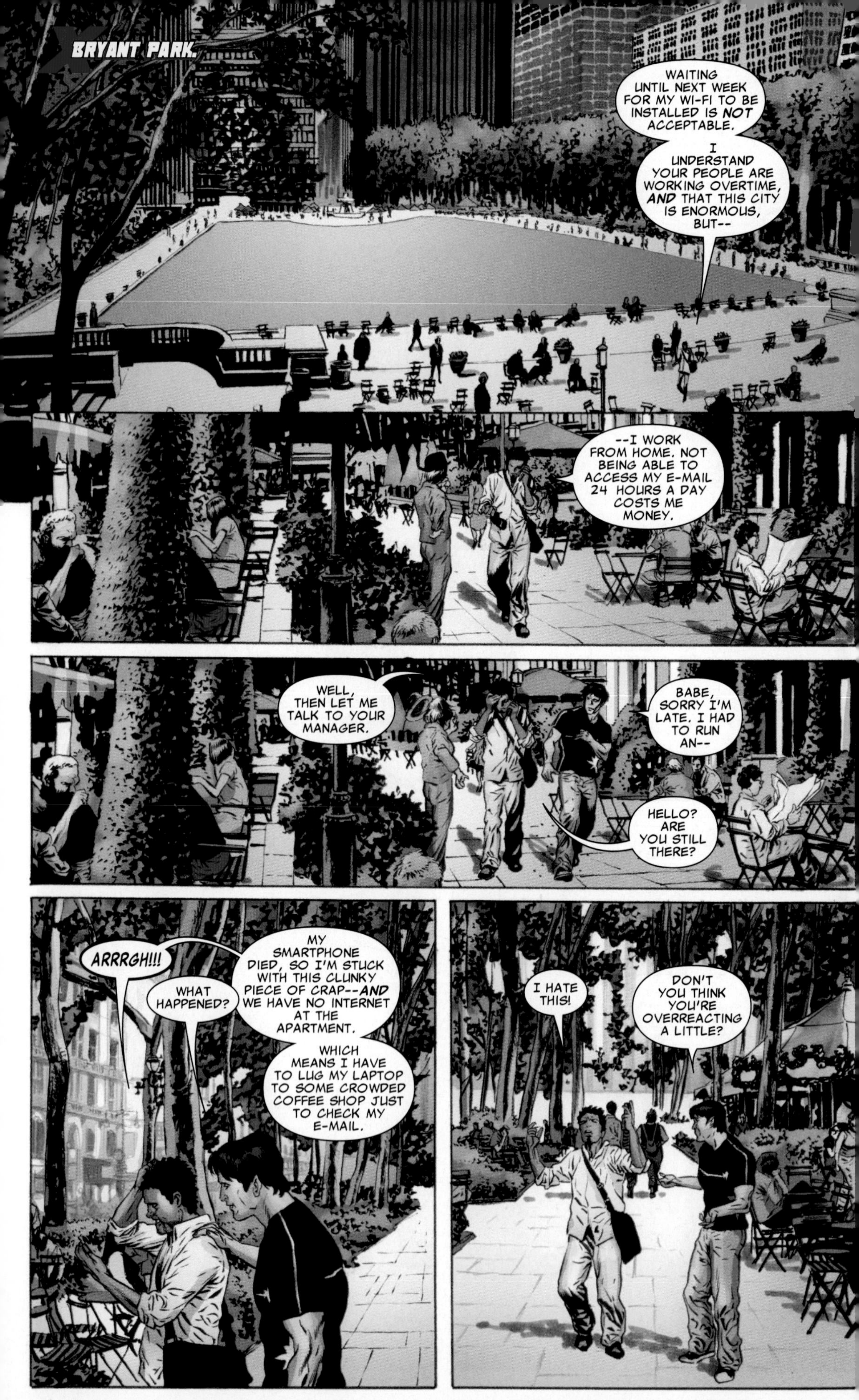
BRYANT PARK.
WAITING UNTIL NEXT WEEK FOR MY WI-FI TO BE INSTALLED IS NOT ACCEPTABLE.
I UNDERSTAND YOUR PEOPLE ARE WORKING OVERTIME, AND THAT THIS CITY IS ENORMOUS, BUT--
--I WORK FROM HOME. NOT BEING ABLE TO ACCESS MY E-MAIL 24 HOURS A DAY COSTS ME MONEY.
WELL, THEN LET ME TALK TO YOUR MANAGER.
BABE, SORRY I'M LATE. I HAD TO RUN AN--
HELLO? ARE YOU STILL THERE?
ARRRGH!!!
WHAT HAPPENED?
MY SMARTPHONE DIED, SO I'M STUCK WITH THIS CLUNKY PIECE OF CRAP--AND WE HAVE NO INTERNET AT THE APARTMENT.
WHICH MEANS I HAVE TO LUG MY LAPTOP TO SOME CROWDED COFFEE SHOP JUST TO CHECK MY E-MAIL.
I HATE THIS!
DON'T YOU THINK YOU'RE OVERREACTING A LITTLE?

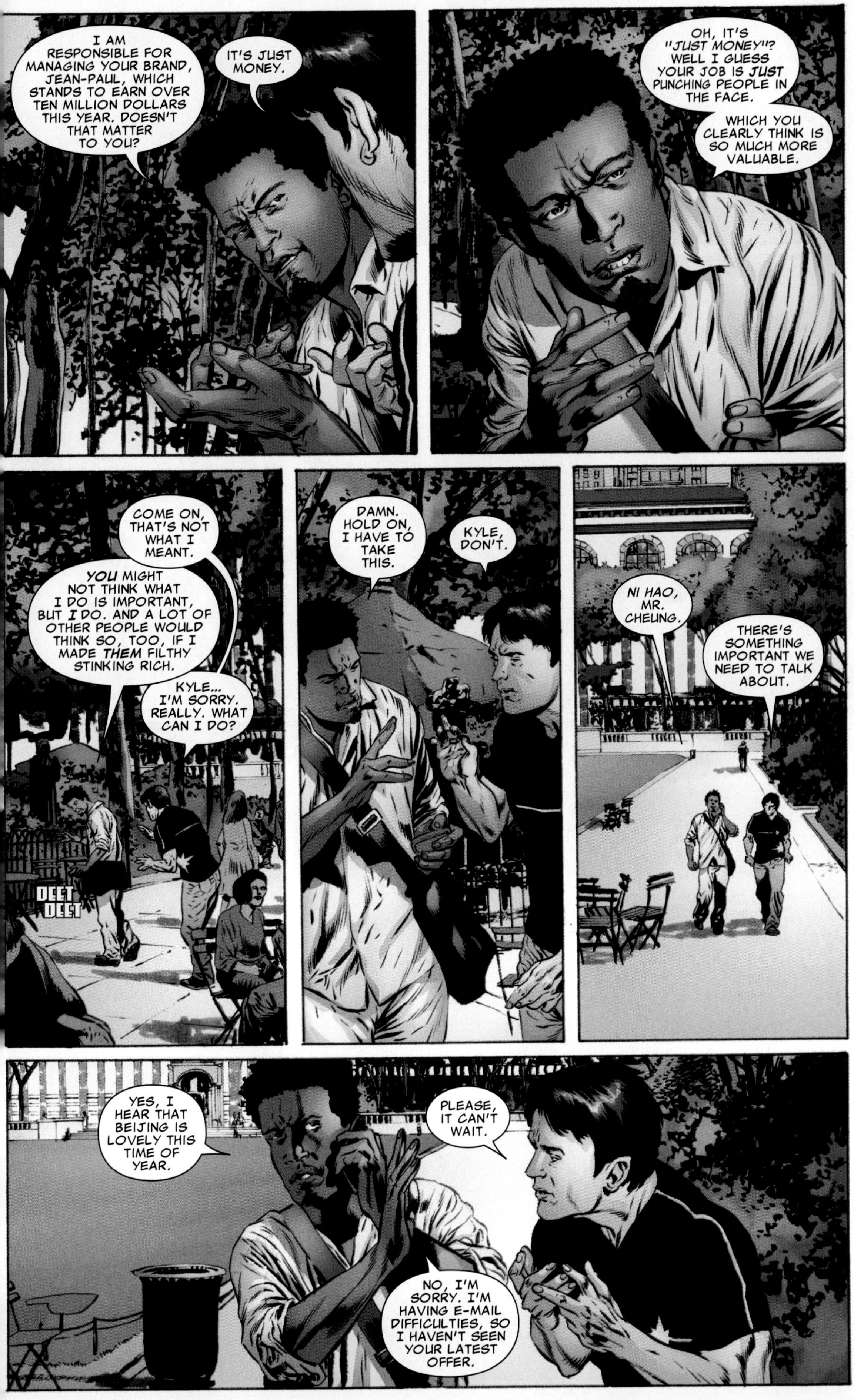
I AM RESPONSIBLE FOR MANAGING YOUR BRAND, JEAN-PAUL, WHICH STANDS TO EARN OVER TEN MILLION DOLLARS THIS YEAR. DOESN'T THAT MATTER TO YOU?
IT'S JUST MONEY.
OH, IT'S "JUST MONEY"? WELL I GUESS YOUR JOB IS JUST PUNCHING PEOPLE IN THE FACE.
WHICH YOU CLEARLY THINK IS SO MUCH MORE VALUABLE.
COME ON, THAT'S NOT WHAT I MEANT.
YOU MIGHT NOT THINK WHAT I DO IS IMPORTANT, BUT I DO. AND A LOT OF OTHER PEOPLE WOULD THINK SO, TOO, IF I MADE THEM FILTHY STINKING RICH.
KYLE... I'M SORRY. REALLY. WHAT CAN I DO?
DEET DEET
DAMN. HOLD ON, I HAVE TO TAKE THIS.
KYLE, DON'T.
NI HAO, MR. CHEUNG.
THERE'S SOMETHING IMPORTANT WE NEED TO TALK ABOUT.
YES, I HEAR THAT BEIJING IS LOVELY THIS TIME OF YEAR.
PLEASE, IT CAN'T WAIT.
NO, I'M SORRY. I'M HAVING E-MAIL DIFFICULTIES, SO I HAVEN'T SEEN YOUR LATEST OFFER.

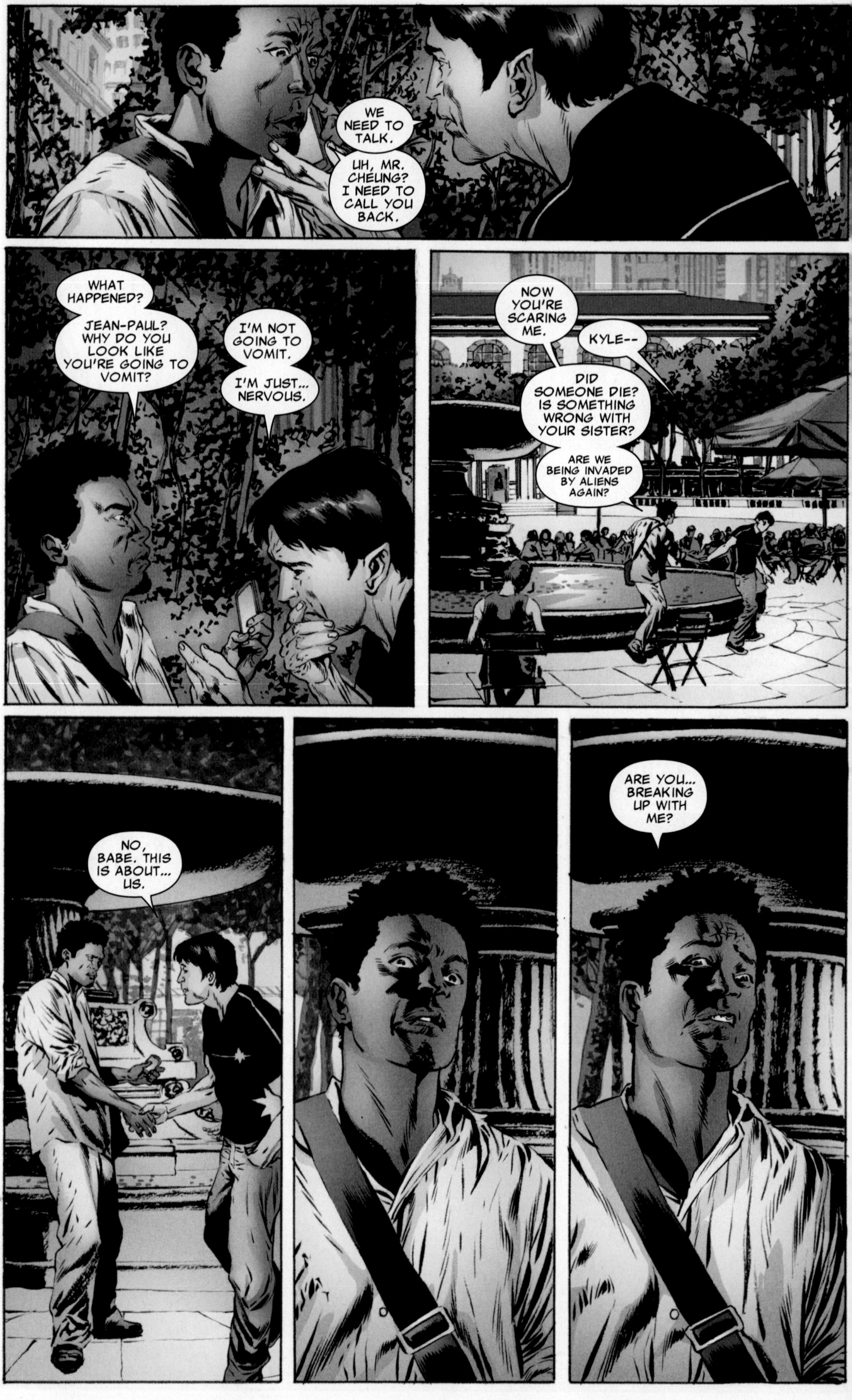
WE NEED TO TALK.
UH, MR. CHEUNG? I NEED TO CALL YOU BACK.
WHAT HAPPENED?
JEAN-PAUL? WHY DO YOU LOOK LIKE YOU'RE GOING TO VOMIT?
I'M NOT GOING TO VOMIT.
I'M JUST... NERVOUS.
NOW YOU'RE SCARING ME.
KYLE--
DID SOMEONE DIE? IS SOMETHING WRONG WITH YOUR SISTER?
ARE WE BEING INVADED BY ALIENS AGAIN?
NO, BABE. THIS IS ABOUT... US.
ARE YOU... BREAKING UP WITH ME?

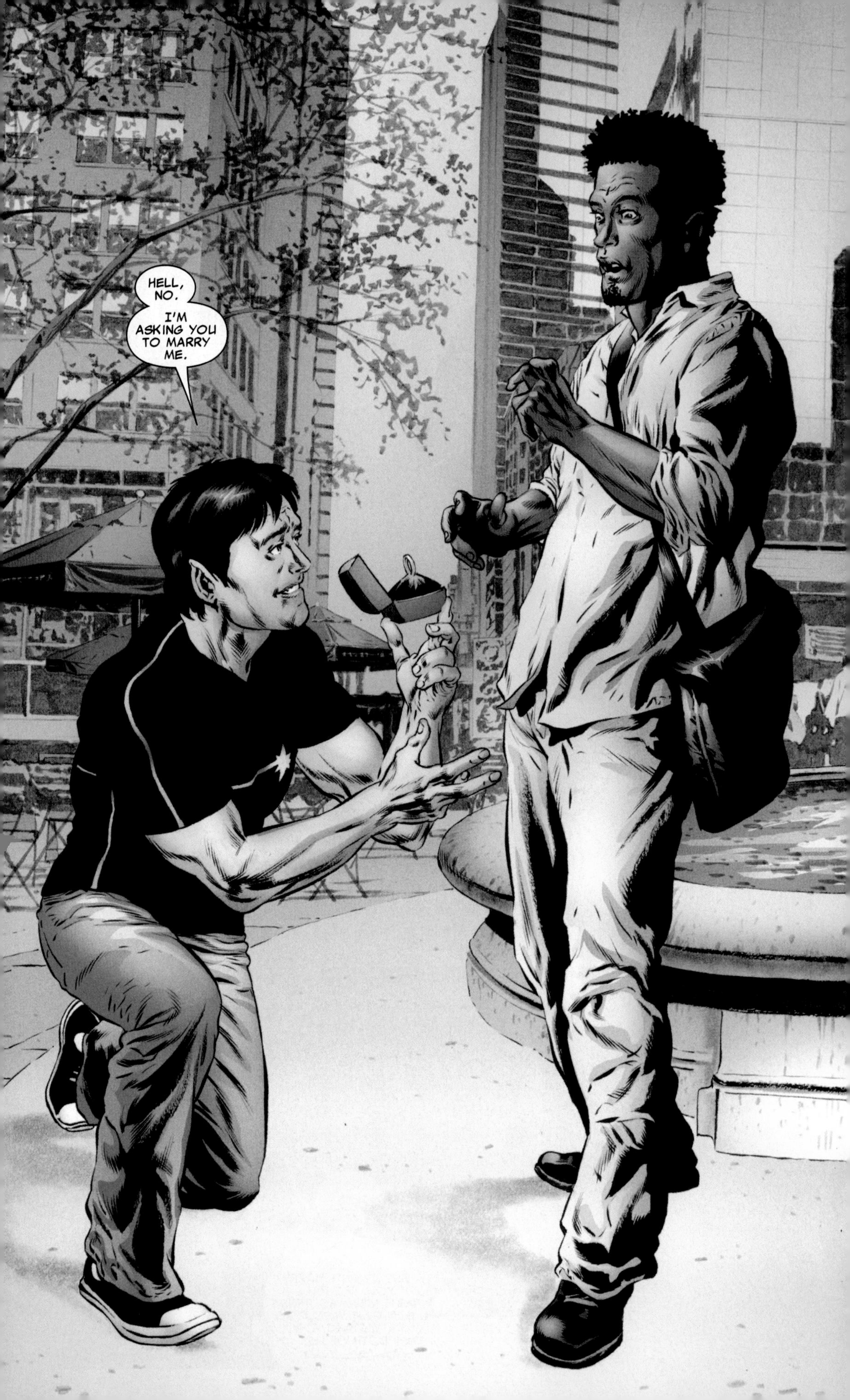
HELL, NO.
I'M ASKING YOU TO MARRY ME.

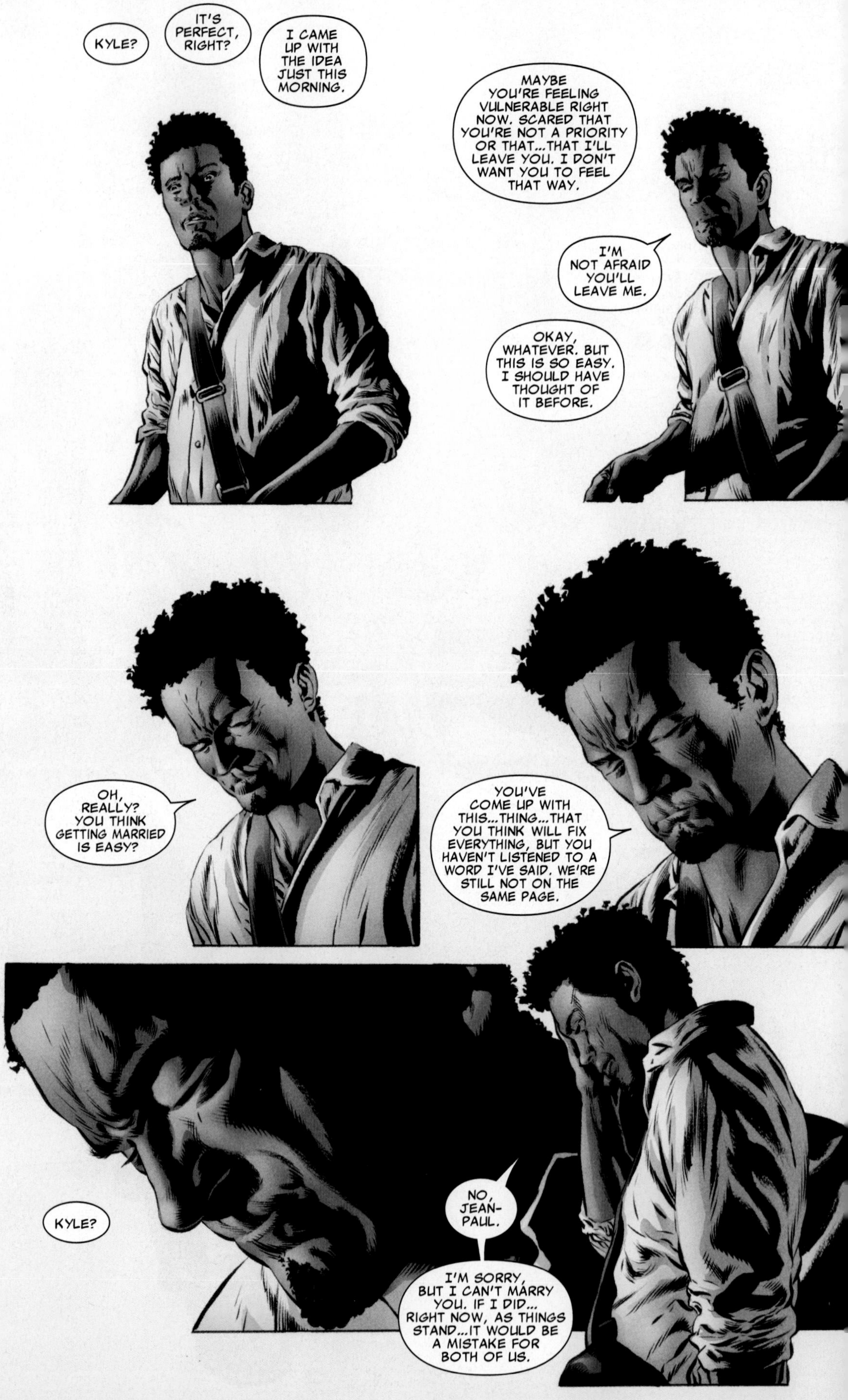
KYLE?
IT'S PERFECT, RIGHT?
I CAME UP WITH THE IDEA JUST THIS MORNING.
MAYBE YOU'RE FEELING VULNERABLE RIGHT NOW. SCARED THAT YOU'RE NOT A PRIORITY OR THAT...THAT I'LL LEAVE YOU. I DON'T WANT YOU TO FEEL THAT WAY.
I'M NOT AFRAID YOU'LL LEAVE ME.
OKAY, WHATEVER. BUT THIS IS SO EASY. I SHOULD HAVE THOUGHT OF IT BEFORE.
OH, REALLY? YOU THINK GETTING MARRIED IS EASY?
YOU'VE COME UP WITH THIS...THING...THAT YOU THINK WILL FIX EVERYTHING, BUT YOU HAVEN'T LISTENED TO A WORD I'VE SAID. WE'RE STILL NOT ON THE SAME PAGE.
KYLE?
NO, JEAN-PAUL.
I'M SORRY, BUT I CAN'T MARRY YOU. IF I DID... RIGHT NOW, AS THINGS STAND...IT WOULD BE A MISTAKE FOR BOTH OF US.

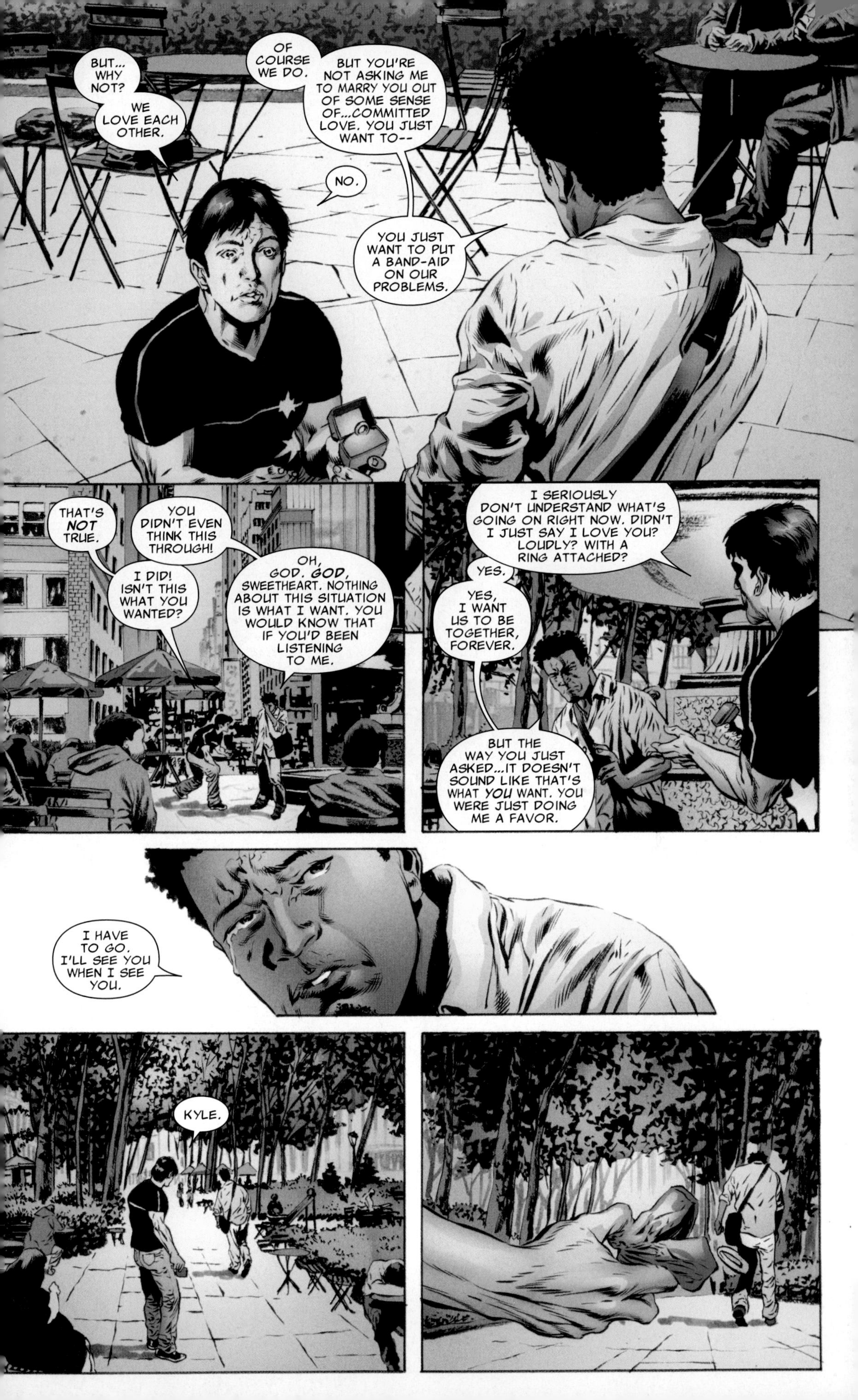
BUT... WHY NOT?
WE LOVE EACH OTHER.
OF COURSE WE DO.
BUT YOU'RE NOT ASKING ME TO MARRY YOU OUT OF SOME SENSE OF...COMMITTED LOVE. YOU JUST WANT TO--
NO.
YOU JUST WANT TO PUT A BAND-AID ON OUR PROBLEMS.
THAT'S NOT TRUE.
YOU DIDN'T EVEN THINK THIS THROUGH!
I DID! ISN'T THIS WHAT YOU WANTED?
OH, GOD. GOD, SWEETHEART. NOTHING ABOUT THIS SITUATION IS WHAT I WANT. YOU WOULD KNOW THAT IF YOU'D BEEN LISTENING TO ME.
I SERIOUSLY DON'T UNDERSTAND WHAT'S GOING ON RIGHT NOW. DIDN'T I JUST SAY I LOVE YOU? LOUDLY? WITH A RING ATTACHED?
YES.
YES, I WANT US TO BE TOGETHER, FOREVER.
BUT THE WAY YOU JUST ASKED...IT DOESN'T SOUND LIKE THAT'S WHAT YOU WANT. YOU WERE JUST DOING ME A FAVOR.
I HAVE TO GO. I'LL SEE YOU WHEN I SEE YOU.
KYLE.

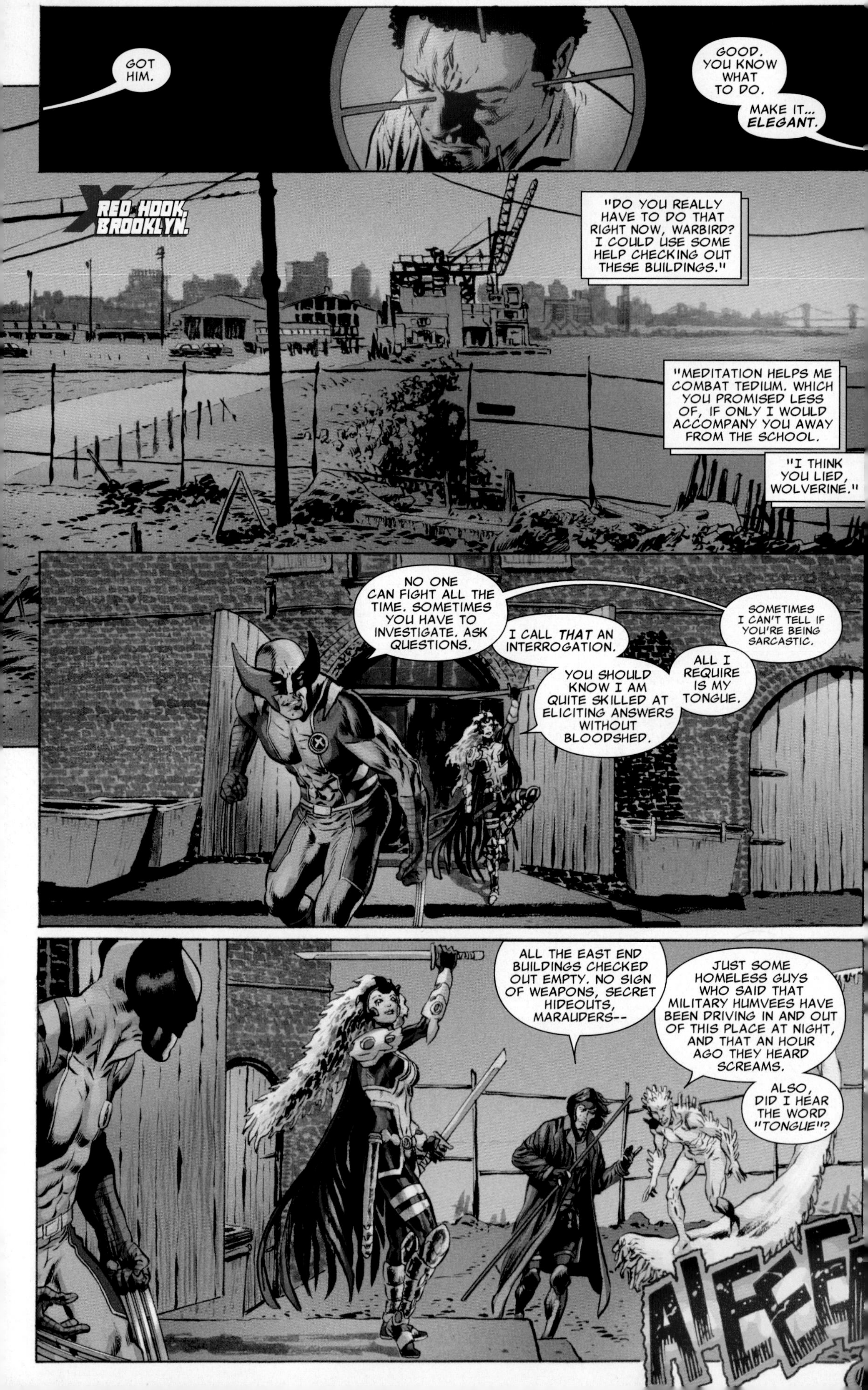
GOT HIM.
GOOD. YOU KNOW WHAT TO DO.
MAKE IT... ELEGANT.
RED HOOK, BROOKLYN.
"DO YOU REALLY HAVE TO DO THAT RIGHT NOW, WARBIRD? I COULD USE SOME HELP CHECKING OUT THESE BUILDINGS."
"MEDITATION HELPS ME COMBAT TEDIUM. WHICH YOU PROMISED LESS OF, IF ONLY I WOULD ACCOMPANY YOU AWAY FROM THE SCHOOL.
"I THINK YOU LIED, WOLVERINE."
NO ONE CAN FIGHT ALL THE TIME. SOMETIMES YOU HAVE TO INVESTIGATE. ASK QUESTIONS.
I CALL THAT AN INTERROGATION.
YOU SHOULD KNOW I AM QUITE SKILLED AT ELICITING ANSWERS WITHOUT BLOODSHED.
ALL I REQUIRE IS MY TONGUE.
SOMETIMES I CAN'T TELL IF YOU'RE BEING SARCASTIC.
ALL THE EAST END BUILDINGS CHECKED OUT EMPTY. NO SIGN OF WEAPONS, SECRET HIDEOUTS, MARAUDERS--
JUST SOME HOMELESS GUYS WHO SAID THAT MILITARY HUMVEES HAVE BEEN DRIVING IN AND OUT OF THIS PLACE AT NIGHT, AND THAT AN HOUR AGO THEY HEARD SCREAMS.
ALSO, DID I HEAR THE WORD "TONGUE"?
AIEEE

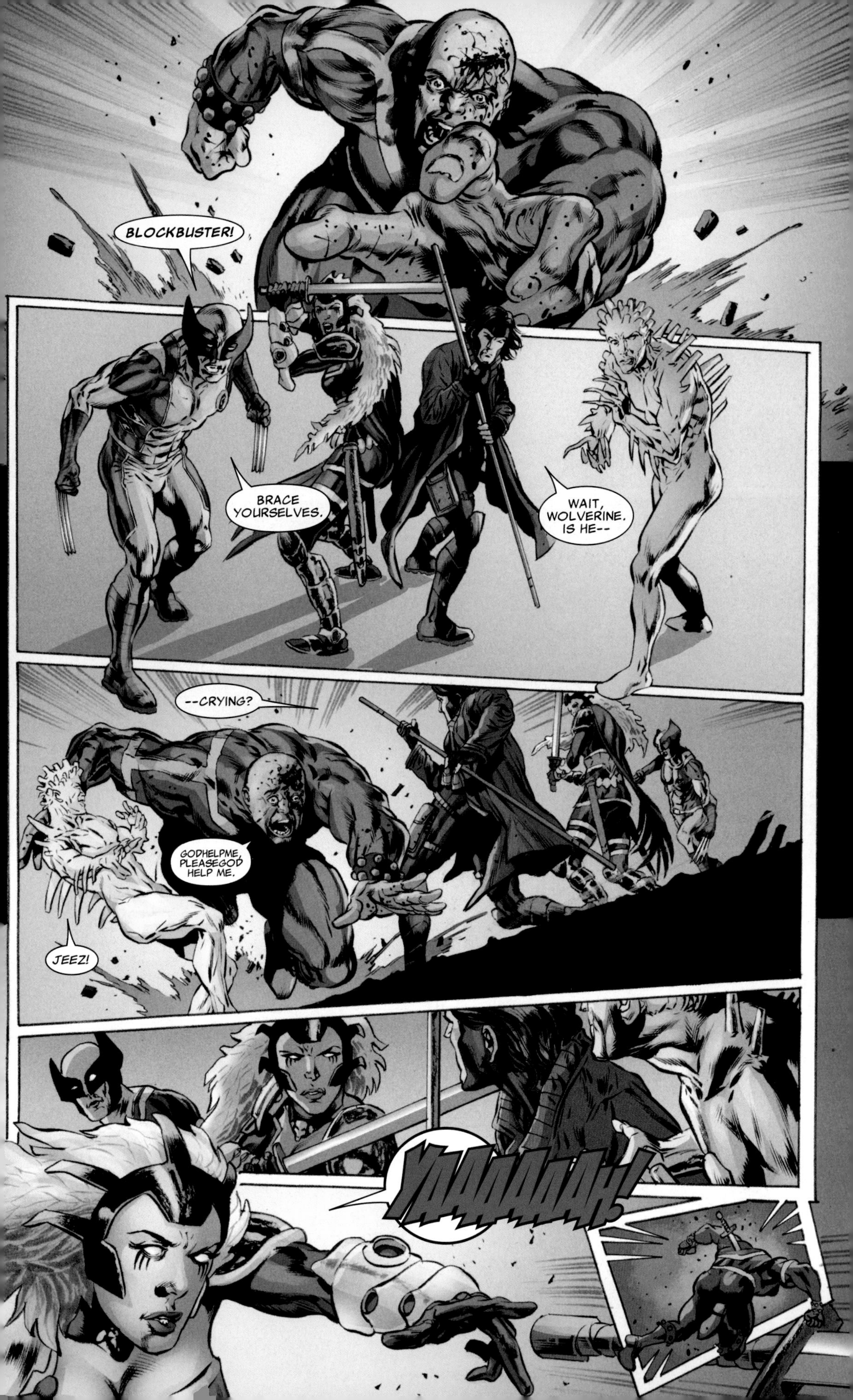
BLOCKBUSTER!
BRACE YOURSELVES.
WAIT, WOLVERINE. IS HE--
--CRYING?
GODHELPME, PLEASEGOD HELP ME.
JEEZ!
YAAAAAAH!

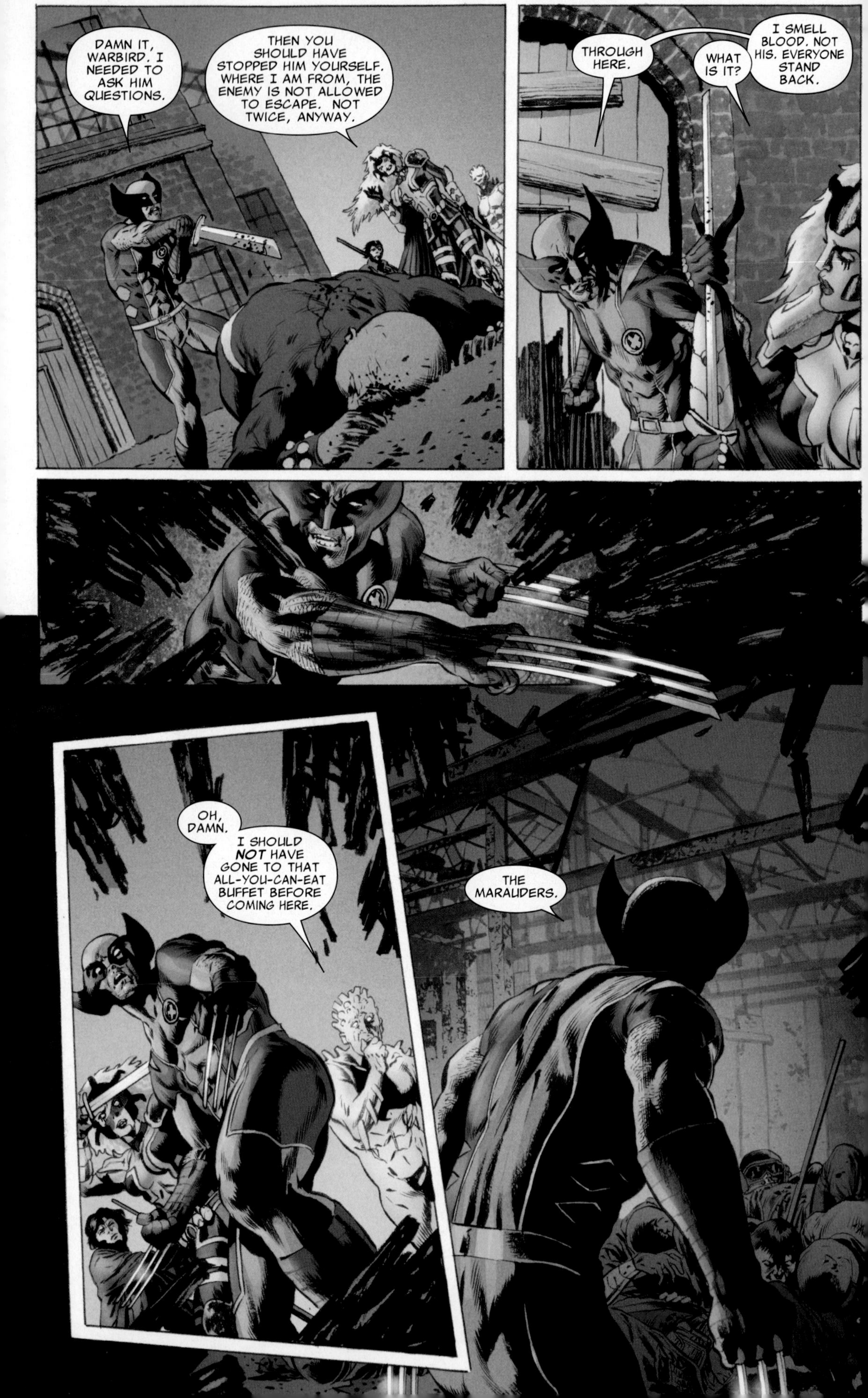
DAMN IT, WARBIRD. I NEEDED TO ASK HIM QUESTIONS.
THEN YOU SHOULD HAVE STOPPED HIM YOURSELF. WHERE I AM FROM, THE ENEMY IS NOT ALLOWED TO ESCAPE. NOT TWICE, ANYWAY.
THROUGH HERE.
WHAT IS IT?
I SMELL BLOOD. NOT HIS. EVERYONE STAND BACK.
OH, DAMN.
I SHOULD NOT HAVE GONE TO THAT ALL-YOU-CAN-EAT BUFFET BEFORE COMING HERE.
THE MARAUDERS.

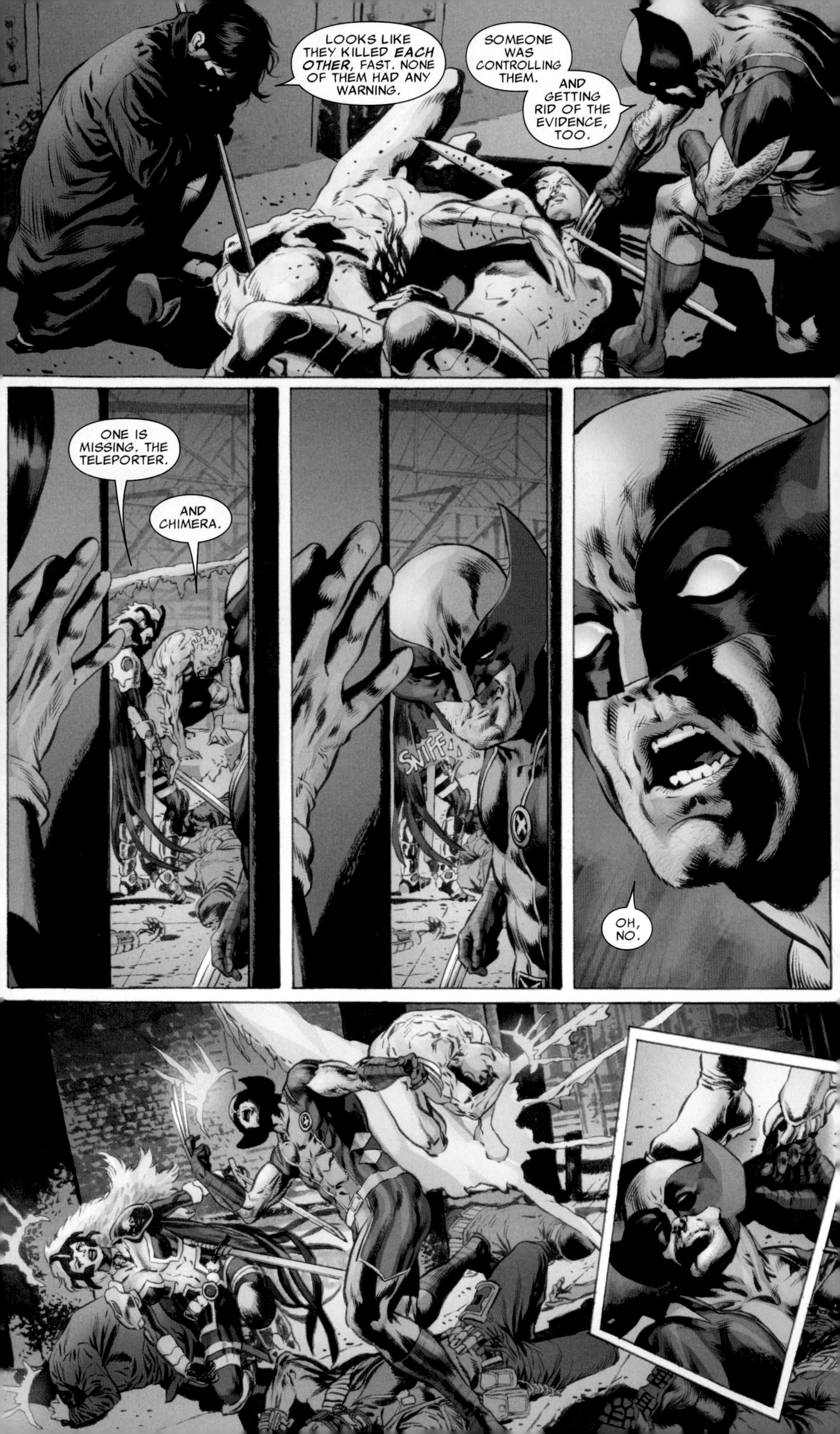
LOOKS LIKE THEY KILLED EACH OTHER, FAST. NONE OF THEM HAD ANY WARNING.
SOMEONE WAS CONTROLLING THEM.
AND GETTING RID OF THE EVIDENCE, TOO.
ONE IS MISSING. THE TELEPORTER.
AND CHIMERA.
SNIFF
OH, NO.

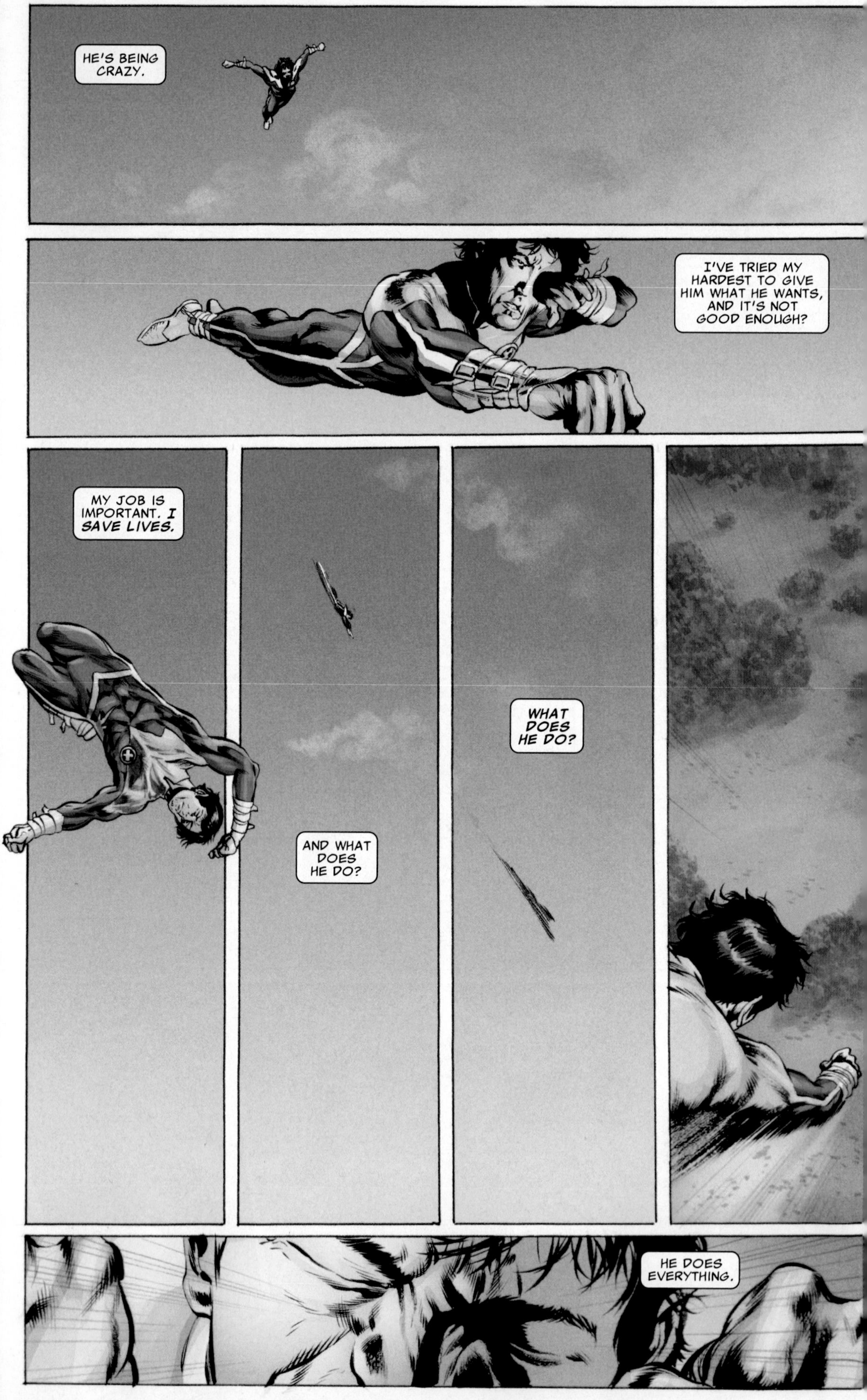
HE'S BEING CRAZY.
I'VE TRIED MY HARDEST TO GIVE HIM WHAT HE WANTS, AND IT'S NOT GOOD ENOUGH?
MY JOB IS IMPORTANT. I SAVE LIVES.
AND WHAT DOES HE DO?
WHAT DOES HE DO?
HE DOES EVERYTHING.

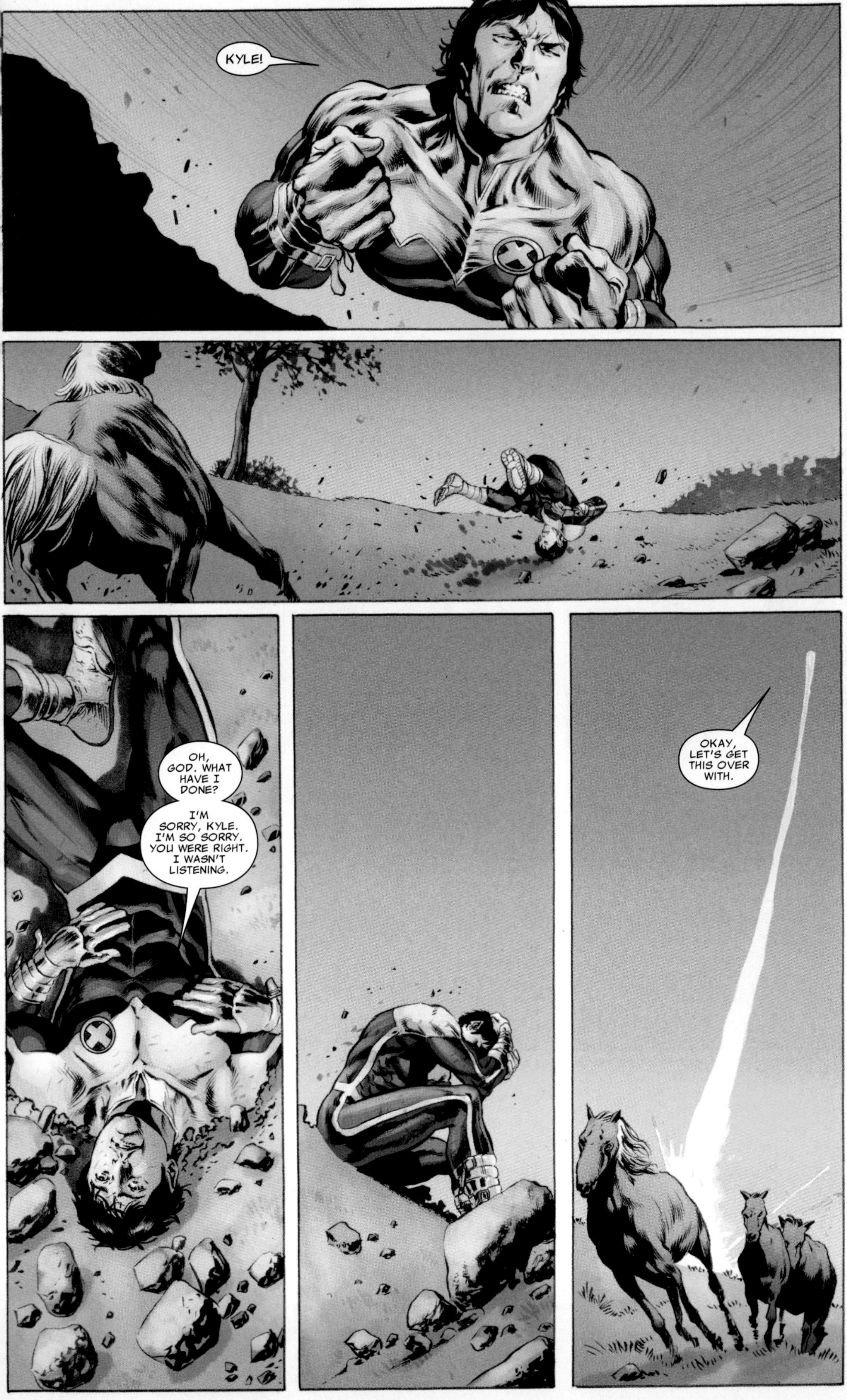
KYLE!
OH, GOD. WHAT HAVE I DONE?
I'M SORRY, KYLE. I'M SO SORRY. YOU WERE RIGHT. I WASN'T LISTENING.
OKAY, LET'S GET THIS OVER WITH.

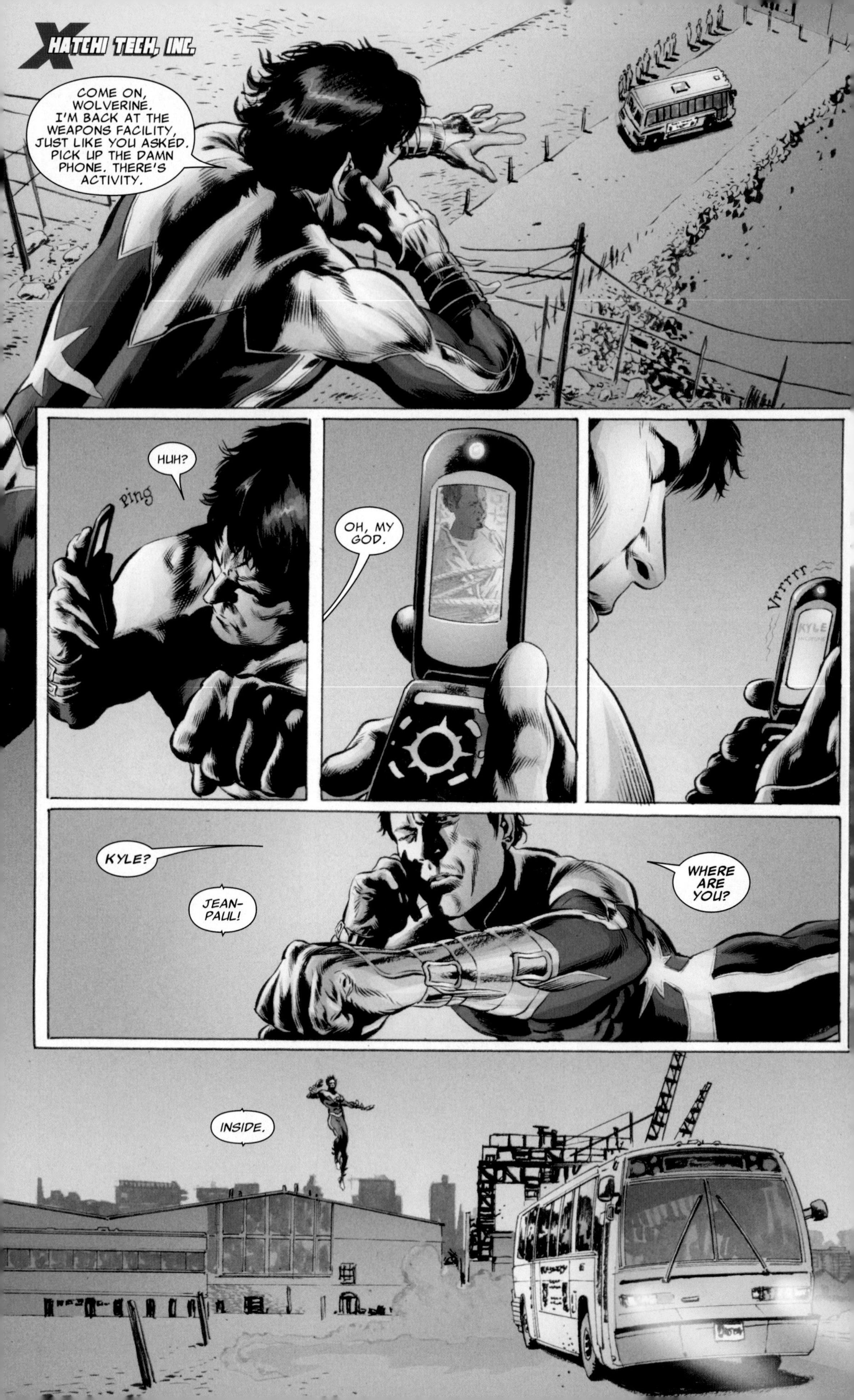
HATCHI TECH, INC.
COME ON, WOLVERINE. I'M BACK AT THE WEAPONS FACILITY, JUST LIKE YOU ASKED. PICK UP THE DAMN PHONE. THERE'S ACTIVITY.
HUH?
Ping
OH, MY GOD.
Vrrrrr
KYLE
KYLE?
JEAN-PAUL!
WHERE ARE YOU?
INSIDE.

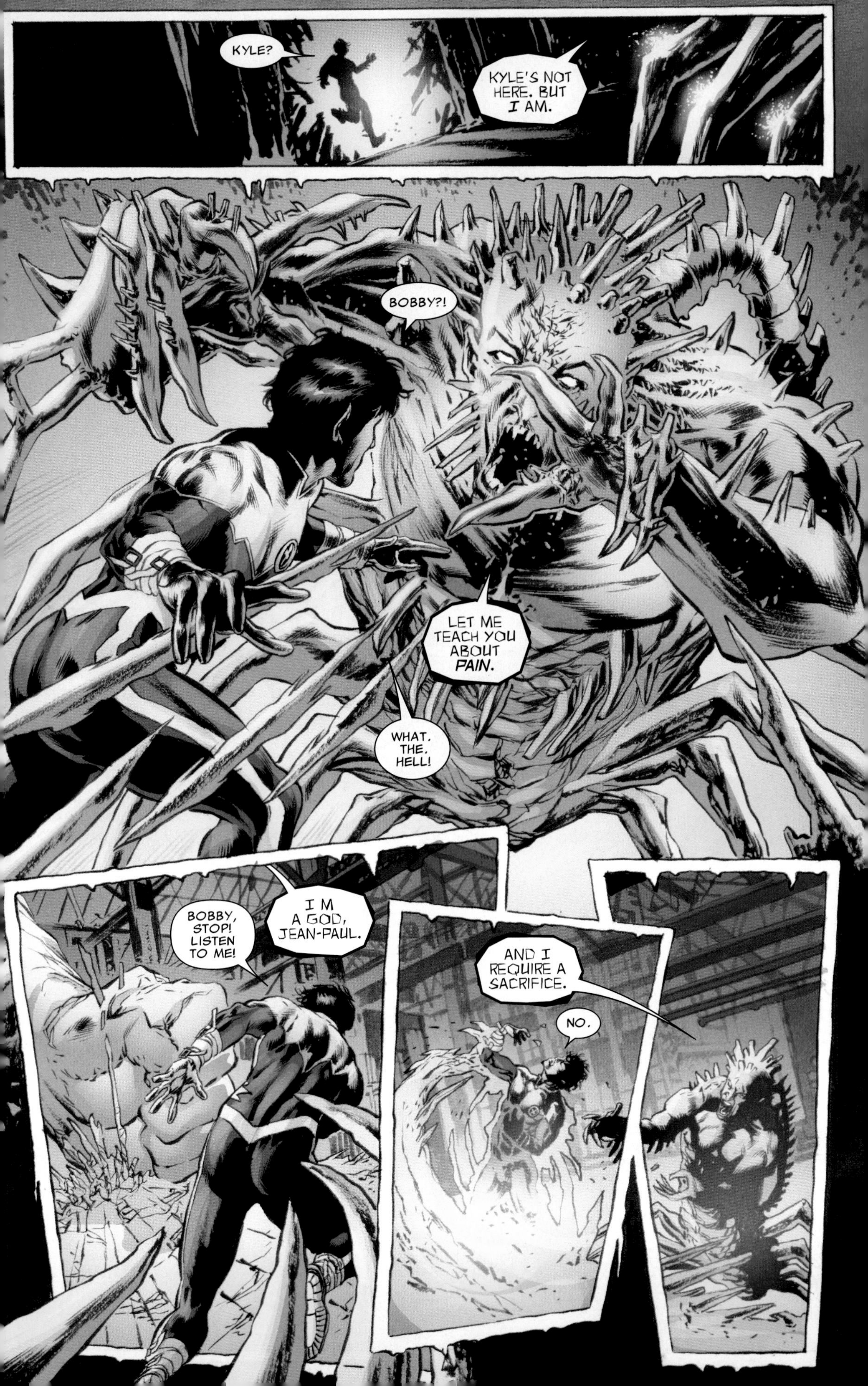
KYLE?
KYLE'S NOT HERE. BUT I AM.
BOBBY?!
LET ME TEACH YOU ABOUT PAIN.
WHAT. THE. HELL!
BOBBY, STOP! LISTEN TO ME!
I M A GOD, JEAN-PAUL.
AND I REQUIRE A SACRIFICE.
NO.

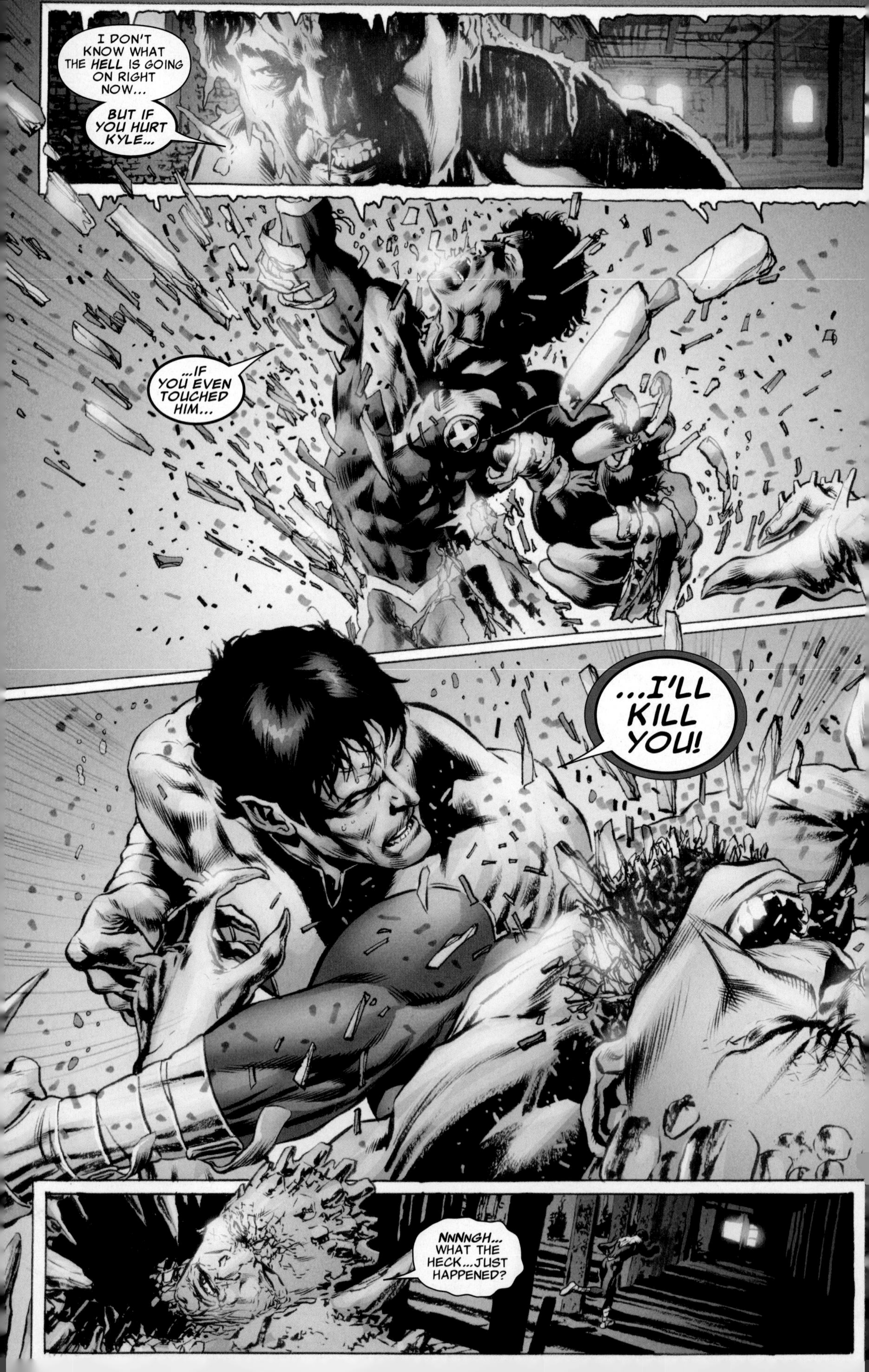

I DON'T KNOW WHAT THE HELL IS GOING ON RIGHT NOW...
BUT IF YOU HURT KYLE...
...IF YOU EVEN TOUCHED HIM...
...I'LL KILL YOU!
NNNNGH... WHAT THE HECK...JUST HAPPENED?

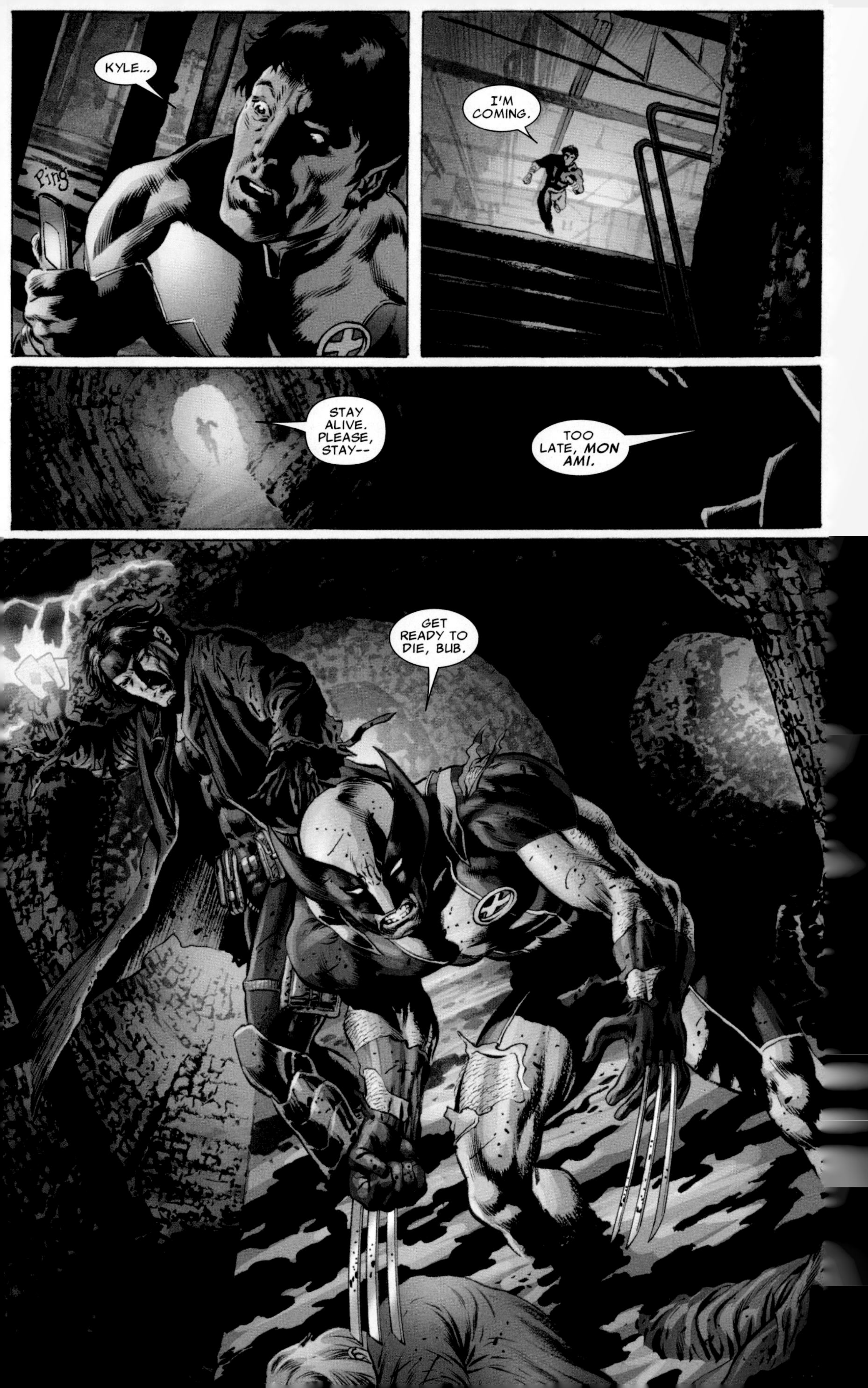
KYLE...
PING
I'M COMING.
STAY ALIVE. PLEASE, STAY--
TOO LATE, MON AMI.
GET READY TO DIE, BUB.

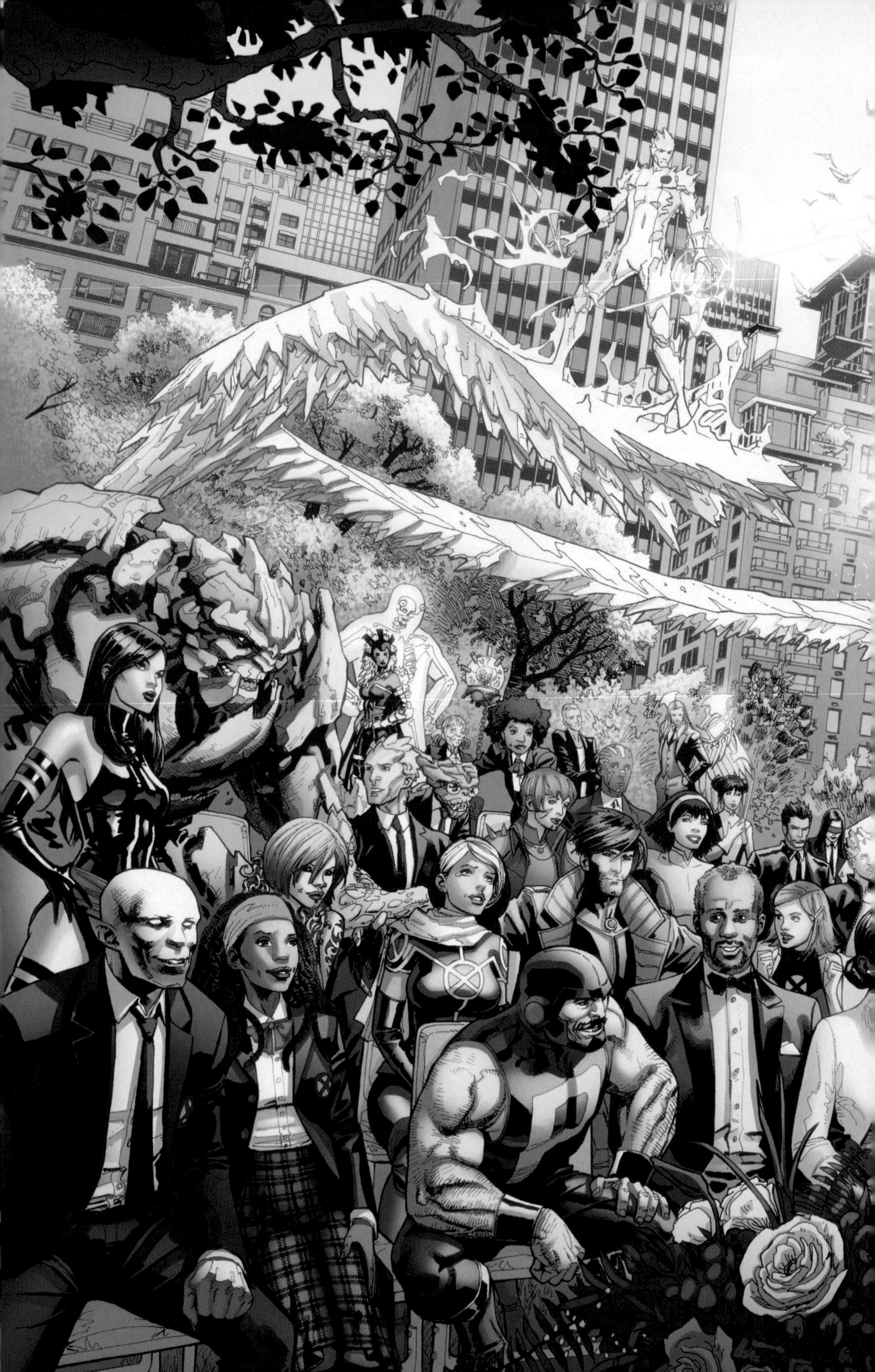

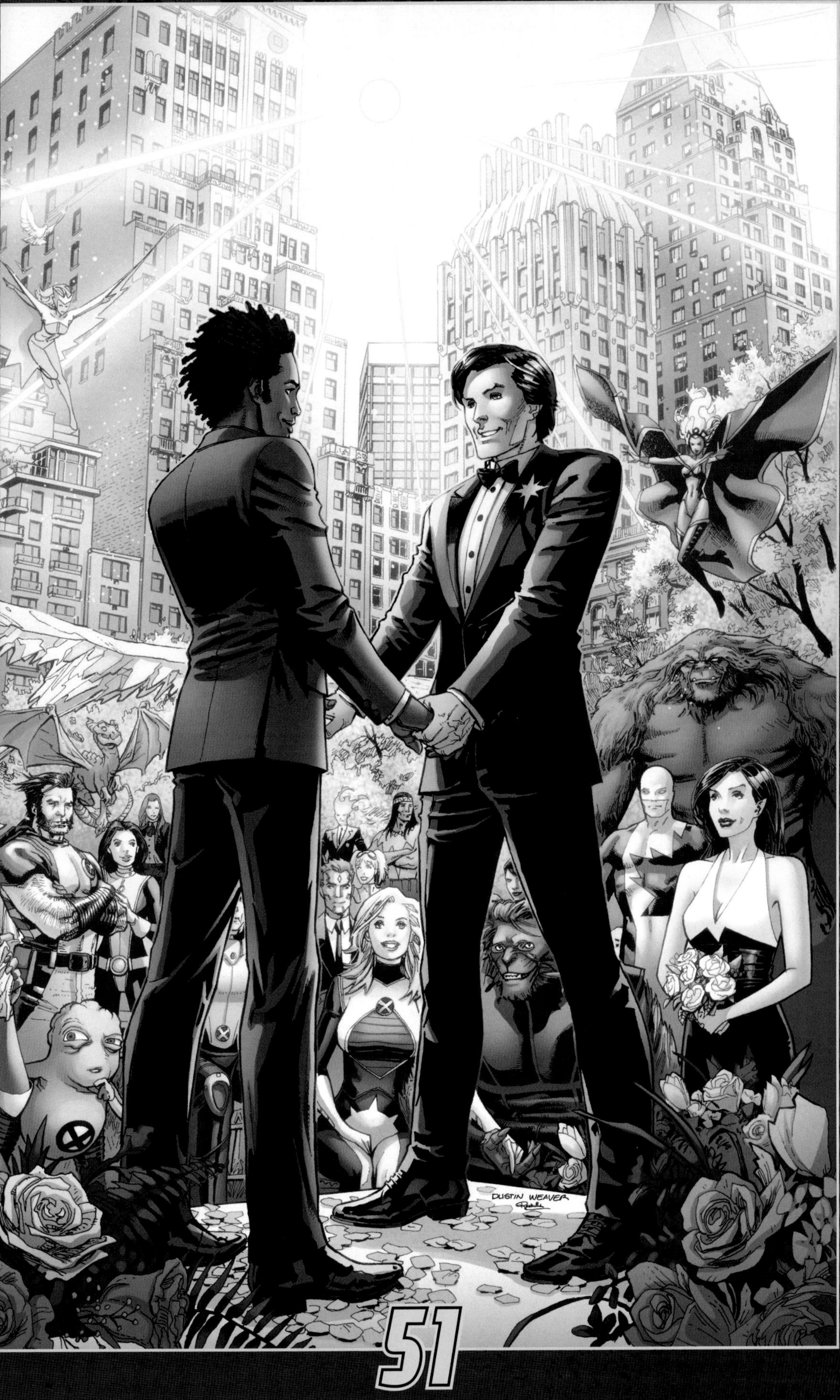
DUSTIN WEAVER
51

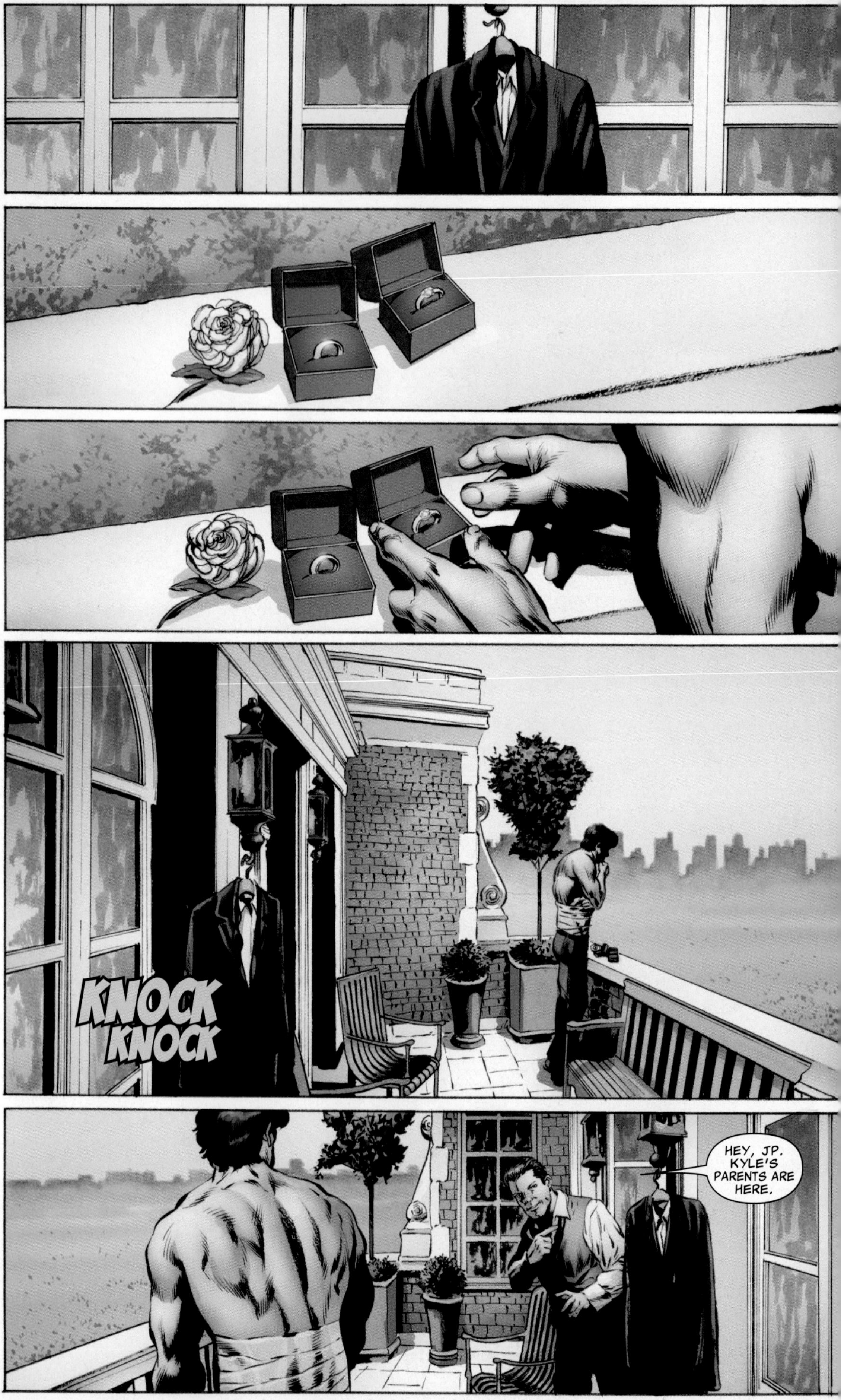
KNOCK
KNOCK
HEY, JP. KYLE'S PARENTS ARE HERE.

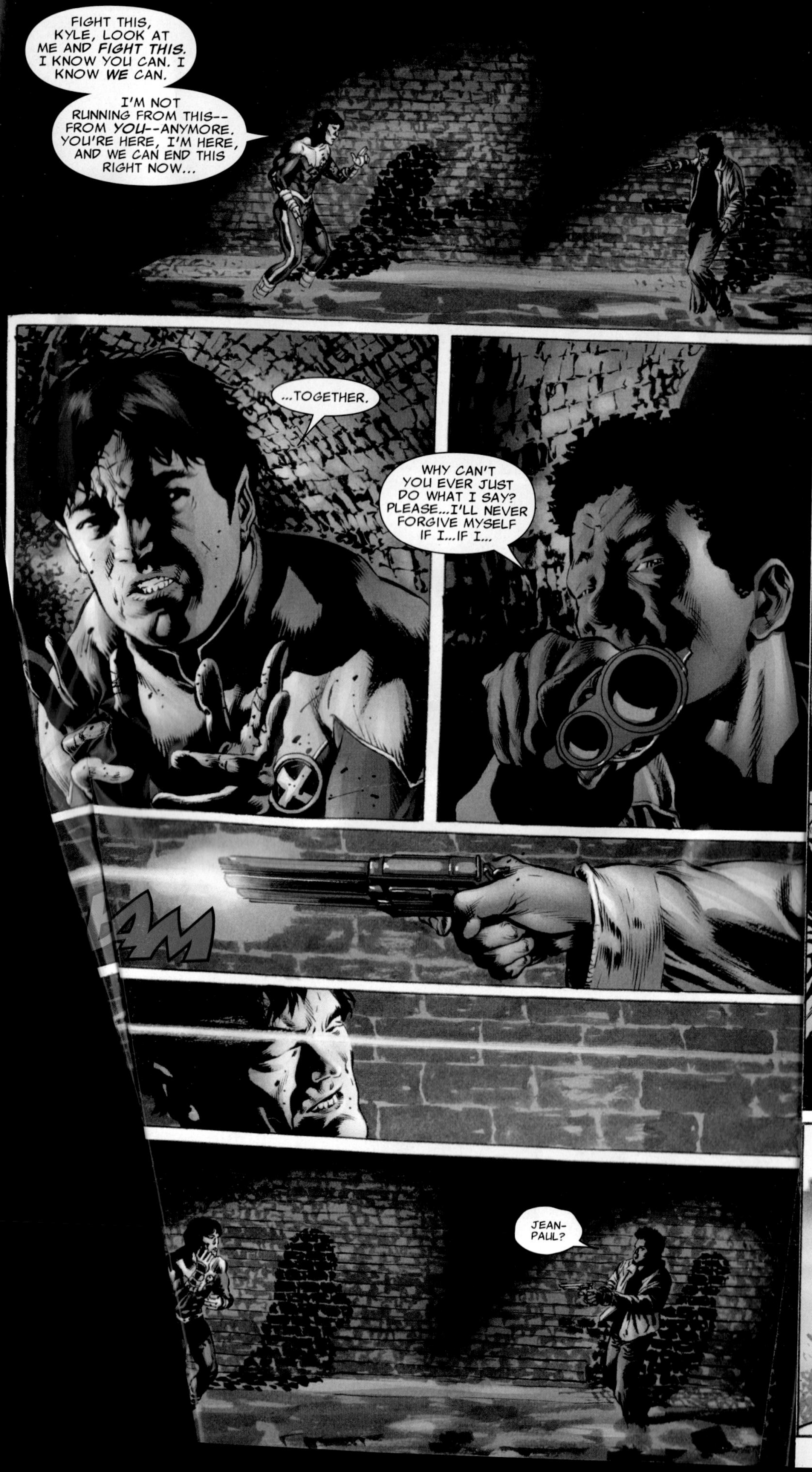

FIGHT THIS, KYLE, LOOK AT ME AND FIGHT THIS. I KNOW YOU CAN. I KNOW WE CAN.
I'M NOT RUNNING FROM THIS--FROM YOU--ANYMORE. YOU'RE HERE, I'M HERE, AND WE CAN END THIS RIGHT NOW...
...TOGETHER.
WHY CAN'T YOU EVER JUST DO WHAT I SAY? PLEASE...I'LL NEVER FORGIVE MYSELF IF I...IF I...
JEAN-PAUL?

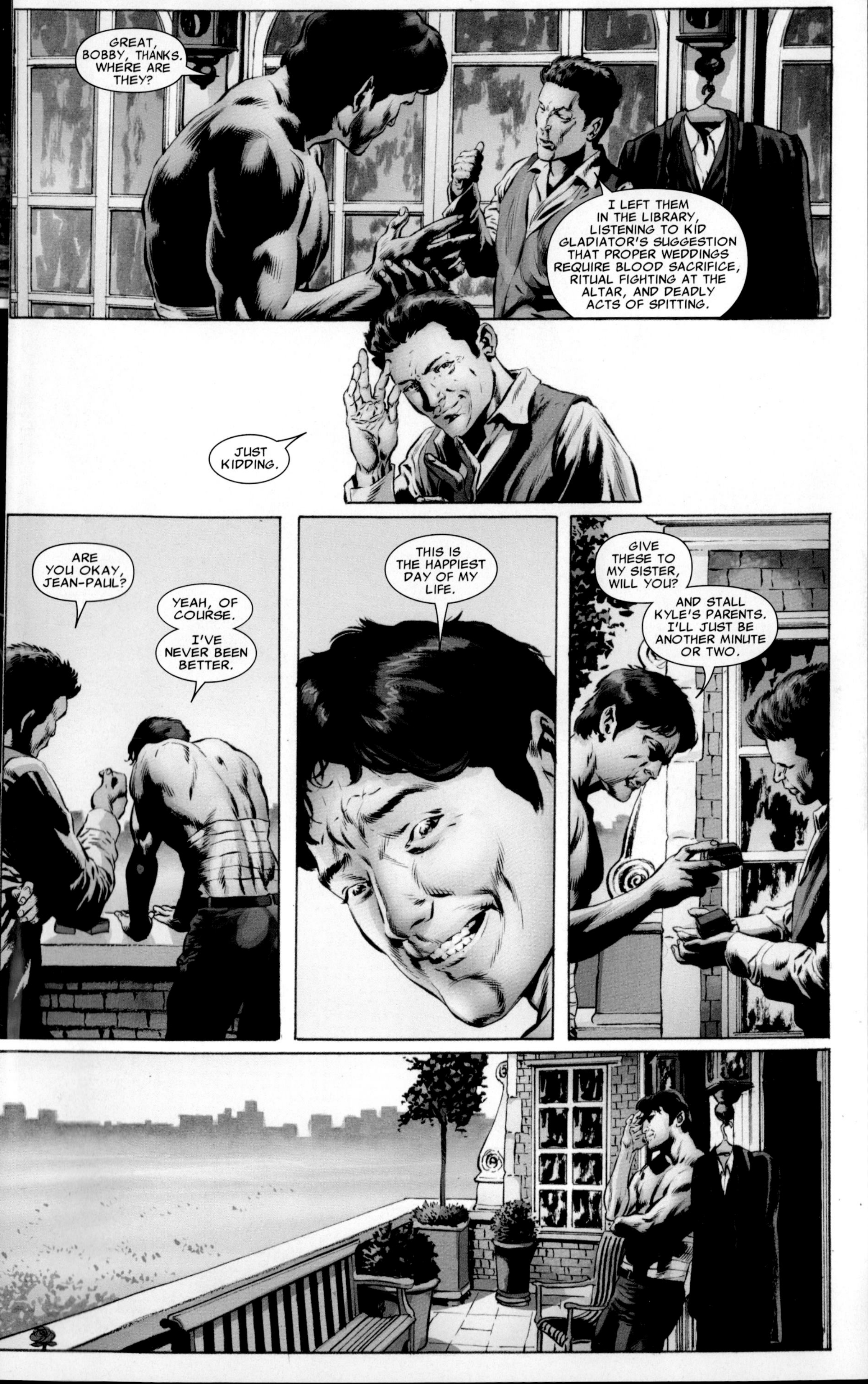

GREAT, BOBBY, THANKS. WHERE ARE THEY?
I LEFT THEM IN THE LIBRARY, LISTENING TO KID GLADIATOR'S SUGGESTION THAT PROPER WEDDINGS REQUIRE BLOOD SACRIFICE, RITUAL FIGHTING AT THE ALTAR, AND DEADLY ACTS OF SPITTING.
JUST KIDDING.
ARE YOU OKAY, JEAN-PAUL?
YEAH, OF COURSE.
I'VE NEVER BEEN BETTER.
THIS IS THE HAPPIEST DAY OF MY LIFE.
GIVE THESE TO MY SISTER, WILL YOU?
AND STALL KYLE'S PARENTS. I'LL JUST BE ANOTHER MINUTE OR TWO.

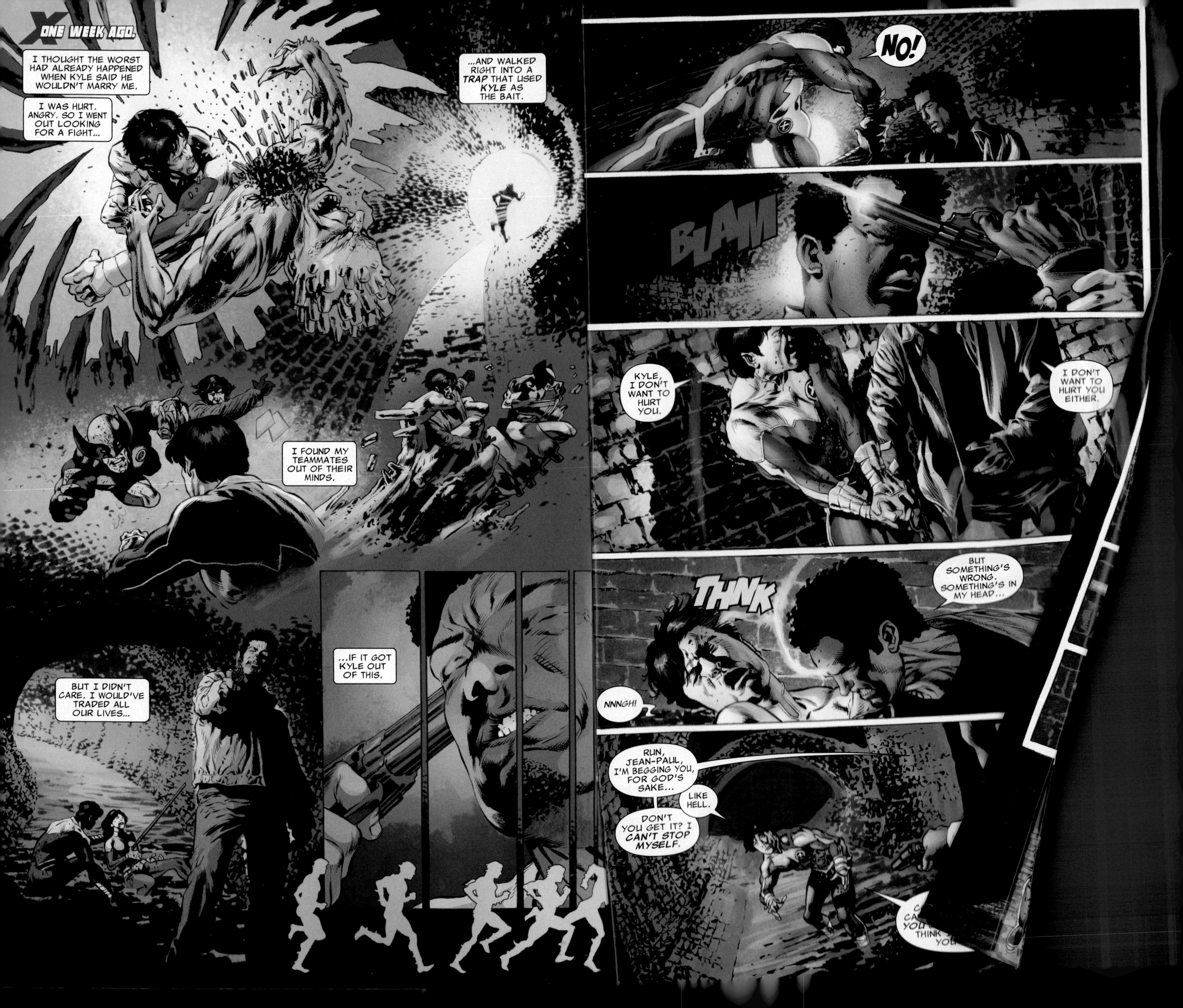

ONE WEEK AGO.
I THOUGHT THE WORST HAD ALREADY HAPPENED WHEN KYLE SAID HE WOULDN'T MARRY ME.
I WAS HURT. ANGRY. SO I WENT OUT LOOKING FOR A FIGHT...
...AND WALKED RIGHT INTO A TRAP THAT USED KYLE AS THE BAIT.
I FOUND MY TEAMMATES OUT OF THEIR MINDS.
BUT I DIDN'T CARE. I WOULD'VE TRADED ALL OUR LIVES...
...IF IT GOT KYLE OUT OF THIS.
NO!
BLAM
KYLE, I DON'T WANT TO HURT YOU.
I DON'T WANT TO HURT YOU EITHER.
THNK
BUT SOMETHING'S WRONG. SOMETHING'S IN MY HEAD...
NNNGH!
RUN, JEAN-PAUL, I'M BEGGING YOU, FOR GOD'S SAKE...
LIKE HELL.
DON'T YOU GET IT? I CAN'T STOP MYSELF.

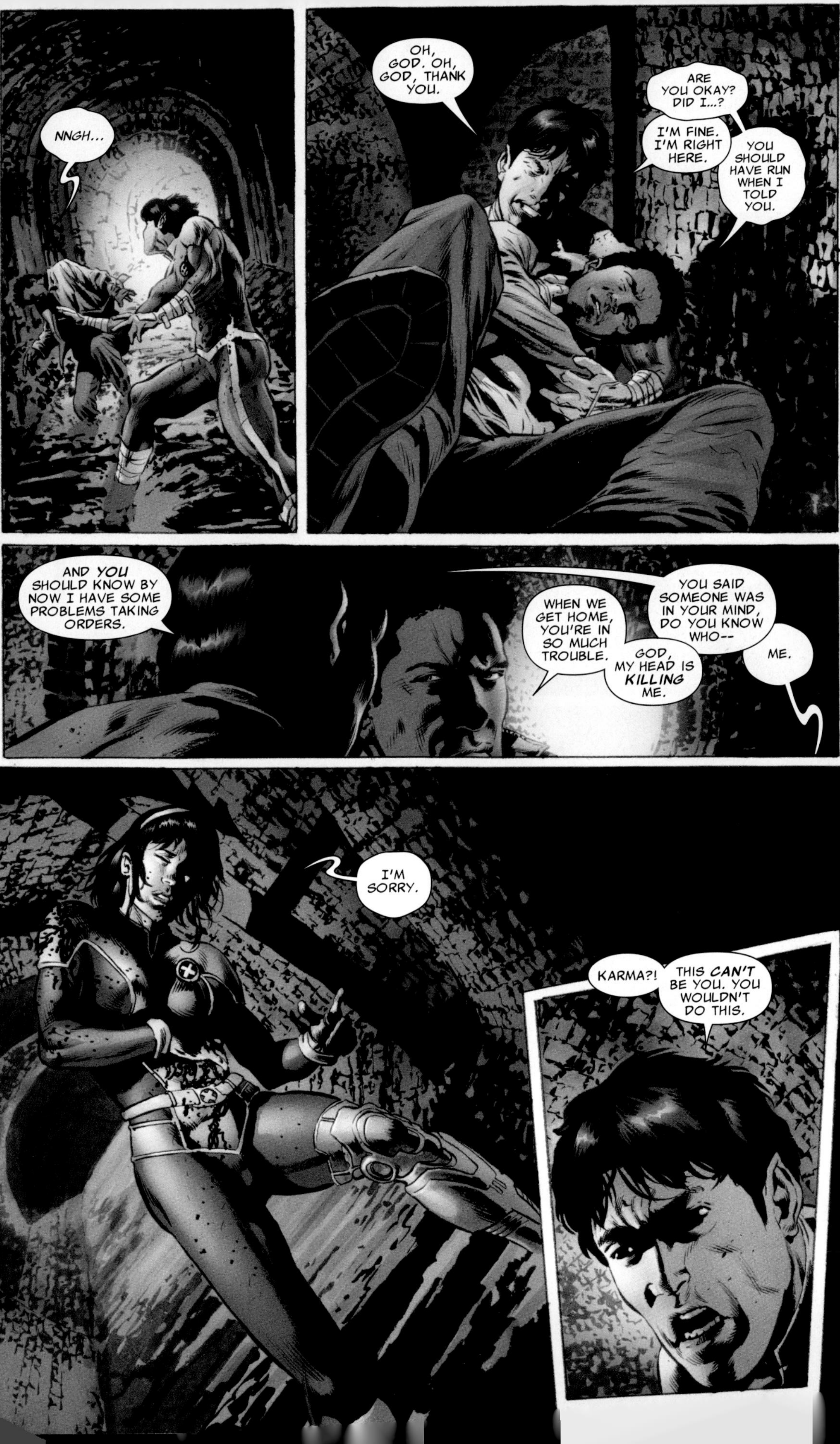
NNGH...
OH, GOD. OH, GOD, THANK YOU.
ARE YOU OKAY? DID I...?
I'M FINE. I'M RIGHT HERE.
YOU SHOULD HAVE RUN WHEN I TOLD YOU.
AND YOU SHOULD KNOW BY NOW I HAVE SOME PROBLEMS TAKING ORDERS.
WHEN WE GET HOME, YOU'RE IN SO MUCH TROUBLE.
YOU SAID SOMEONE WAS IN YOUR MIND, DO YOU KNOW WHO--
GOD, MY HEAD IS KILLING ME.
ME.
I'M SORRY.
KARMA?!
THIS CAN'T BE YOU. YOU WOULDN'T DO THIS.

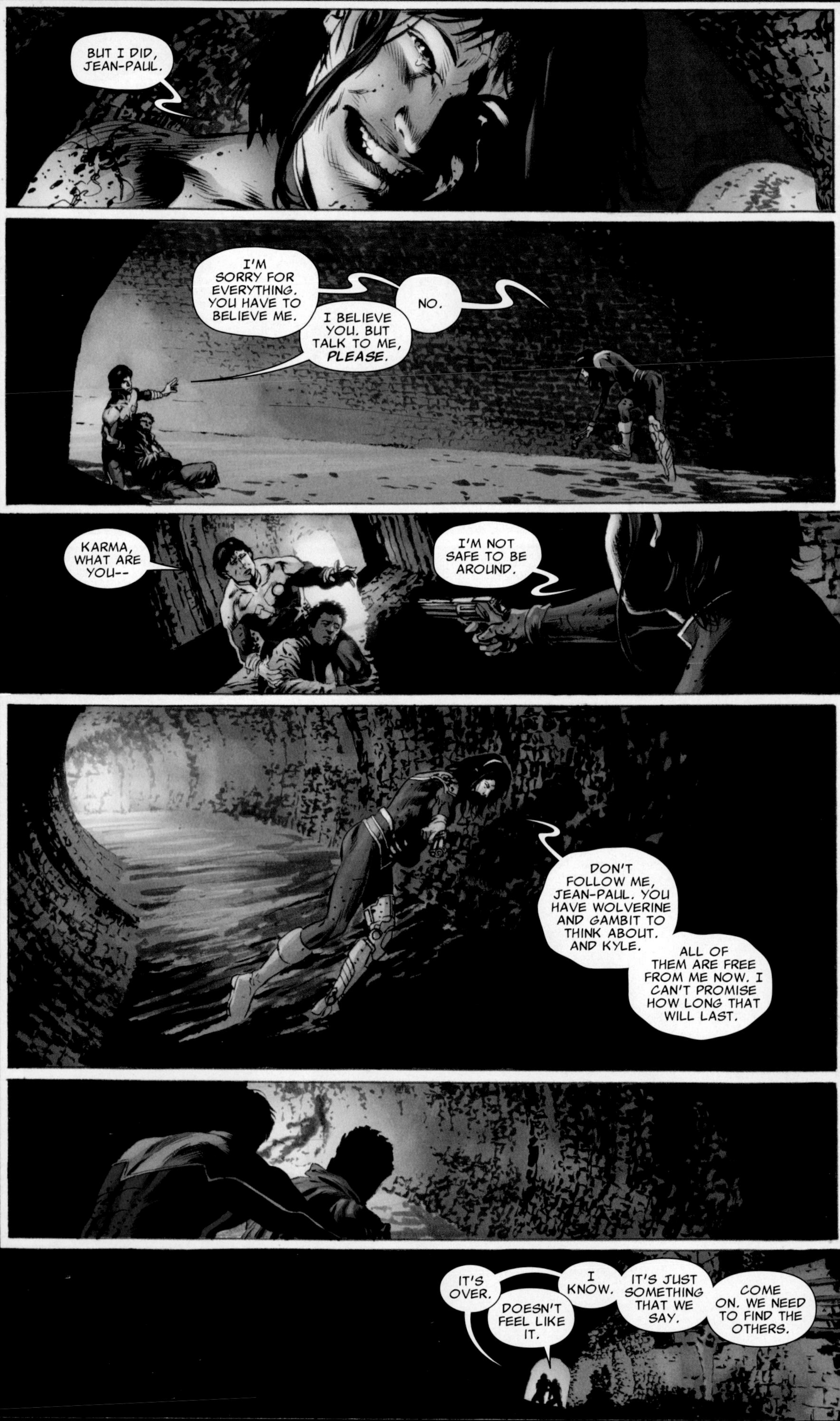
BUT I DID, JEAN-PAUL.
I'M SORRY FOR EVERYTHING. YOU HAVE TO BELIEVE ME.
NO.
I BELIEVE YOU. BUT TALK TO ME, PLEASE.
KARMA, WHAT ARE YOU--
I'M NOT SAFE TO BE AROUND.
DON'T FOLLOW ME, JEAN-PAUL. YOU HAVE WOLVERINE AND GAMBIT TO THINK ABOUT. AND KYLE.
ALL OF THEM ARE FREE FROM ME NOW. I CAN'T PROMISE HOW LONG THAT WILL LAST.
IT'S OVER.
DOESN'T FEEL LIKE IT.
I KNOW.
IT'S JUST SOMETHING THAT WE SAY.
COME ON. WE NEED TO FIND THE OTHERS.

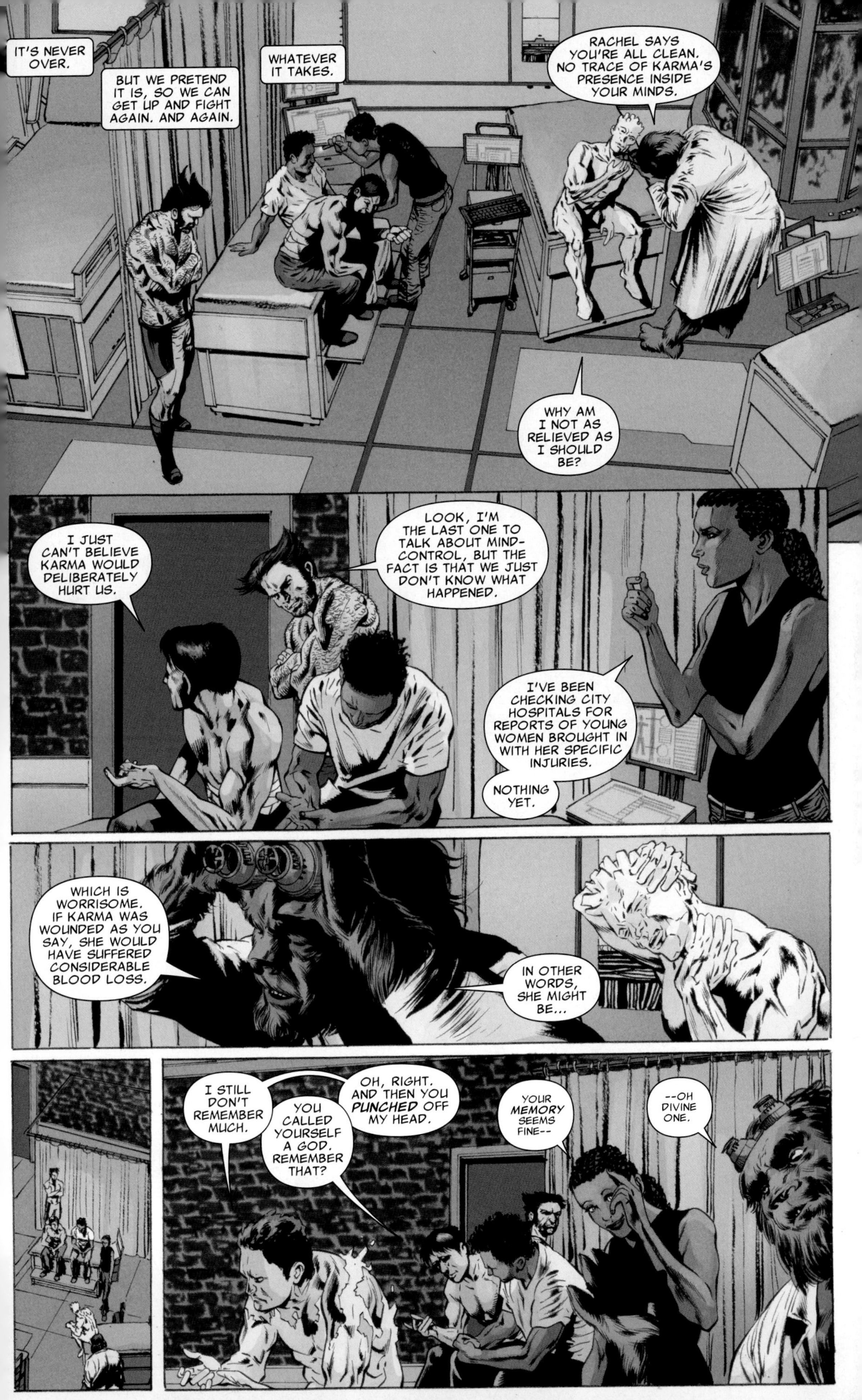

IT'S NEVER OVER.
BUT WE PRETEND IT IS, SO WE CAN GET UP AND FIGHT AGAIN. AND AGAIN.
WHATEVER IT TAKES.
RACHEL SAYS YOU'RE ALL CLEAN. NO TRACE OF KARMA'S PRESENCE INSIDE YOUR MINDS.
WHY AM I NOT AS RELIEVED AS I SHOULD BE?
I JUST CAN'T BELIEVE KARMA WOULD DELIBERATELY HURT US.
LOOK, I'M THE LAST ONE TO TALK ABOUT MIND-CONTROL, BUT THE FACT IS THAT WE JUST DON'T KNOW WHAT HAPPENED.
I'VE BEEN CHECKING CITY HOSPITALS FOR REPORTS OF YOUNG WOMEN BROUGHT IN WITH HER SPECIFIC INJURIES.
NOTHING YET.
WHICH IS WORRISOME. IF KARMA WAS WOUNDED AS YOU SAY, SHE WOULD HAVE SUFFERED CONSIDERABLE BLOOD LOSS.
IN OTHER WORDS, SHE MIGHT BE...
I STILL DON'T REMEMBER MUCH.
YOU CALLED YOURSELF A GOD. REMEMBER THAT?
OH, RIGHT. AND THEN YOU *PUNCHED* OFF MY HEAD.
YOUR *MEMORY* SEEMS FINE--
--OH DIVINE ONE.

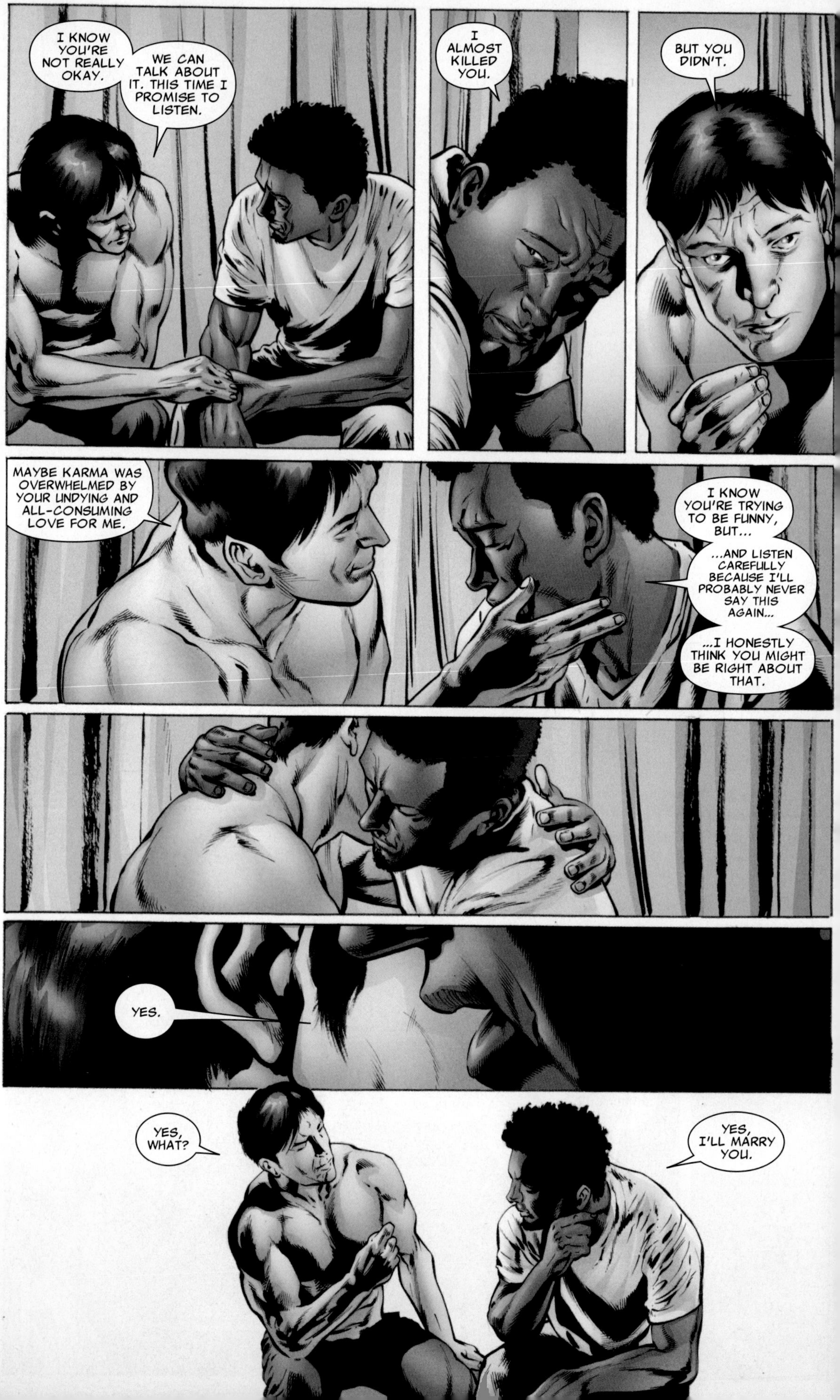
I KNOW YOU'RE NOT REALLY OKAY.
WE CAN TALK ABOUT IT. THIS TIME I PROMISE TO LISTEN.
I ALMOST KILLED YOU.
BUT YOU DIDN'T.
MAYBE KARMA WAS OVERWHELMED BY YOUR UNDYING AND ALL-CONSUMING LOVE FOR ME.
I KNOW YOU'RE TRYING TO BE FUNNY, BUT...
...AND LISTEN CAREFULLY BECAUSE I'LL PROBABLY NEVER SAY THIS AGAIN...
...I HONESTLY THINK YOU MIGHT BE RIGHT ABOUT THAT.
YES.
YES, WHAT?
YES, I'LL MARRY YOU.

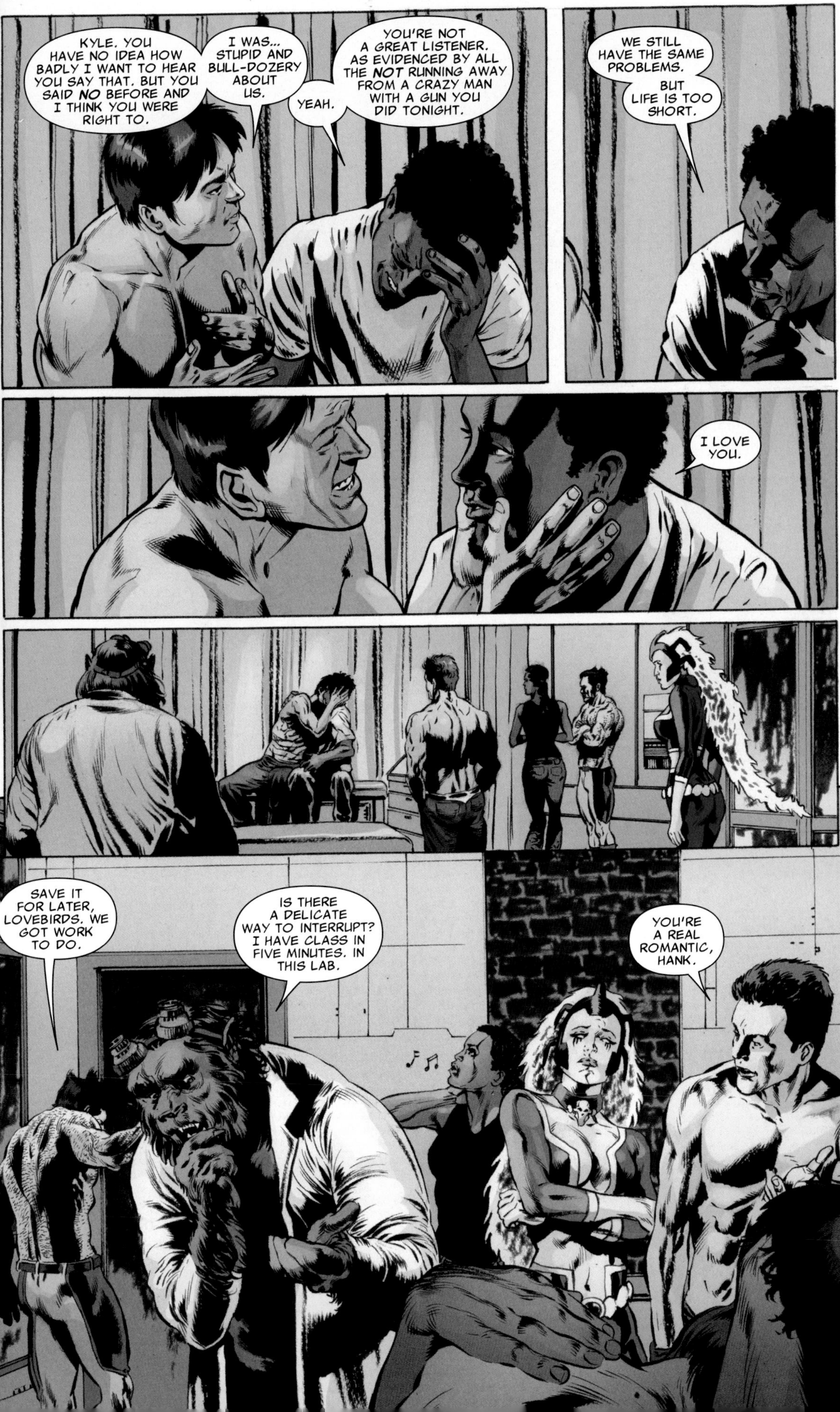
KYLE, YOU HAVE NO IDEA HOW BADLY I WANT TO HEAR YOU SAY THAT. BUT YOU SAID NO BEFORE AND I THINK YOU WERE RIGHT TO.
I WAS... STUPID AND BULL-DOZERY ABOUT US.
YEAH.
YOU'RE NOT A GREAT LISTENER. AS EVIDENCED BY ALL THE NOT RUNNING AWAY FROM A CRAZY MAN WITH A GUN YOU DID TONIGHT.
WE STILL HAVE THE SAME PROBLEMS.
BUT LIFE IS TOO SHORT.
I LOVE YOU.
SAVE IT FOR LATER, LOVEBIRDS. WE GOT WORK TO DO.
IS THERE A DELICATE WAY TO INTERRUPT? I HAVE CLASS IN FIVE MINUTES. IN THIS LAB.
YOU'RE A REAL ROMANTIC, HANK.

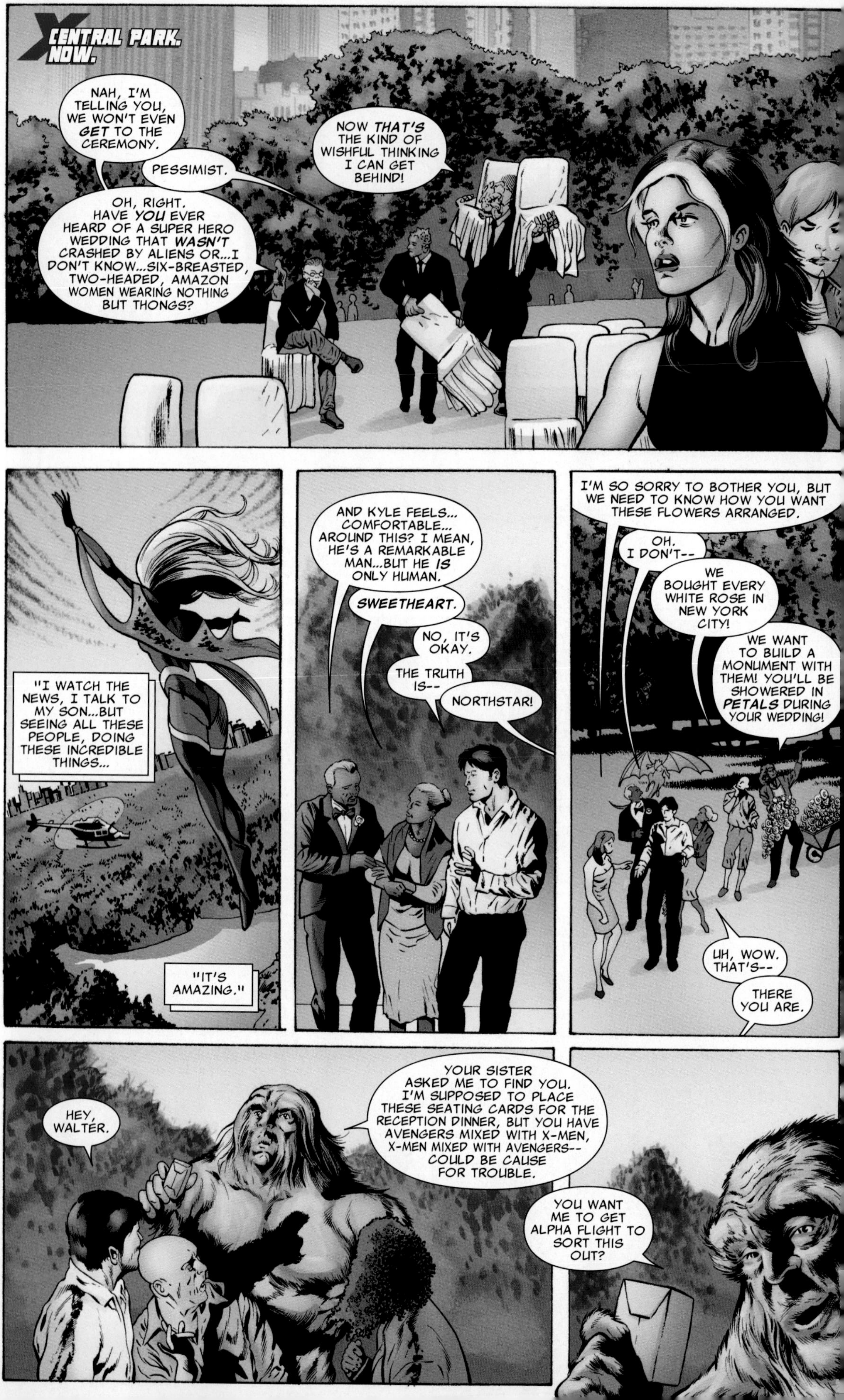
CENTRAL PARK. NOW.
NAH, I'M TELLING YOU, WE WON'T EVEN GET TO THE CEREMONY.
PESSIMIST.
OH, RIGHT. HAVE YOU EVER HEARD OF A SUPER HERO WEDDING THAT WASN'T CRASHED BY ALIENS OR...I DON'T KNOW...SIX-BREASTED, TWO-HEADED, AMAZON WOMEN WEARING NOTHING BUT THONGS?
NOW THAT'S THE KIND OF WISHFUL THINKING I CAN GET BEHIND!
"I WATCH THE NEWS, I TALK TO MY SON...BUT SEEING ALL THESE PEOPLE, DOING THESE INCREDIBLE THINGS...
"IT'S AMAZING."
AND KYLE FEELS... COMFORTABLE... AROUND THIS? I MEAN, HE'S A REMARKABLE MAN...BUT HE IS ONLY HUMAN.
SWEETHEART.
NO, IT'S OKAY.
THE TRUTH IS--
NORTHSTAR!
I'M SO SORRY TO BOTHER YOU, BUT WE NEED TO KNOW HOW YOU WANT THESE FLOWERS ARRANGED.
OH. I DON'T--
WE BOUGHT EVERY WHITE ROSE IN NEW YORK CITY!
WE WANT TO BUILD A MONUMENT WITH THEM! YOU'LL BE SHOWERED IN PETALS DURING YOUR WEDDING!
UH, WOW. THAT'S--
THERE YOU ARE.
HEY, WALTER.
YOUR SISTER ASKED ME TO FIND YOU. I'M SUPPOSED TO PLACE THESE SEATING CARDS FOR THE RECEPTION DINNER, BUT YOU HAVE AVENGERS MIXED WITH X-MEN, X-MEN MIXED WITH AVENGERS--COULD BE CAUSE FOR TROUBLE.
YOU WANT ME TO GET ALPHA FLIGHT TO SORT THIS OUT?

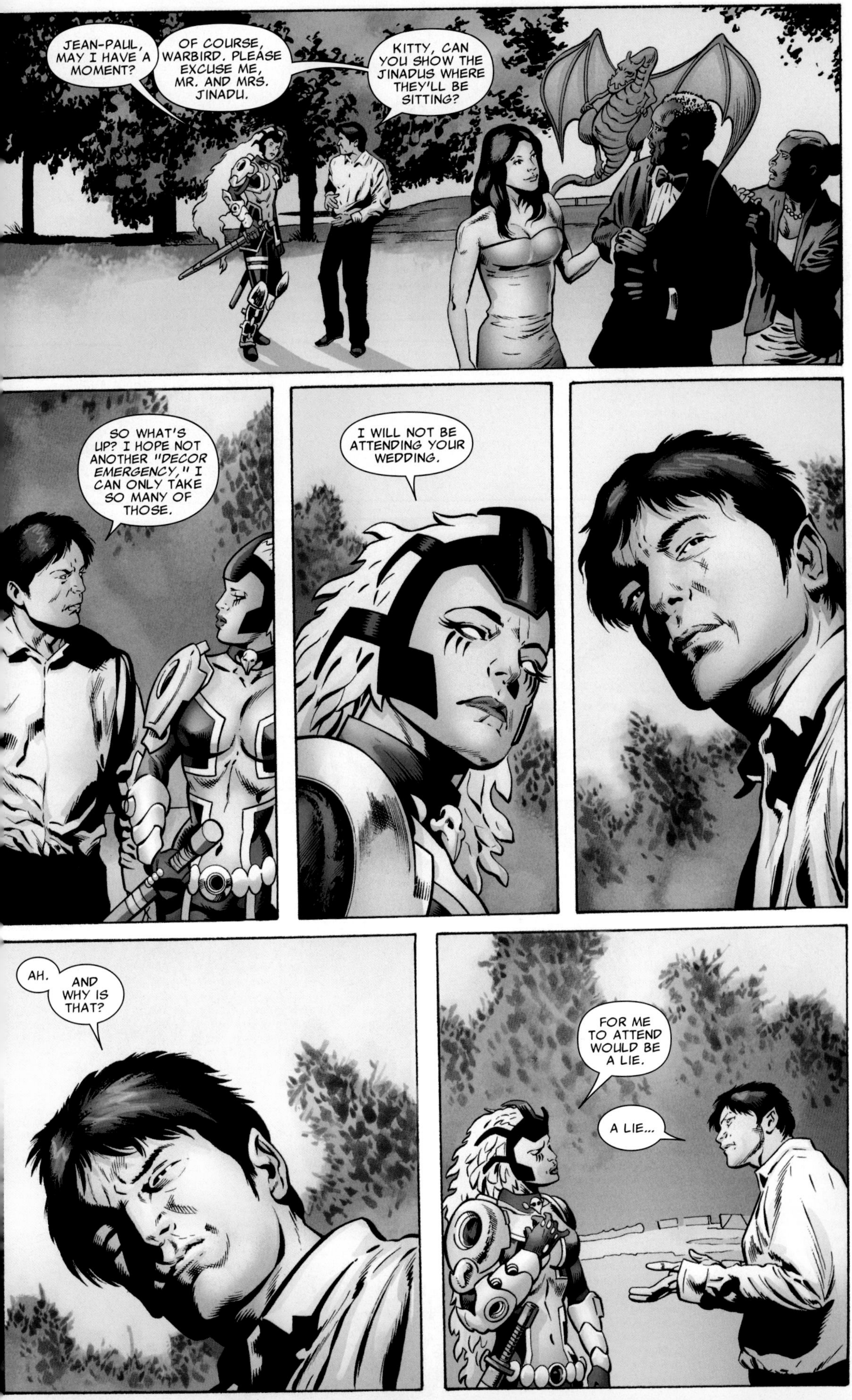
JEAN-PAUL, MAY I HAVE A MOMENT?
OF COURSE, WARBIRD. PLEASE EXCUSE ME, MR. AND MRS. JINADU.
KITTY, CAN YOU SHOW THE JINADUS WHERE THEY'LL BE SITTING?
SO WHAT'S UP? I HOPE NOT ANOTHER "DECOR EMERGENCY," I CAN ONLY TAKE SO MANY OF THOSE.
I WILL NOT BE ATTENDING YOUR WEDDING.
AH.
AND WHY IS THAT?
FOR ME TO ATTEND WOULD BE A LIE.
A LIE...

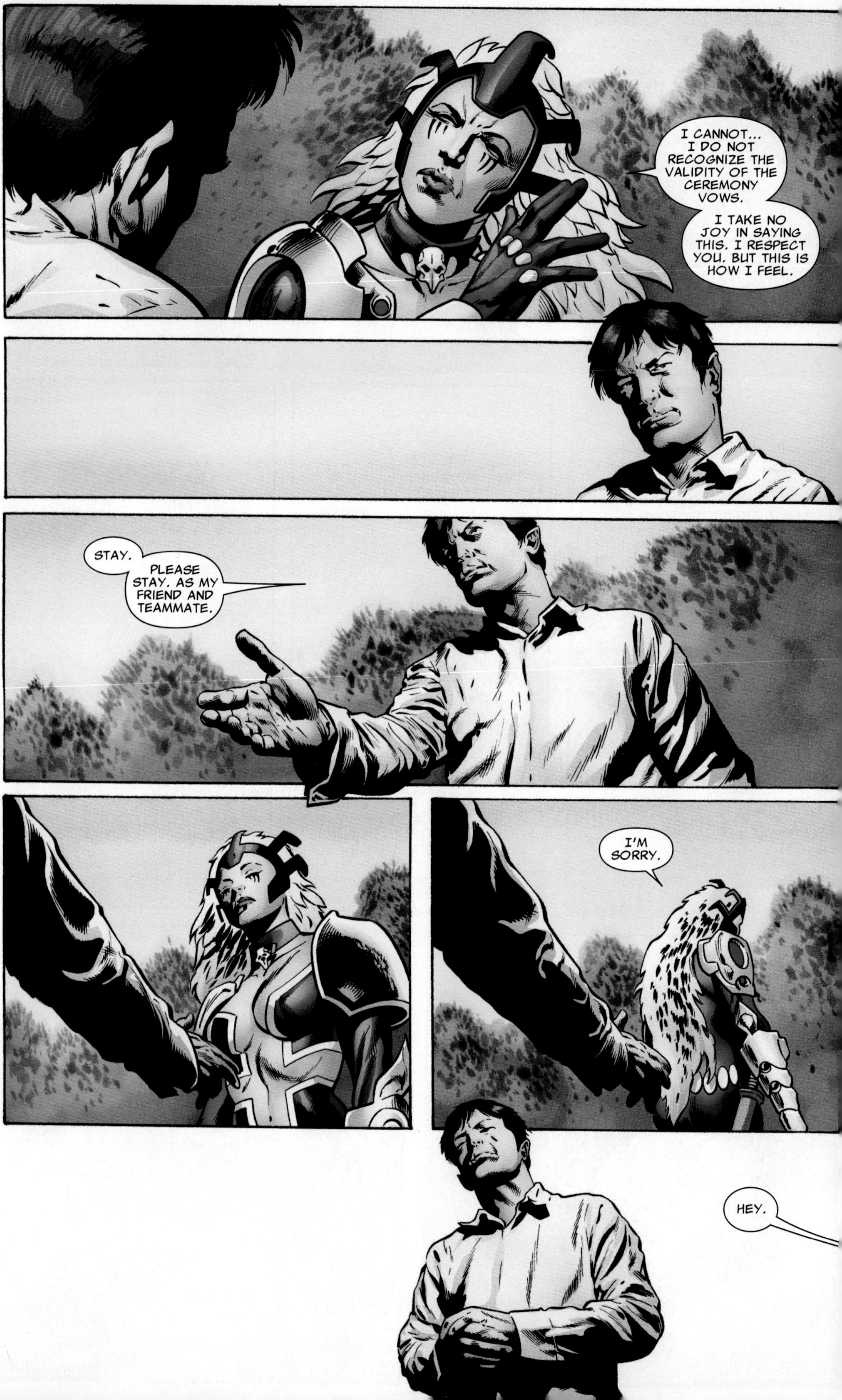
I CANNOT... I DO NOT RECOGNIZE THE VALIDITY OF THE CEREMONY VOWS.
I TAKE NO JOY IN SAYING THIS. I RESPECT YOU. BUT THIS IS HOW I FEEL.
STAY.
PLEASE STAY. AS MY FRIEND AND TEAMMATE.
I'M SORRY.
HEY.

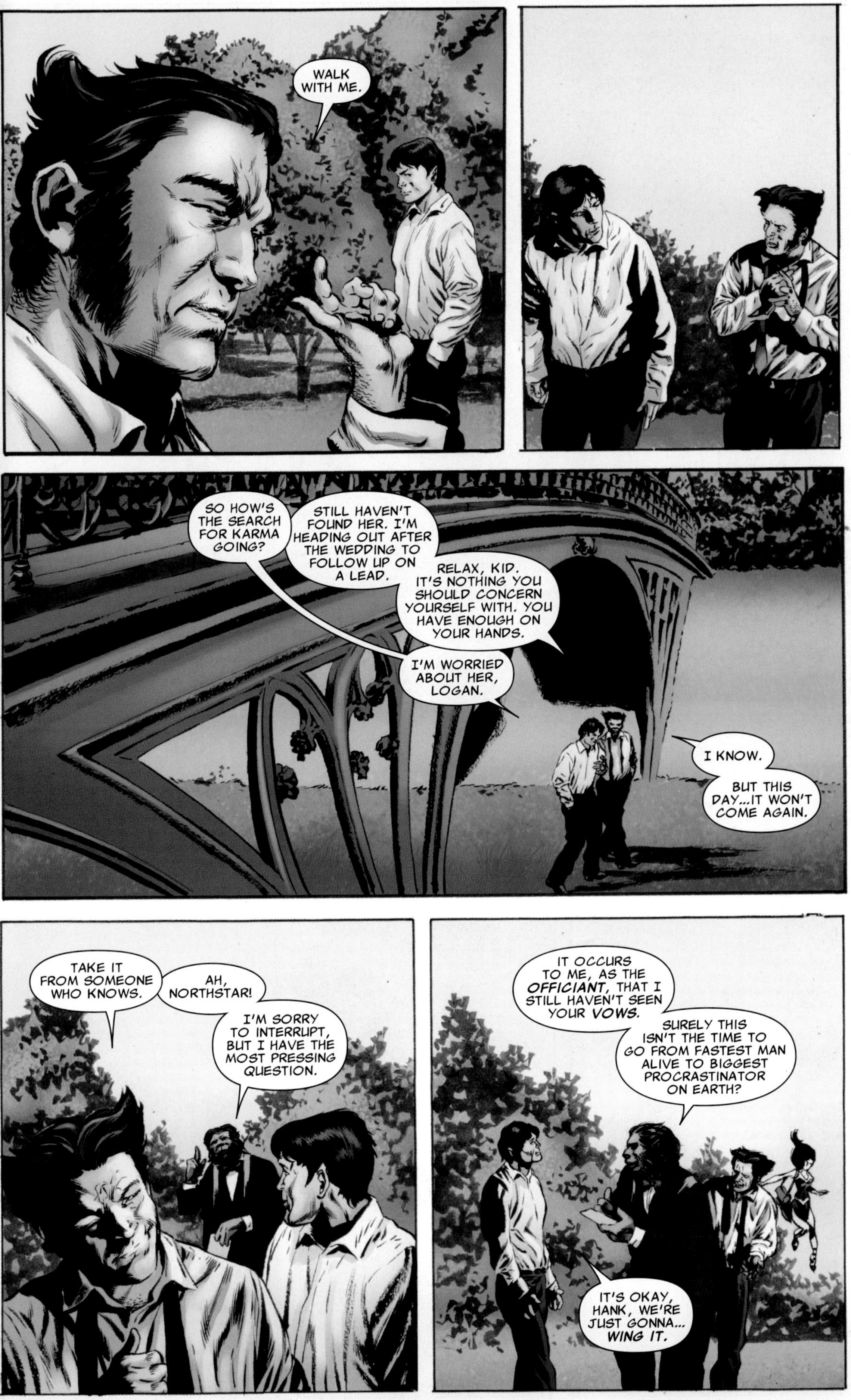
WALK WITH ME.
SO HOW'S THE SEARCH FOR KARMA GOING?
STILL HAVEN'T FOUND HER. I'M HEADING OUT AFTER THE WEDDING TO FOLLOW UP ON A LEAD.
RELAX, KID. IT'S NOTHING YOU SHOULD CONCERN YOURSELF WITH. YOU HAVE ENOUGH ON YOUR HANDS.
I'M WORRIED ABOUT HER, LOGAN.
I KNOW.
BUT THIS DAY...IT WON'T COME AGAIN.
TAKE IT FROM SOMEONE WHO KNOWS.
AH, NORTHSTAR!
I'M SORRY TO INTERRUPT, BUT I HAVE THE MOST PRESSING QUESTION.
IT OCCURS TO ME, AS THE OFFICIANT, THAT I STILL HAVEN'T SEEN YOUR VOWS.
SURELY THIS ISN'T THE TIME TO GO FROM FASTEST MAN ALIVE TO BIGGEST PROCRASTINATOR ON EARTH?
IT'S OKAY, HANK, WE'RE JUST GONNA... WING IT.

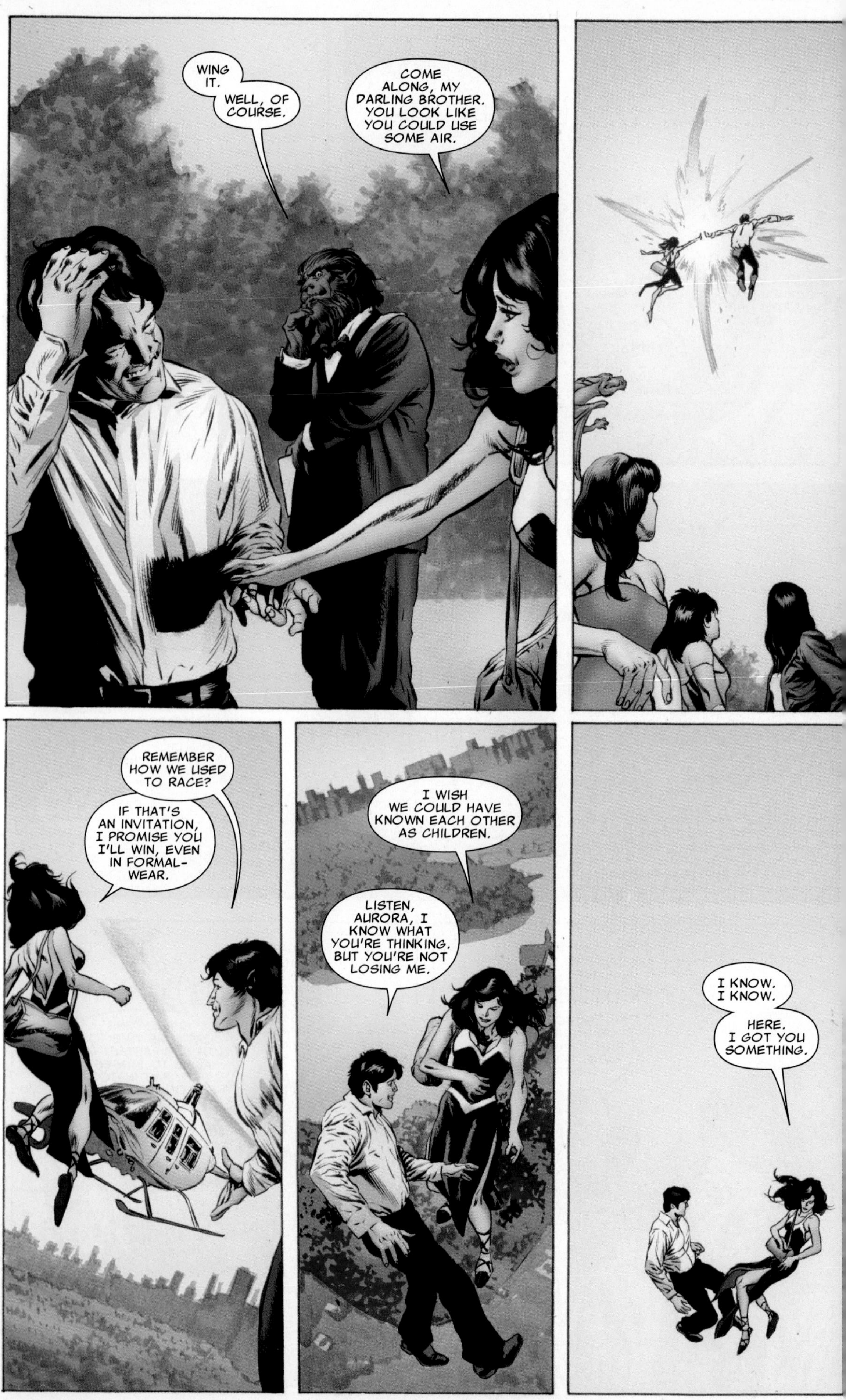
WING IT.
WELL, OF COURSE.
COME ALONG, MY DARLING BROTHER. YOU LOOK LIKE YOU COULD USE SOME AIR.
REMEMBER HOW WE USED TO RACE?
IF THAT'S AN INVITATION, I PROMISE YOU I'LL WIN, EVEN IN FORMAL-WEAR.
I WISH WE COULD HAVE KNOWN EACH OTHER AS CHILDREN.
LISTEN, AURORA, I KNOW WHAT YOU'RE THINKING. BUT YOU'RE NOT LOSING ME.
I KNOW. I KNOW.
HERE. I GOT YOU SOMETHING.

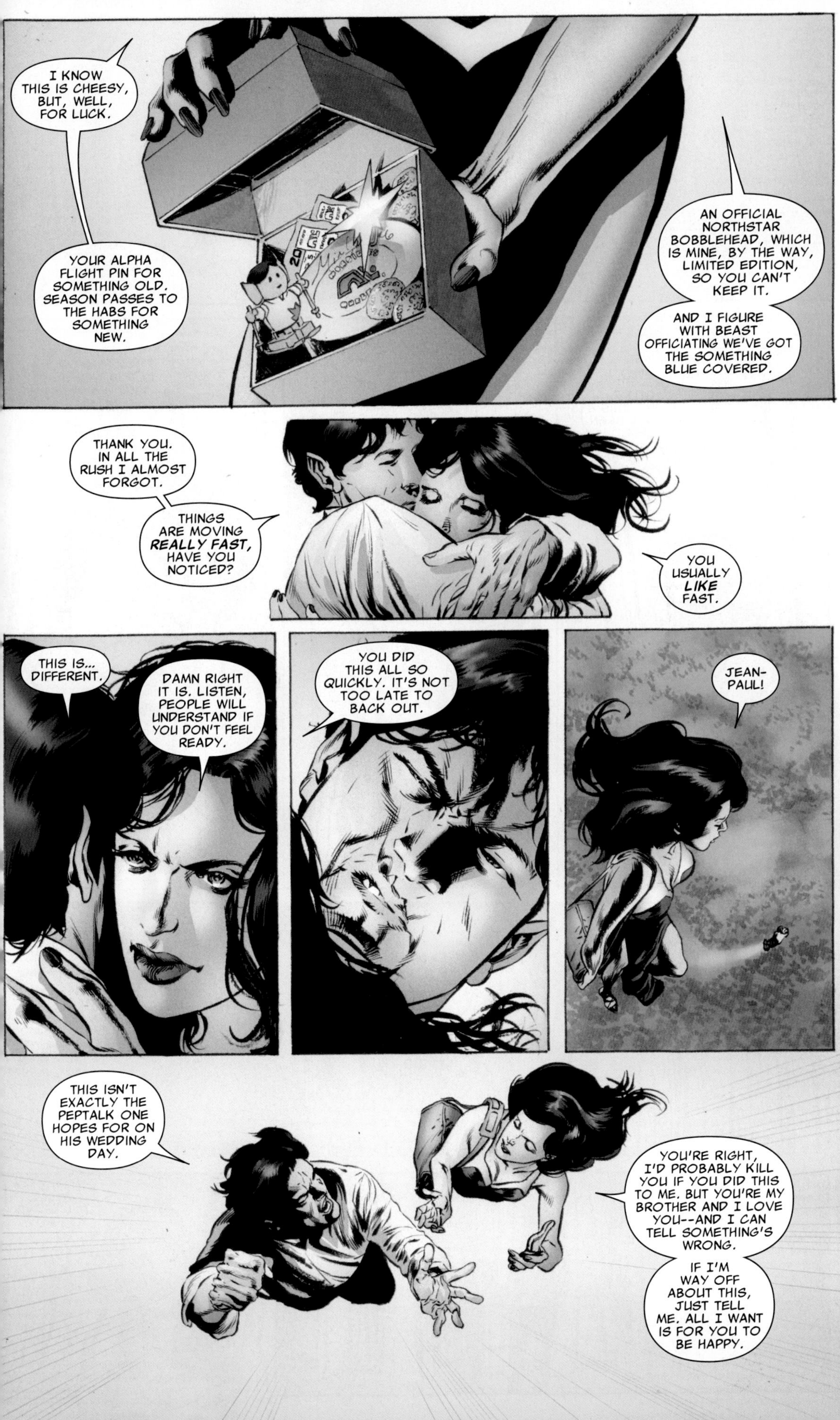
I KNOW THIS IS CHEESY, BUT, WELL, FOR LUCK.
YOUR ALPHA FLIGHT PIN FOR SOMETHING OLD. SEASON PASSES TO THE HABS FOR SOMETHING NEW.
AN OFFICIAL NORTHSTAR BOBBLEHEAD, WHICH IS MINE, BY THE WAY, LIMITED EDITION, SO YOU CAN'T KEEP IT.
AND I FIGURE WITH BEAST OFFICIATING WE'VE GOT THE SOMETHING BLUE COVERED.
THANK YOU. IN ALL THE RUSH I ALMOST FORGOT.
THINGS ARE MOVING REALLY FAST, HAVE YOU NOTICED?
YOU USUALLY LIKE FAST.
THIS IS... DIFFERENT.
DAMN RIGHT IT IS. LISTEN, PEOPLE WILL UNDERSTAND IF YOU DON'T FEEL READY.
YOU DID THIS ALL SO QUICKLY. IT'S NOT TOO LATE TO BACK OUT.
JEAN-PAUL!
THIS ISN'T EXACTLY THE PEPTALK ONE HOPES FOR ON HIS WEDDING DAY.
YOU'RE RIGHT, I'D PROBABLY KILL YOU IF YOU DID THIS TO ME. BUT YOU'RE MY BROTHER AND I LOVE YOU--AND I CAN TELL SOMETHING'S WRONG.
IF I'M WAY OFF ABOUT THIS, JUST TELL ME. ALL I WANT IS FOR YOU TO BE HAPPY.

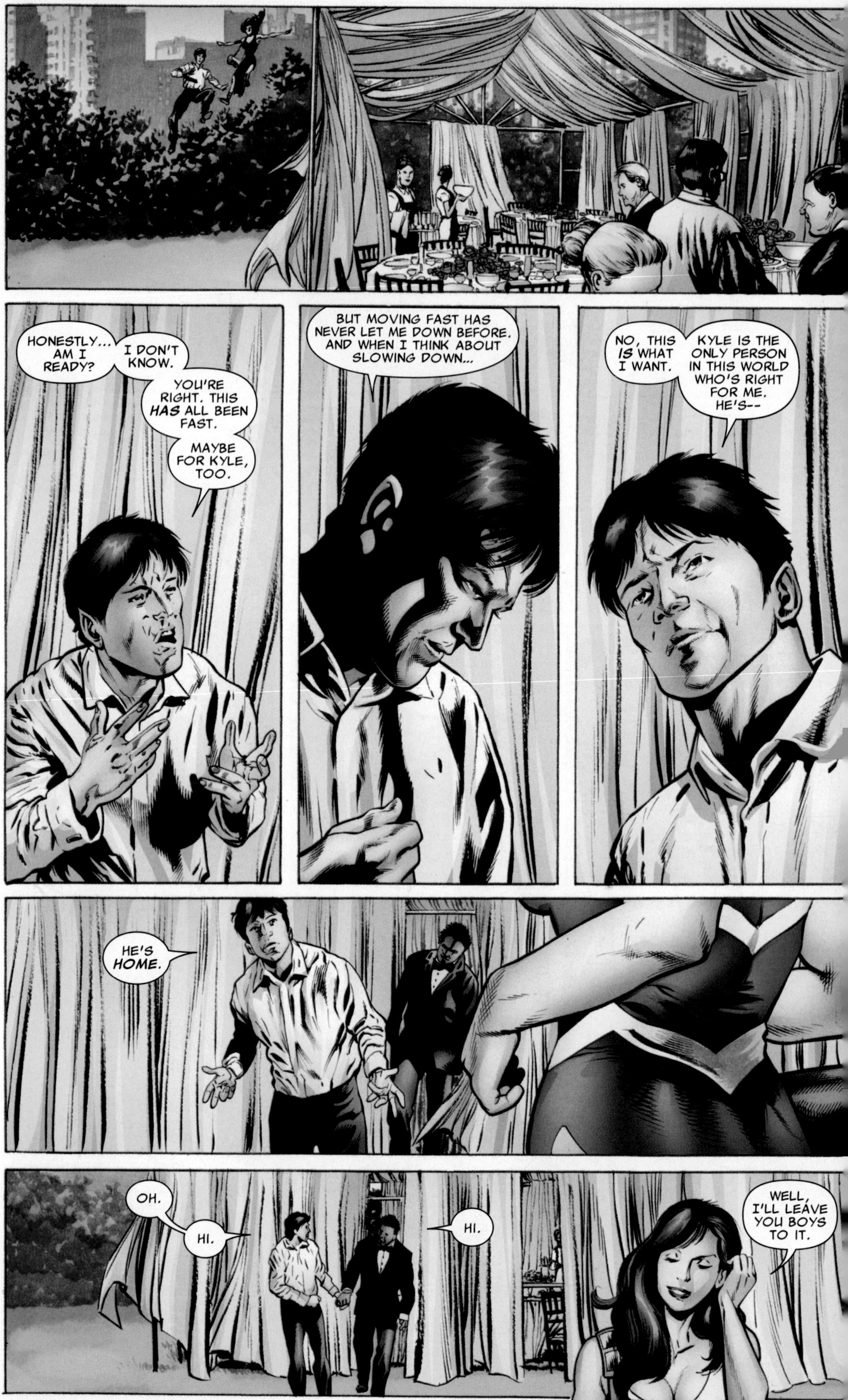
HONESTLY... AM I READY?
I DON'T KNOW.
YOU'RE RIGHT. THIS HAS ALL BEEN FAST.
MAYBE FOR KYLE, TOO.
BUT MOVING FAST HAS NEVER LET ME DOWN BEFORE. AND WHEN I THINK ABOUT SLOWING DOWN...
NO, THIS IS WHAT I WANT.
KYLE IS THE ONLY PERSON IN THIS WORLD WHO'S RIGHT FOR ME. HE'S--
HE'S HOME.
OH.
HI.
HI.
WELL, I'LL LEAVE YOU BOYS TO IT.

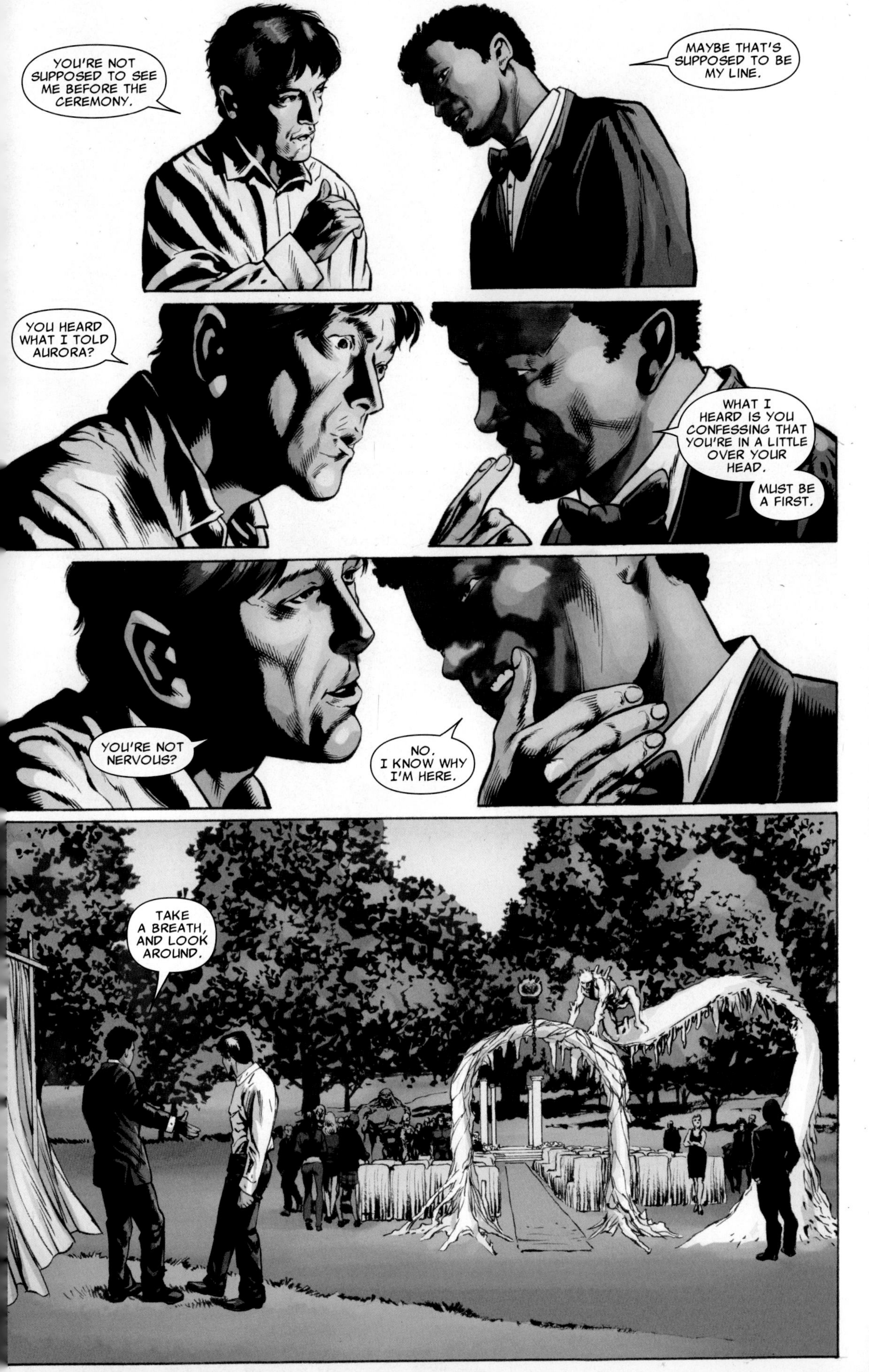

YOU'RE NOT SUPPOSED TO SEE ME BEFORE THE CEREMONY.
MAYBE THAT'S SUPPOSED TO BE MY LINE.
YOU HEARD WHAT I TOLD AURORA?
WHAT I HEARD IS YOU CONFESSING THAT YOU'RE IN A LITTLE OVER YOUR HEAD.
MUST BE A FIRST.
YOU'RE NOT NERVOUS?
NO. I KNOW WHY I'M HERE.
TAKE A BREATH, AND LOOK AROUND.

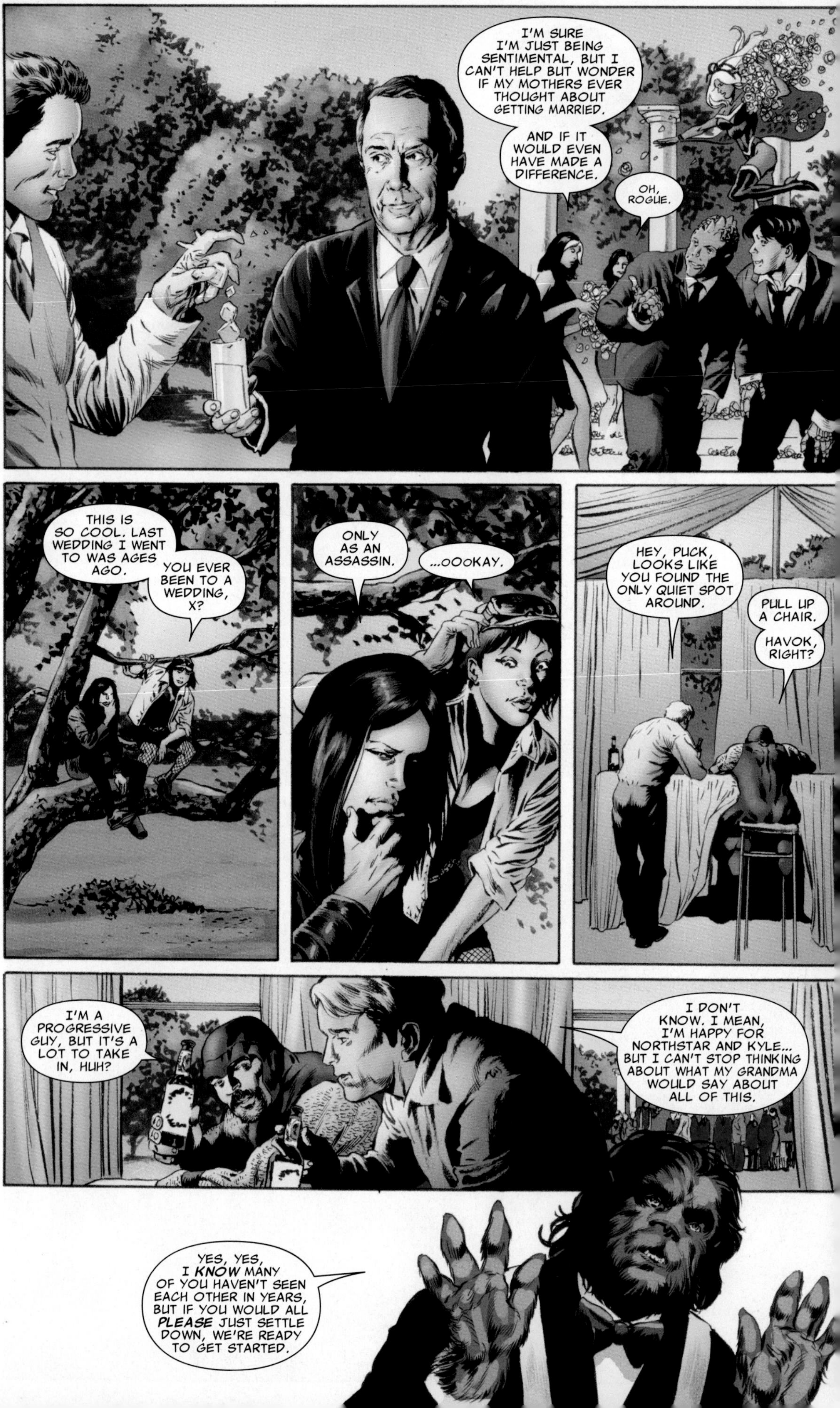
I'M SURE I'M JUST BEING SENTIMENTAL, BUT I CAN'T HELP BUT WONDER IF MY MOTHERS EVER THOUGHT ABOUT GETTING MARRIED.
AND IF IT WOULD EVEN HAVE MADE A DIFFERENCE.
OH, ROGUE.
THIS IS SO COOL. LAST WEDDING I WENT TO WAS AGES AGO.
YOU EVER BEEN TO A WEDDING, X?
ONLY AS AN ASSASSIN.
...OOOKAY.
HEY, PUCK, LOOKS LIKE YOU FOUND THE ONLY QUIET SPOT AROUND.
PULL UP A CHAIR.
HAVOK, RIGHT?
I'M A PROGRESSIVE GUY, BUT IT'S A LOT TO TAKE IN, HUH?
I DON'T KNOW. I MEAN, I'M HAPPY FOR NORTHSTAR AND KYLE... BUT I CAN'T STOP THINKING ABOUT WHAT MY GRANDMA WOULD SAY ABOUT ALL OF THIS.
YES, YES, I *KNOW* MANY OF YOU HAVEN'T SEEN EACH OTHER IN YEARS, BUT IF YOU WOULD ALL *PLEASE* JUST SETTLE DOWN, WE'RE READY TO GET STARTED.

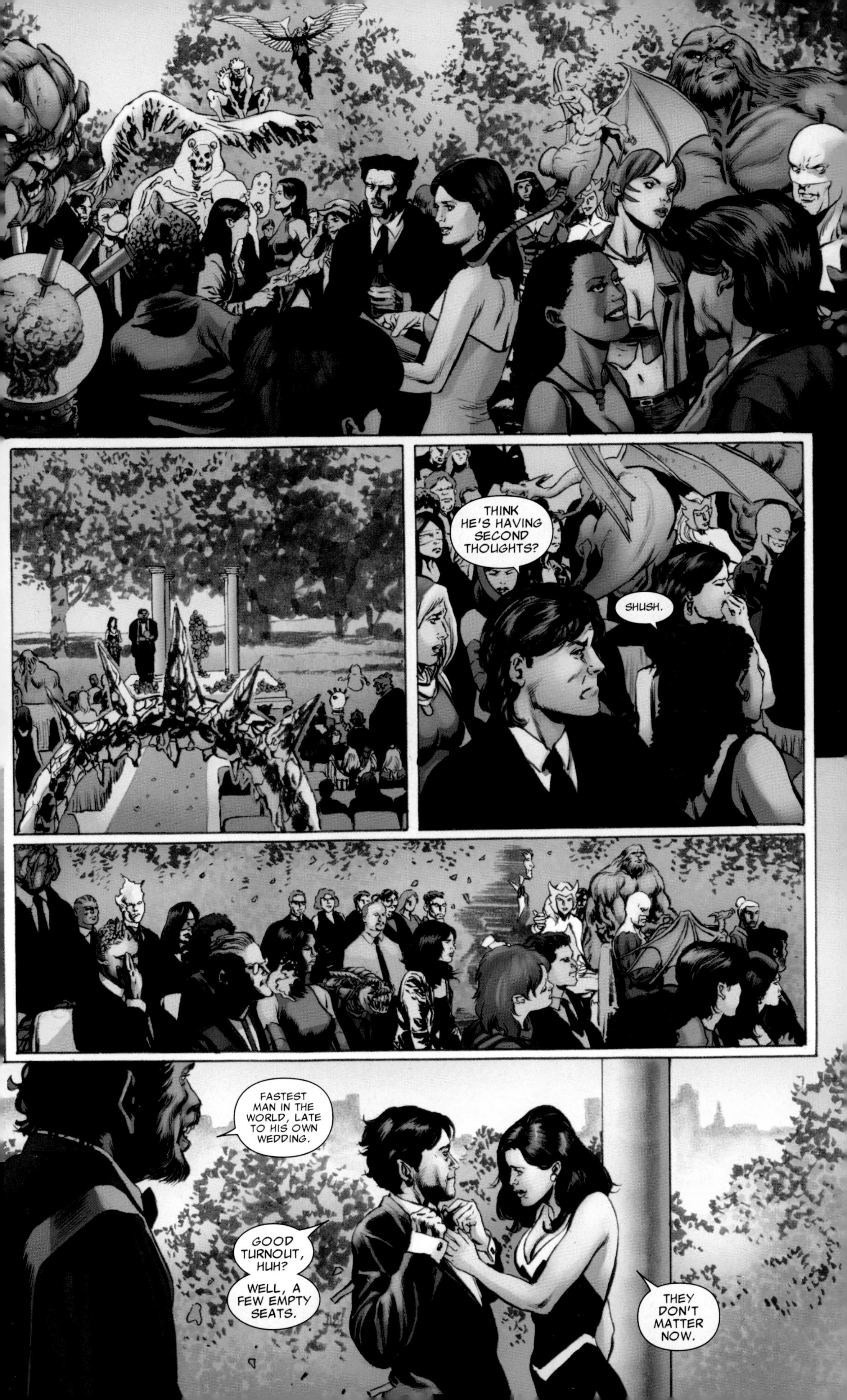
THINK HE'S HAVING SECOND THOUGHTS?
SHUSH.
FASTEST MAN IN THE WORLD, LATE TO HIS OWN WEDDING.
GOOD TURNOUT, HUH?
WELL, A FEW EMPTY SEATS.
THEY DON'T MATTER NOW.

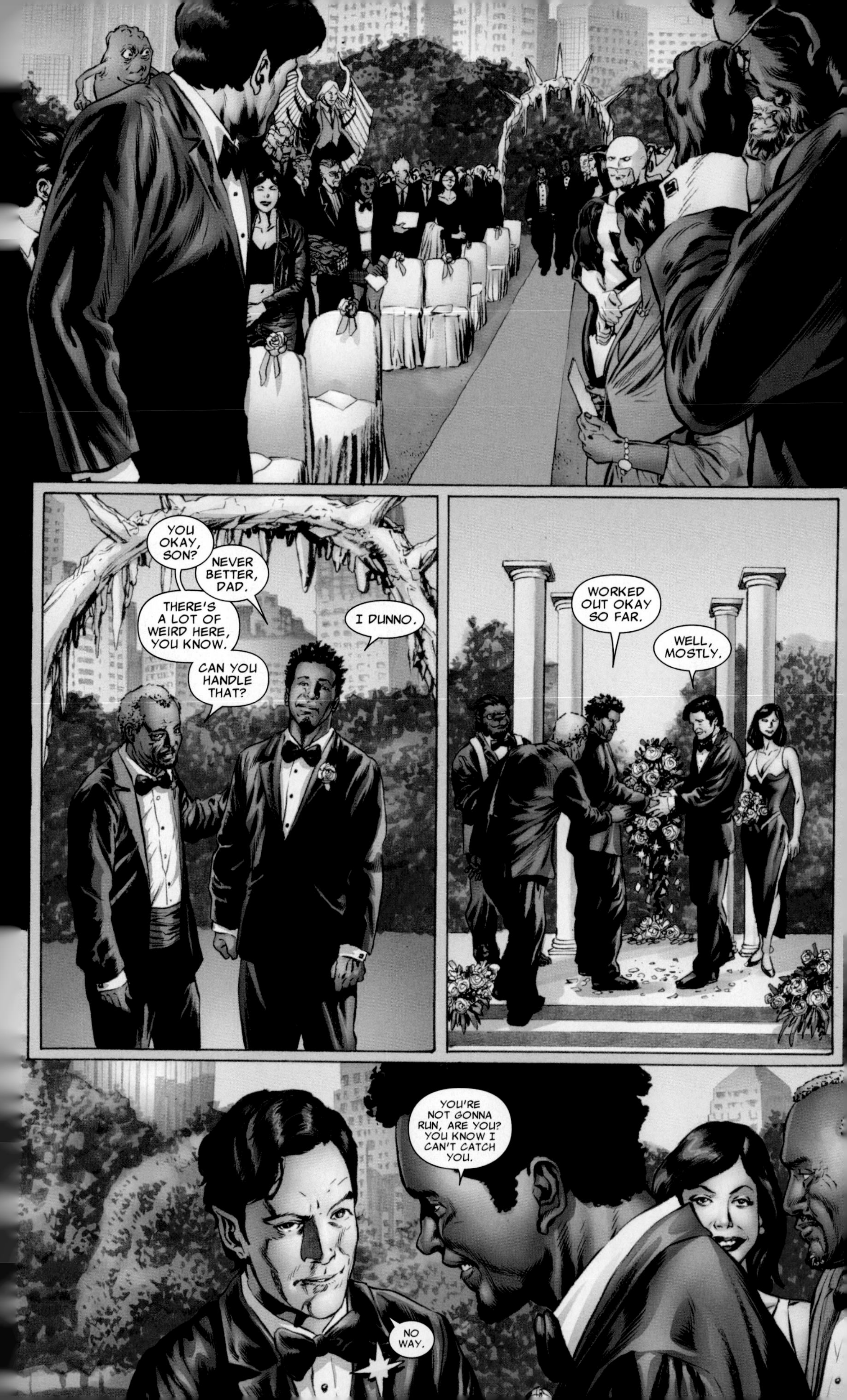
YOU OKAY, SON?
NEVER BETTER, DAD.
THERE'S A LOT OF WEIRD HERE, YOU KNOW.
CAN YOU HANDLE THAT?
I DUNNO.
WORKED OUT OKAY SO FAR.
WELL, MOSTLY.
YOU'RE NOT GONNA RUN, ARE YOU? YOU KNOW I CAN'T CATCH YOU.
NO WAY.

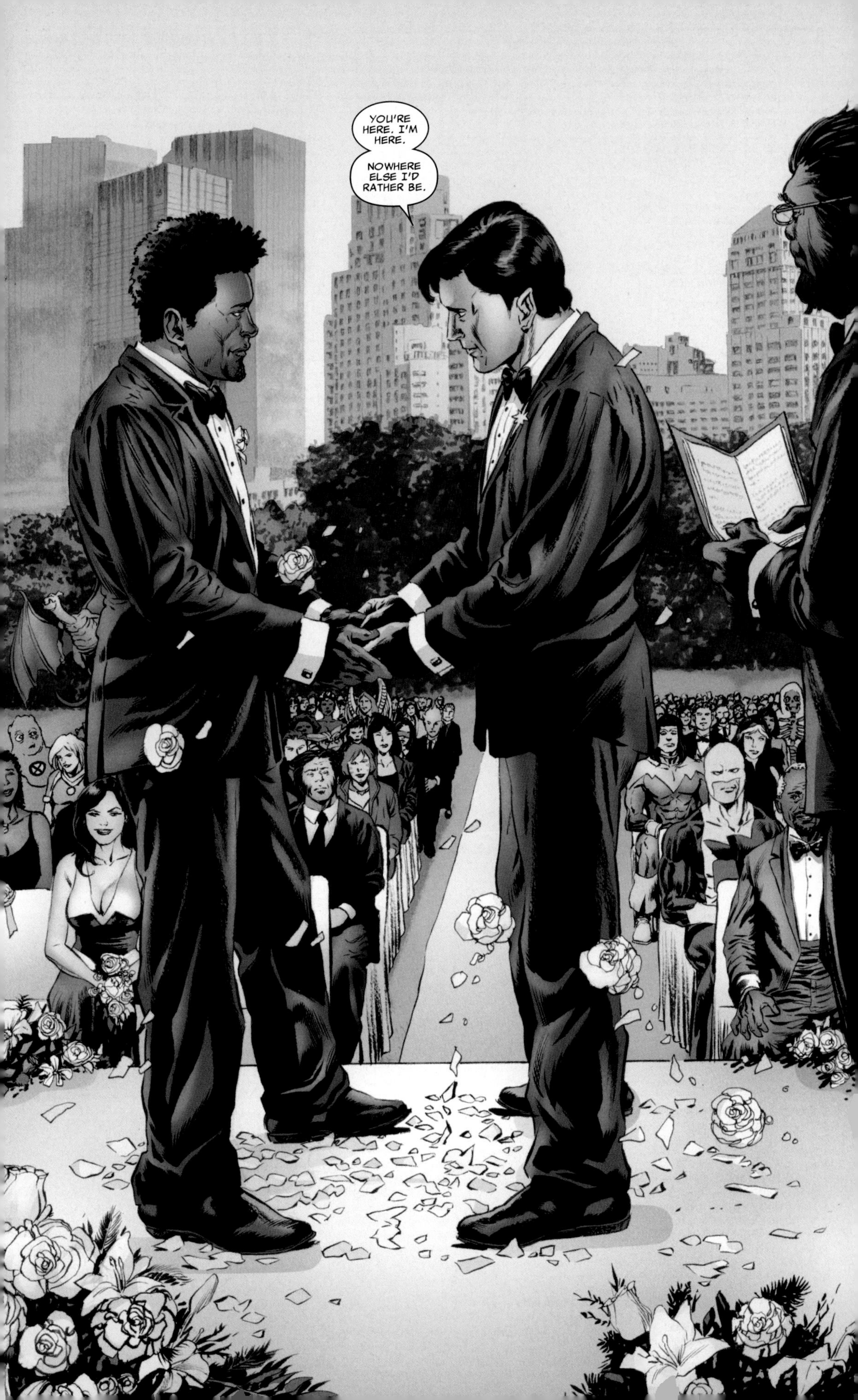
YOU'RE HERE. I'M HERE.
NOWHERE ELSE I'D RATHER BE.

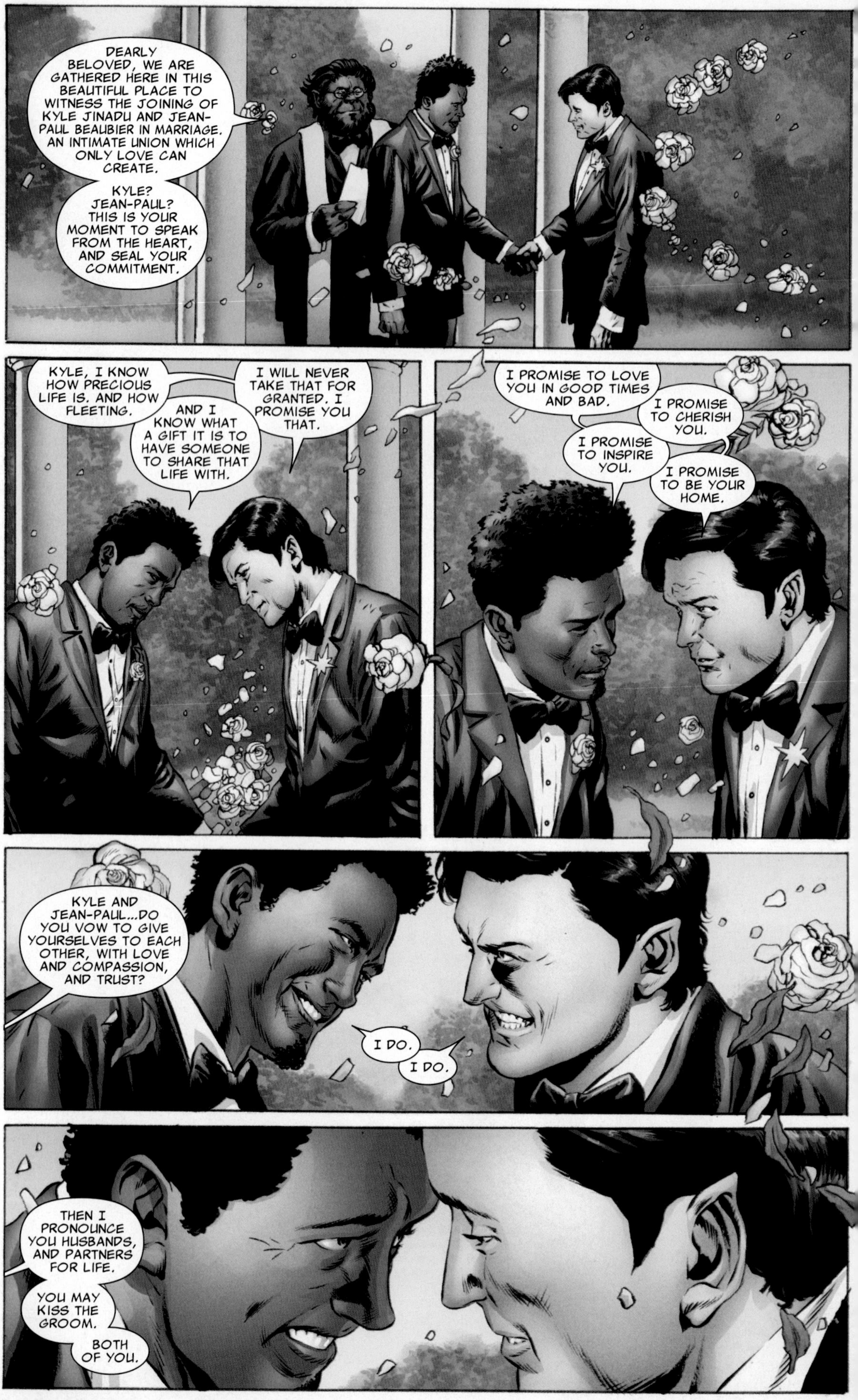
DEARLY BELOVED, WE ARE GATHERED HERE IN THIS BEAUTIFUL PLACE TO WITNESS THE JOINING OF KYLE JINADU AND JEAN-PAUL BEAUBIER IN MARRIAGE. AN INTIMATE UNION WHICH ONLY LOVE CAN CREATE.
KYLE? JEAN-PAUL? THIS IS YOUR MOMENT TO SPEAK FROM THE HEART, AND SEAL YOUR COMMITMENT.
KYLE, I KNOW HOW PRECIOUS LIFE IS. AND HOW FLEETING.
AND I KNOW WHAT A GIFT IT IS TO HAVE SOMEONE TO SHARE THAT LIFE WITH.
I WILL NEVER TAKE THAT FOR GRANTED. I PROMISE YOU THAT.
I PROMISE TO LOVE YOU IN GOOD TIMES AND BAD.
I PROMISE TO CHERISH YOU.
I PROMISE TO INSPIRE YOU.
I PROMISE TO BE YOUR HOME.
KYLE AND JEAN-PAUL...DO YOU VOW TO GIVE YOURSELVES TO EACH OTHER, WITH LOVE AND COMPASSION, AND TRUST?
I DO.
I DO.
THEN I PRONOUNCE YOU HUSBANDS, AND PARTNERS FOR LIFE.
YOU MAY KISS THE GROOM.
BOTH OF YOU.

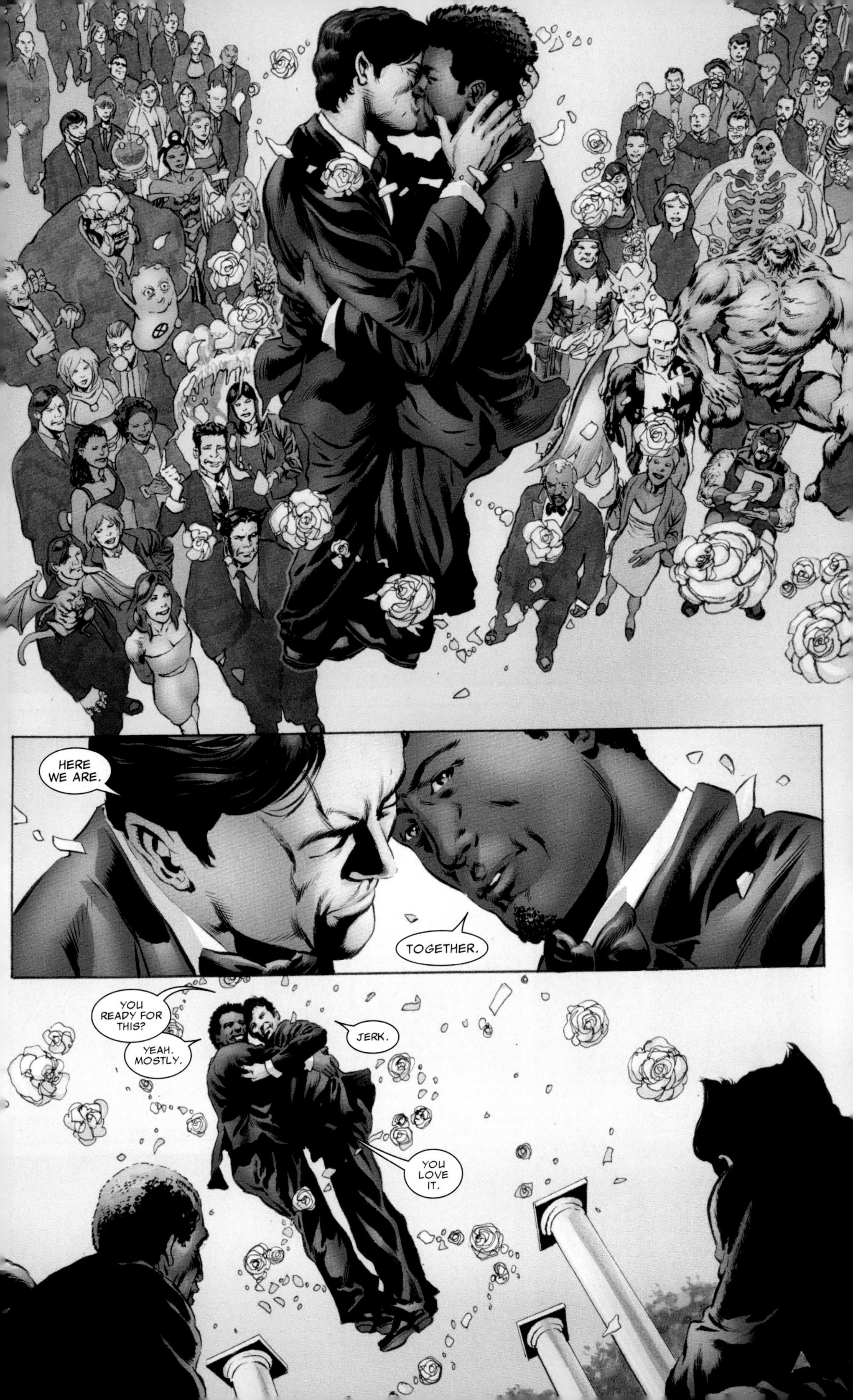
HERE WE ARE.
TOGETHER.
YOU READY FOR THIS?
YEAH. MOSTLY.
JERK.
YOU LOVE IT.

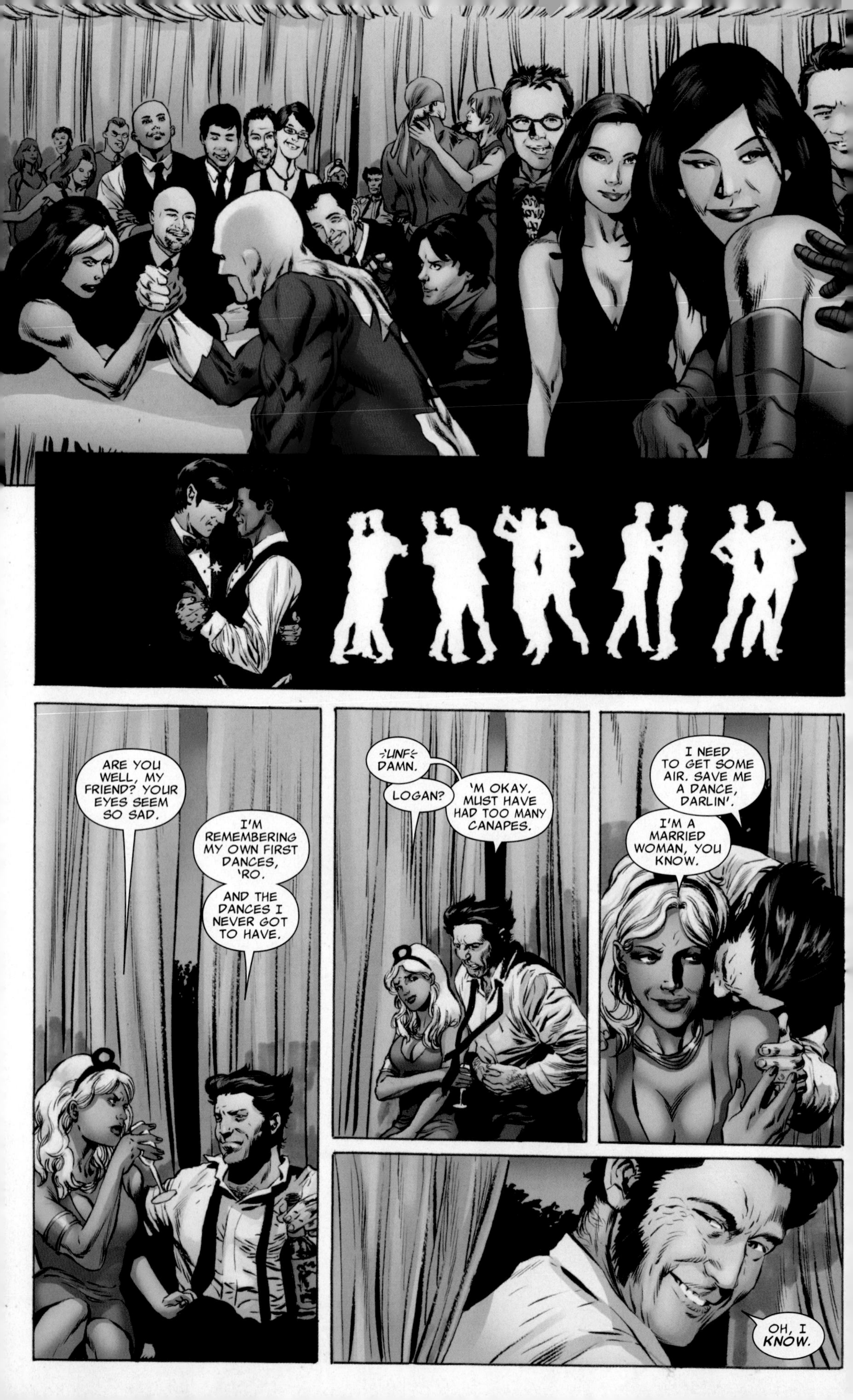
ARE YOU WELL, MY FRIEND? YOUR EYES SEEM SO SAD.
I'M REMEMBERING MY OWN FIRST DANCES, 'RO.
AND THE DANCES I NEVER GOT TO HAVE.
-UNF- DAMN.
LOGAN?
'M OKAY. MUST HAVE HAD TOO MANY CANAPES.
I NEED TO GET SOME AIR. SAVE ME A DANCE, DARLIN'.
I'M A MARRIED WOMAN, YOU KNOW.
OH, I KNOW.

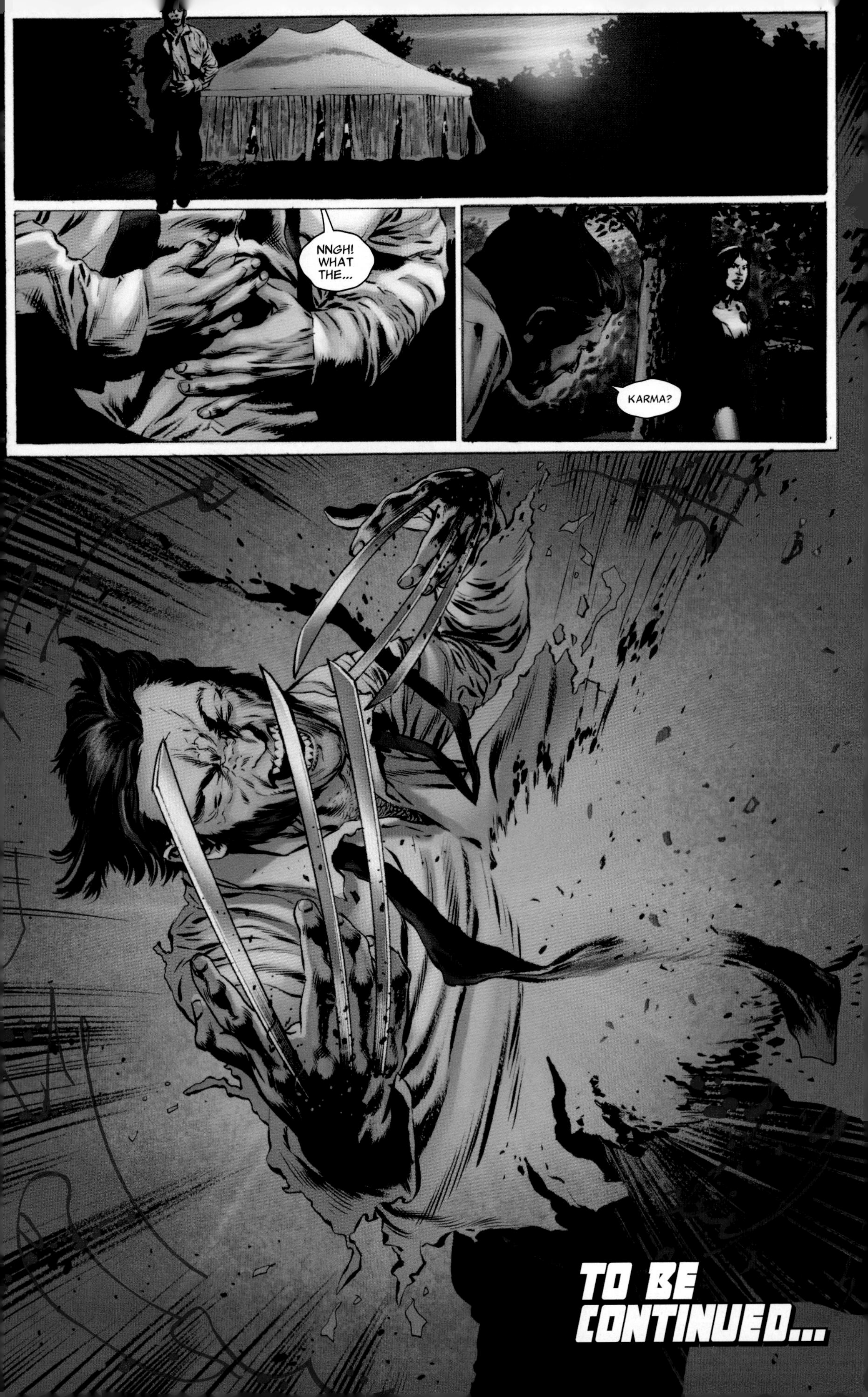
NNGH! WHAT THE...
KARMA?
TO BE CONTINUED...

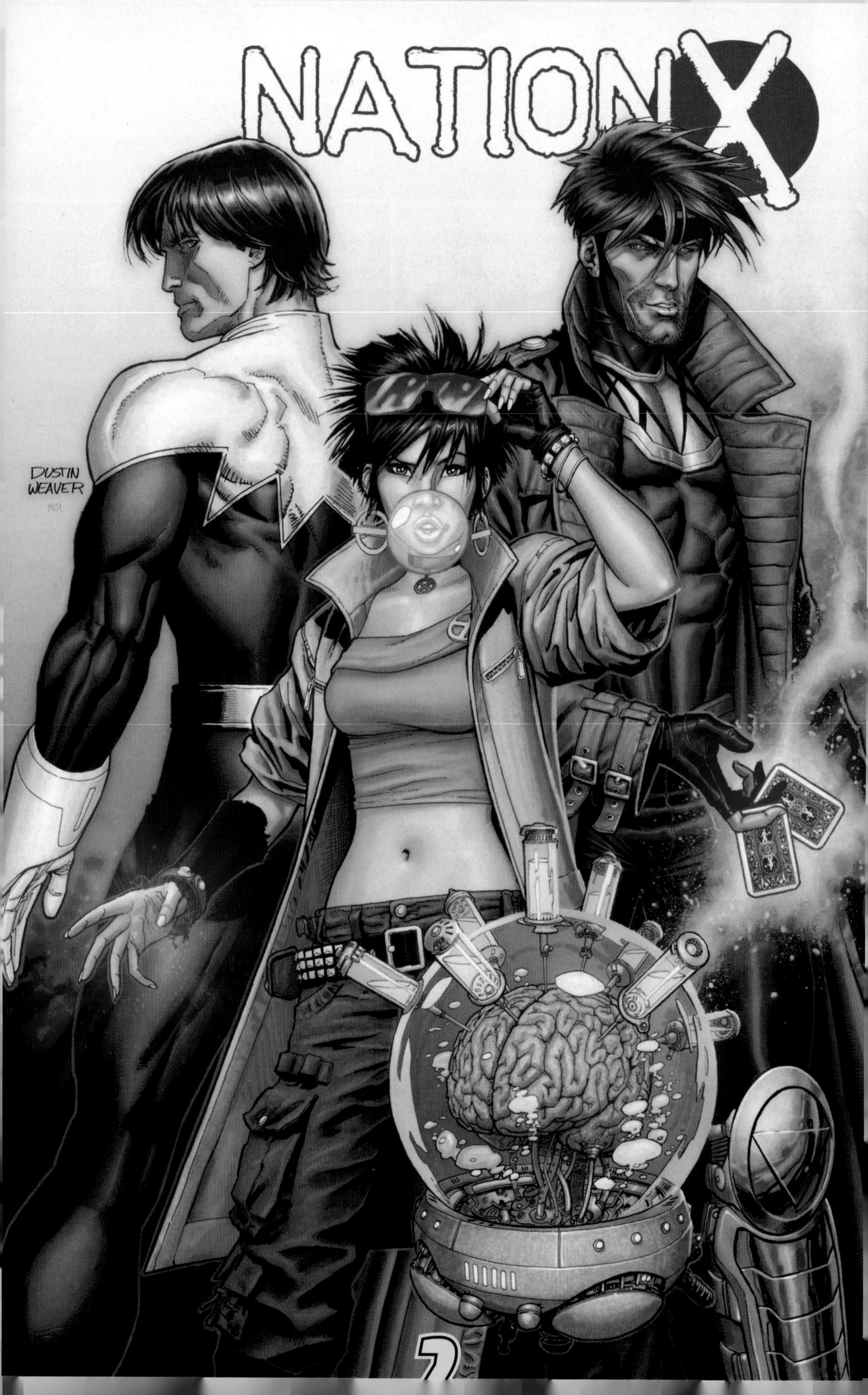
NATION X
DUSTIN WEAVER

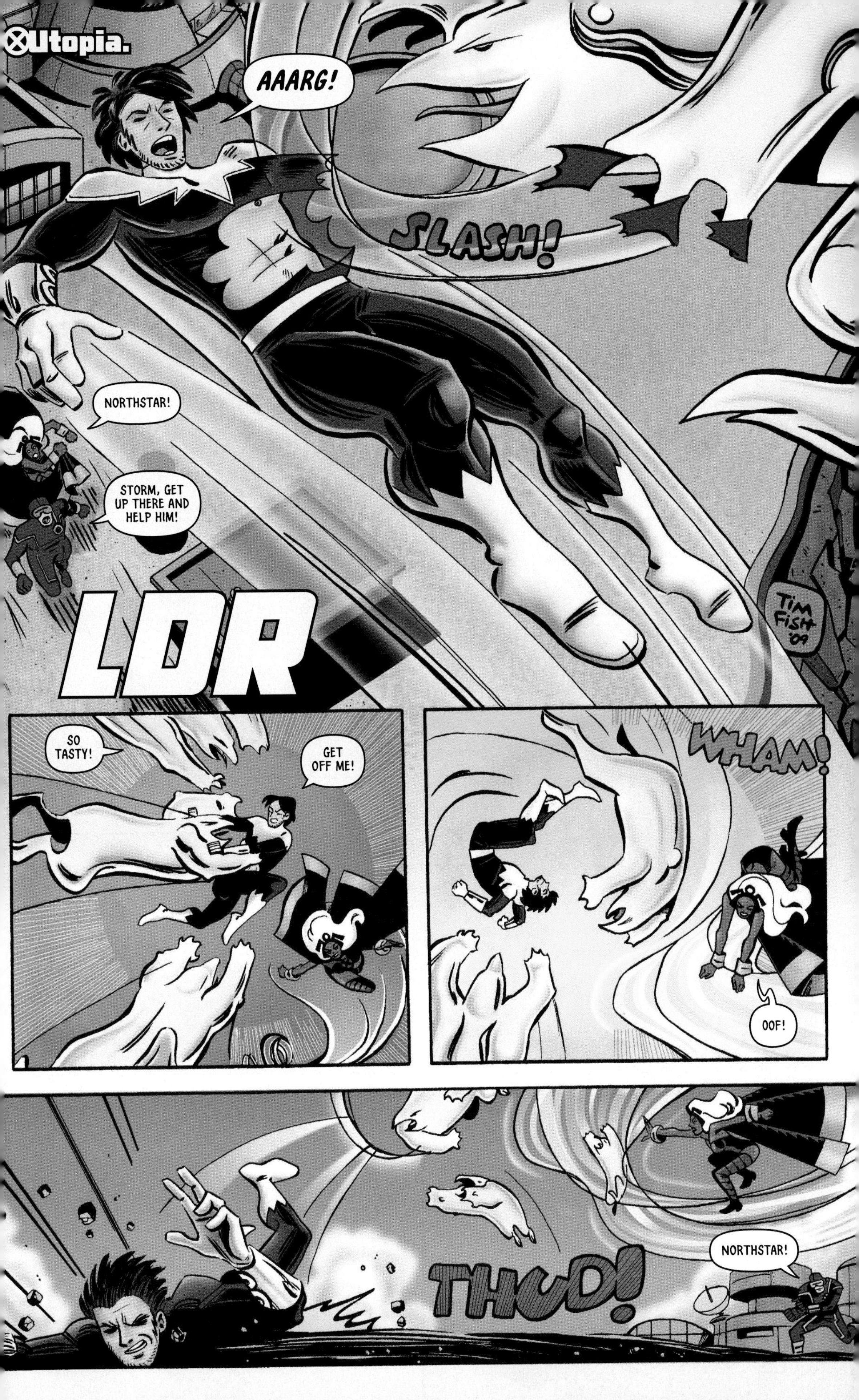
AAARG!
SLASH!
NORTHSTAR!
STORM, GET UP THERE AND HELP HIM!
LDR
TIM FISH '09
SO TASTY!
GET OFF ME!
WHAM!
OOF!
THUD!
NORTHSTAR!

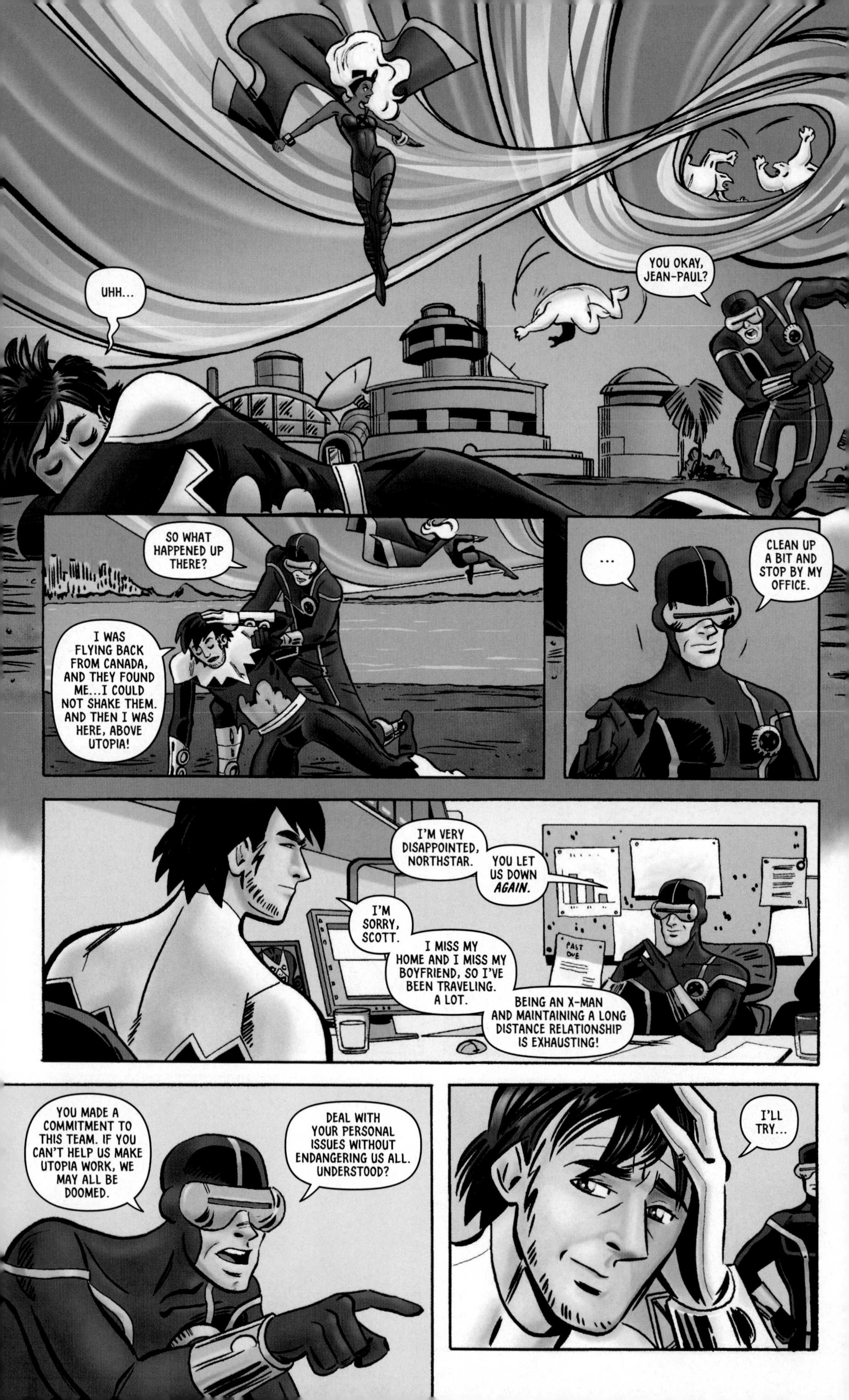

UHH...
YOU OKAY, JEAN-PAUL?
SO WHAT HAPPENED UP THERE?
I WAS FLYING BACK FROM CANADA, AND THEY FOUND ME...I COULD NOT SHAKE THEM. AND THEN I WAS HERE, ABOVE UTOPIA!
...
CLEAN UP A BIT AND STOP BY MY OFFICE.
I'M VERY DISAPPOINTED, NORTHSTAR.
YOU LET US DOWN *AGAIN.*
I'M SORRY, SCOTT.
I MISS MY HOME AND I MISS MY BOYFRIEND, SO I'VE BEEN TRAVELING. A LOT.
BEING AN X-MAN AND MAINTAINING A LONG DISTANCE RELATIONSHIP IS EXHAUSTING!
PAST DUE
YOU MADE A COMMITMENT TO THIS TEAM. IF YOU CAN'T HELP US MAKE UTOPIA WORK, WE MAY ALL BE DOOMED.
DEAL WITH YOUR PERSONAL ISSUES WITHOUT ENDANGERING US ALL. UNDERSTOOD?
I'LL TRY...

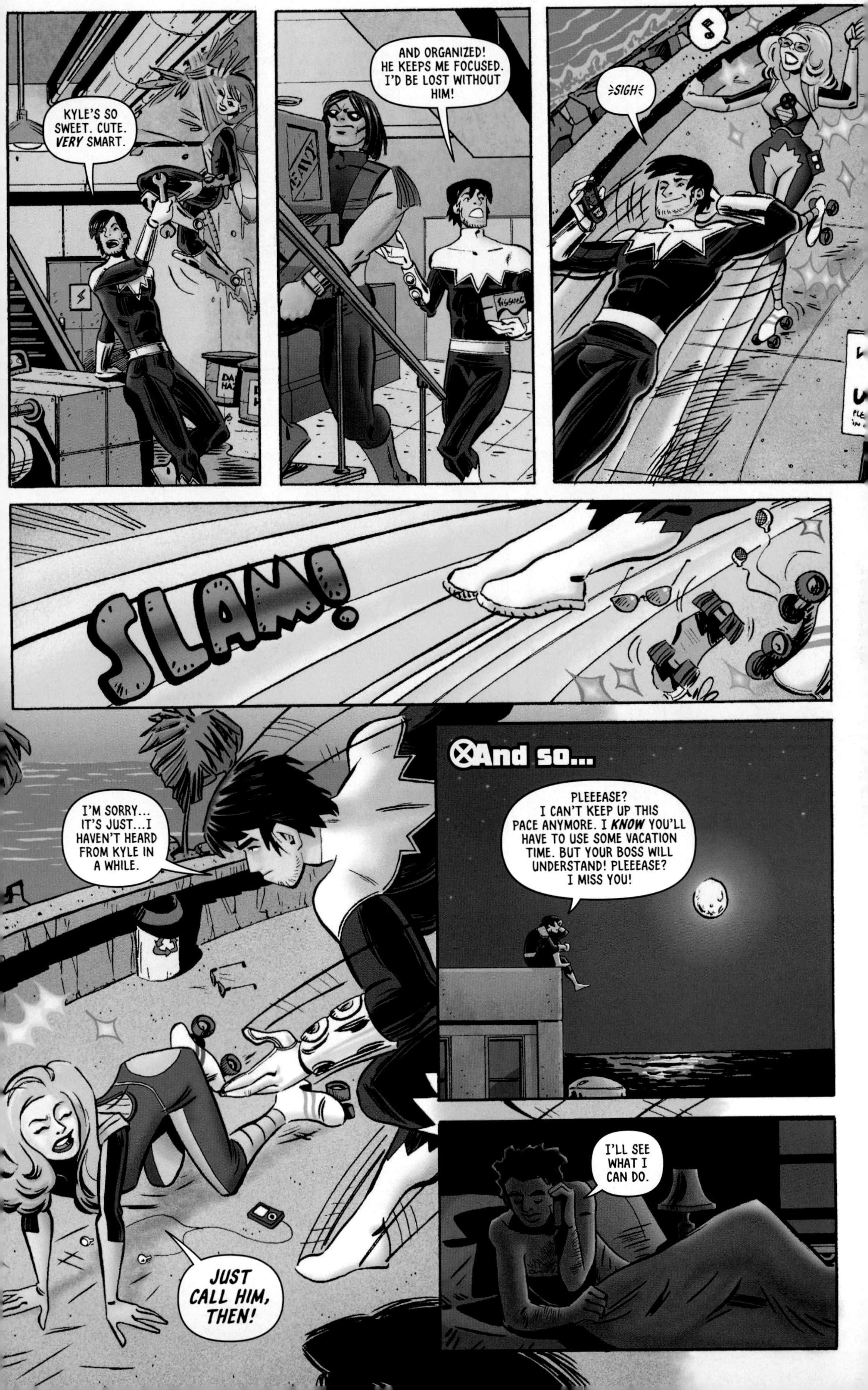
KYLE'S SO SWEET. CUTE. VERY SMART.
AND ORGANIZED! HE KEEPS ME FOCUSED. I'D BE LOST WITHOUT HIM!
HEAVY
SIGH
SLAM!
I'M SORRY... IT'S JUST...I HAVEN'T HEARD FROM KYLE IN A WHILE.
JUST CALL HIM, THEN!
And so...
PLEEEASE? I CAN'T KEEP UP THIS PACE ANYMORE. I KNOW YOU'LL HAVE TO USE SOME VACATION TIME. BUT YOUR BOSS WILL UNDERSTAND! PLEEEASE? I MISS YOU!
I'LL SEE WHAT I CAN DO.

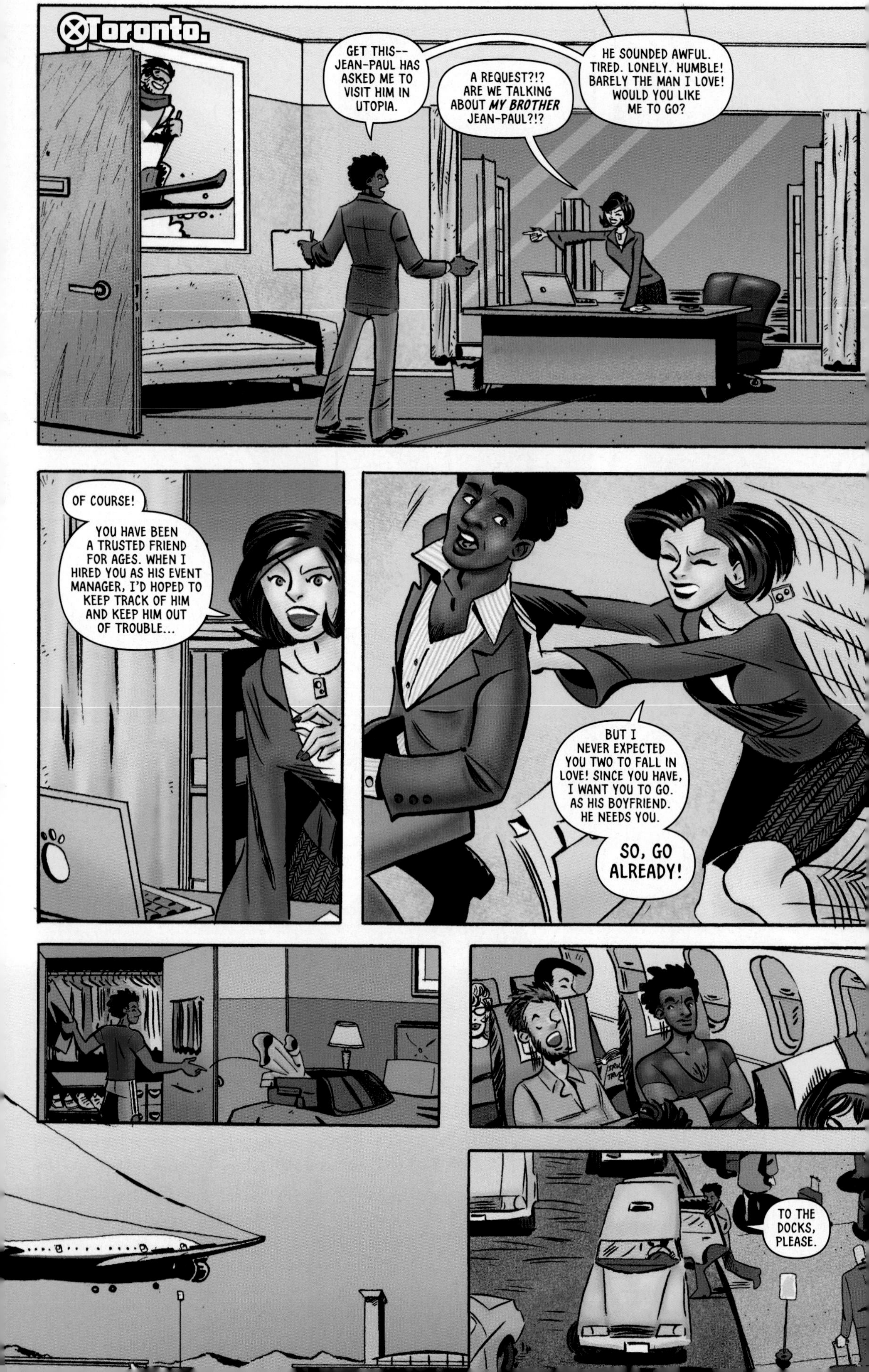
Toronto.
GET THIS-- JEAN-PAUL HAS ASKED ME TO VISIT HIM IN UTOPIA.
A REQUEST?!? ARE WE TALKING ABOUT MY BROTHER JEAN-PAUL?!?
HE SOUNDED AWFUL. TIRED. LONELY. HUMBLE! BARELY THE MAN I LOVE! WOULD YOU LIKE ME TO GO?
OF COURSE!
YOU HAVE BEEN A TRUSTED FRIEND FOR AGES. WHEN I HIRED YOU AS HIS EVENT MANAGER, I'D HOPED TO KEEP TRACK OF HIM AND KEEP HIM OUT OF TROUBLE...
BUT I NEVER EXPECTED YOU TWO TO FALL IN LOVE! SINCE YOU HAVE, I WANT YOU TO GO. AS HIS BOYFRIEND. HE NEEDS YOU.
SO, GO ALREADY!
TO THE DOCKS, PLEASE.

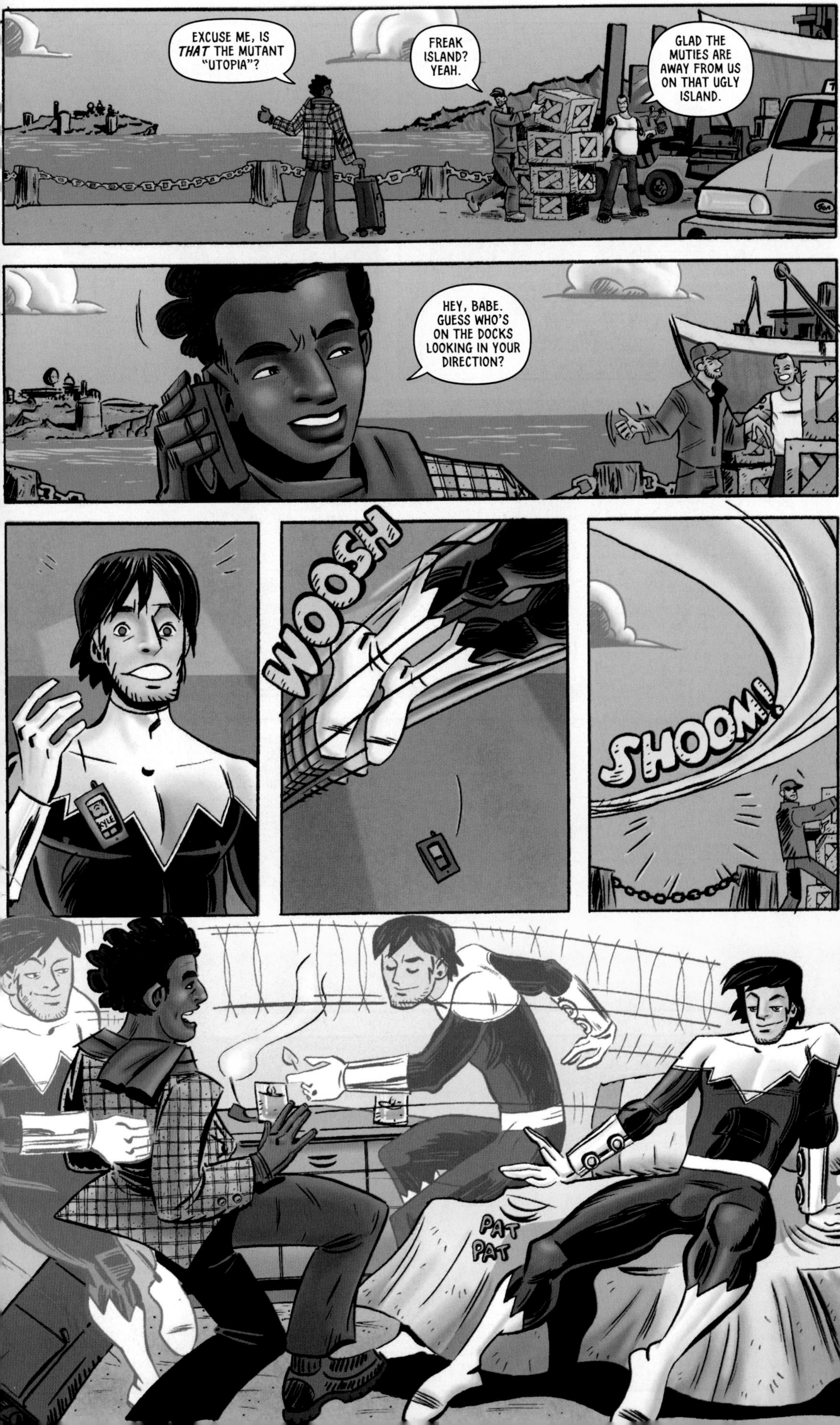
EXCUSE ME, IS *THAT* THE MUTANT "UTOPIA"?
FREAK ISLAND? YEAH.
GLAD THE MUTIES ARE AWAY FROM US ON THAT UGLY ISLAND.
HEY, BABE. GUESS WHO'S ON THE DOCKS LOOKING IN YOUR DIRECTION?
KYLE
WOOSH
SHOOM!
PAT PAT

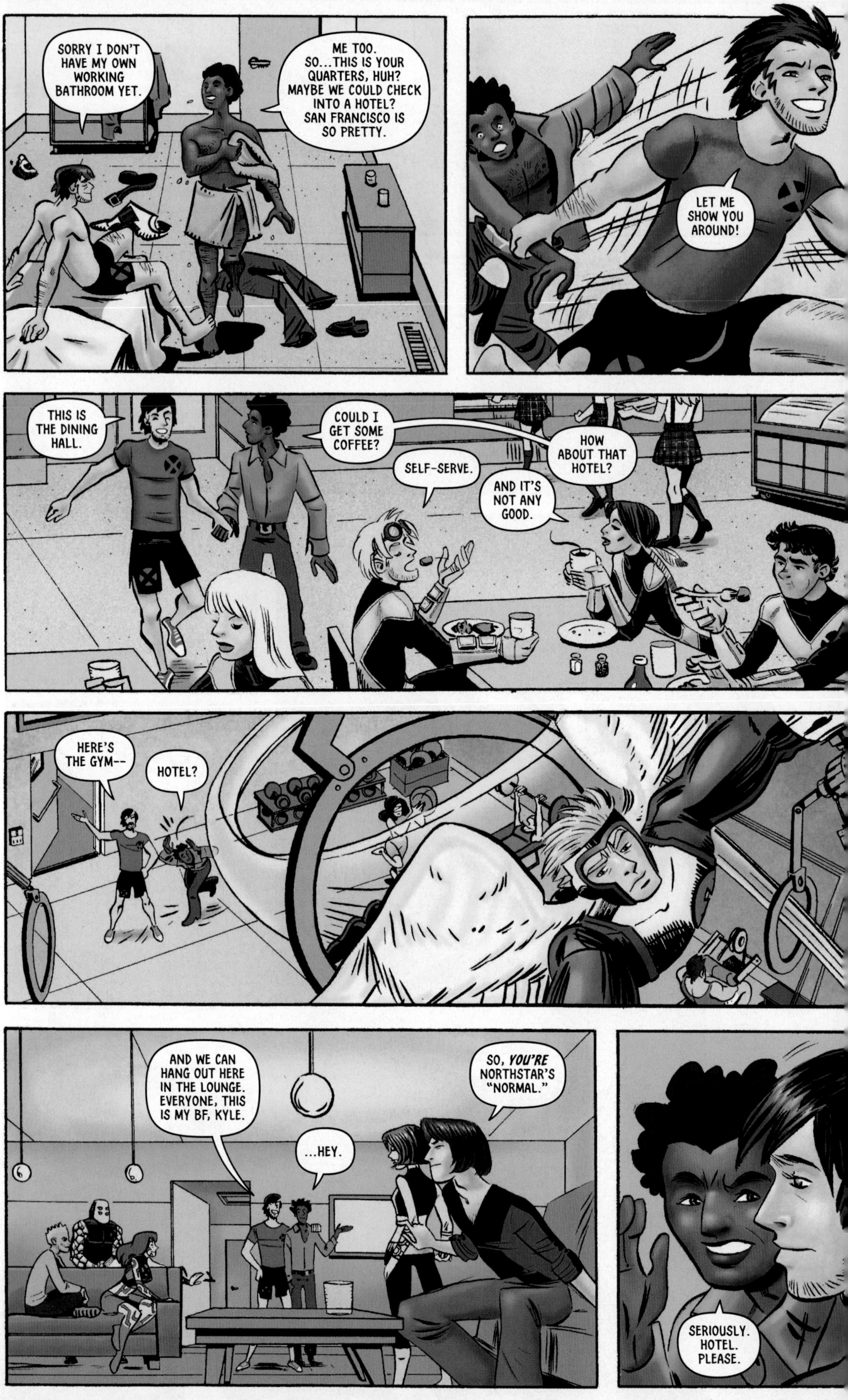
SORRY I DON'T HAVE MY OWN WORKING BATHROOM YET.
ME TOO. SO...THIS IS YOUR QUARTERS, HUH? MAYBE WE COULD CHECK INTO A HOTEL? SAN FRANCISCO IS SO PRETTY.
LET ME SHOW YOU AROUND!
THIS IS THE DINING HALL.
COULD I GET SOME COFFEE?
SELF-SERVE.
HOW ABOUT THAT HOTEL?
AND IT'S NOT ANY GOOD.
HERE'S THE GYM--
HOTEL?
AND WE CAN HANG OUT HERE IN THE LOUNGE. EVERYONE, THIS IS MY BF, KYLE.
...HEY.
SO, YOU'RE NORTHSTAR'S "NORMAL."
SERIOUSLY. HOTEL. PLEASE.

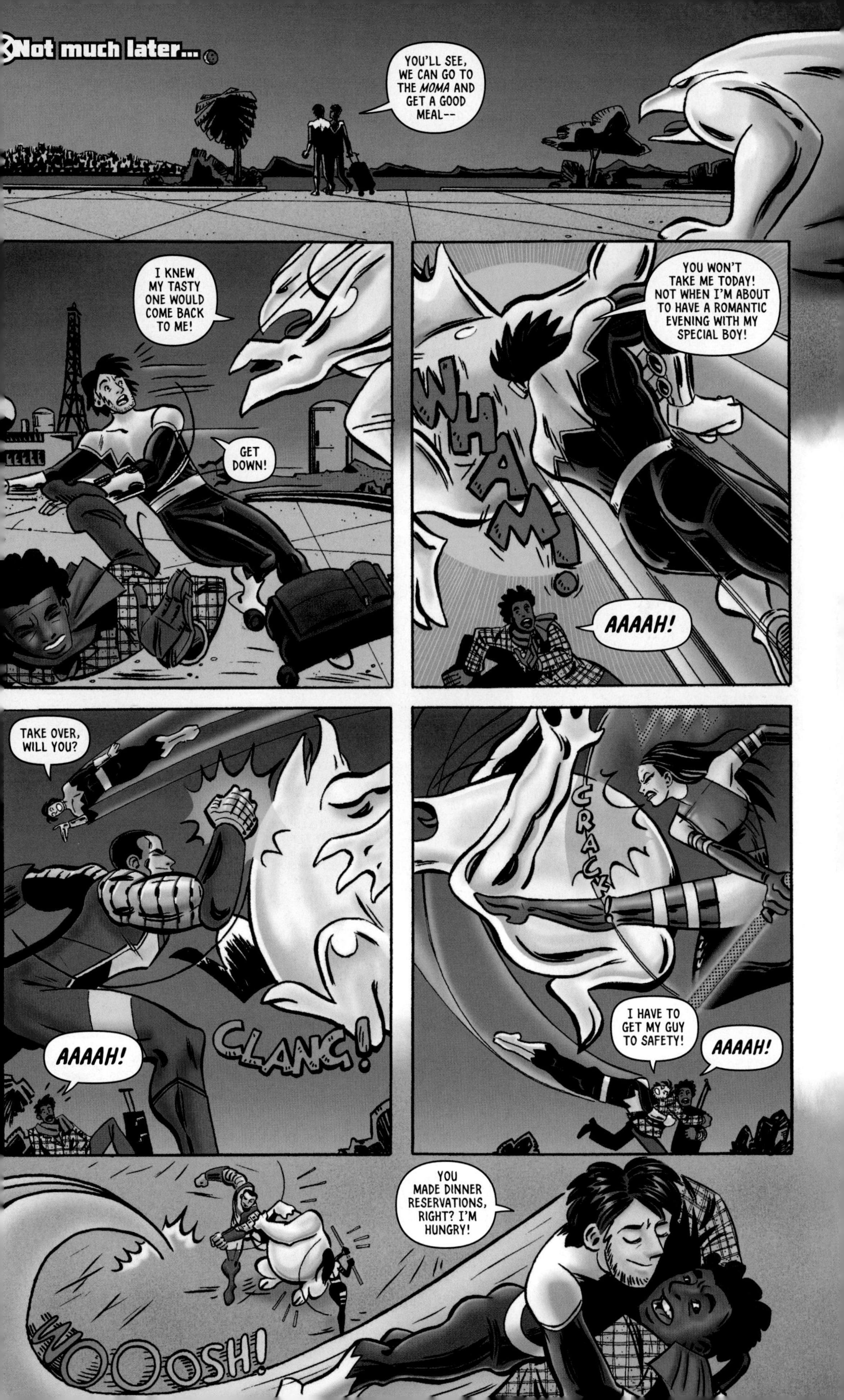
Not much later...
YOU'LL SEE, WE CAN GO TO THE *MOMA* AND GET A GOOD MEAL--
I KNEW MY TASTY ONE WOULD COME BACK TO ME!
GET DOWN!
YOU WON'T TAKE ME TODAY! NOT WHEN I'M ABOUT TO HAVE A ROMANTIC EVENING WITH MY SPECIAL BOY!
WHAM!
AAAAH!
TAKE OVER, WILL YOU?
CLANG!
AAAAH!
CRACK!
I HAVE TO GET MY GUY TO SAFETY!
AAAAH!
YOU MADE DINNER RESERVATIONS, RIGHT? I'M HUNGRY!
WOOOOSH!

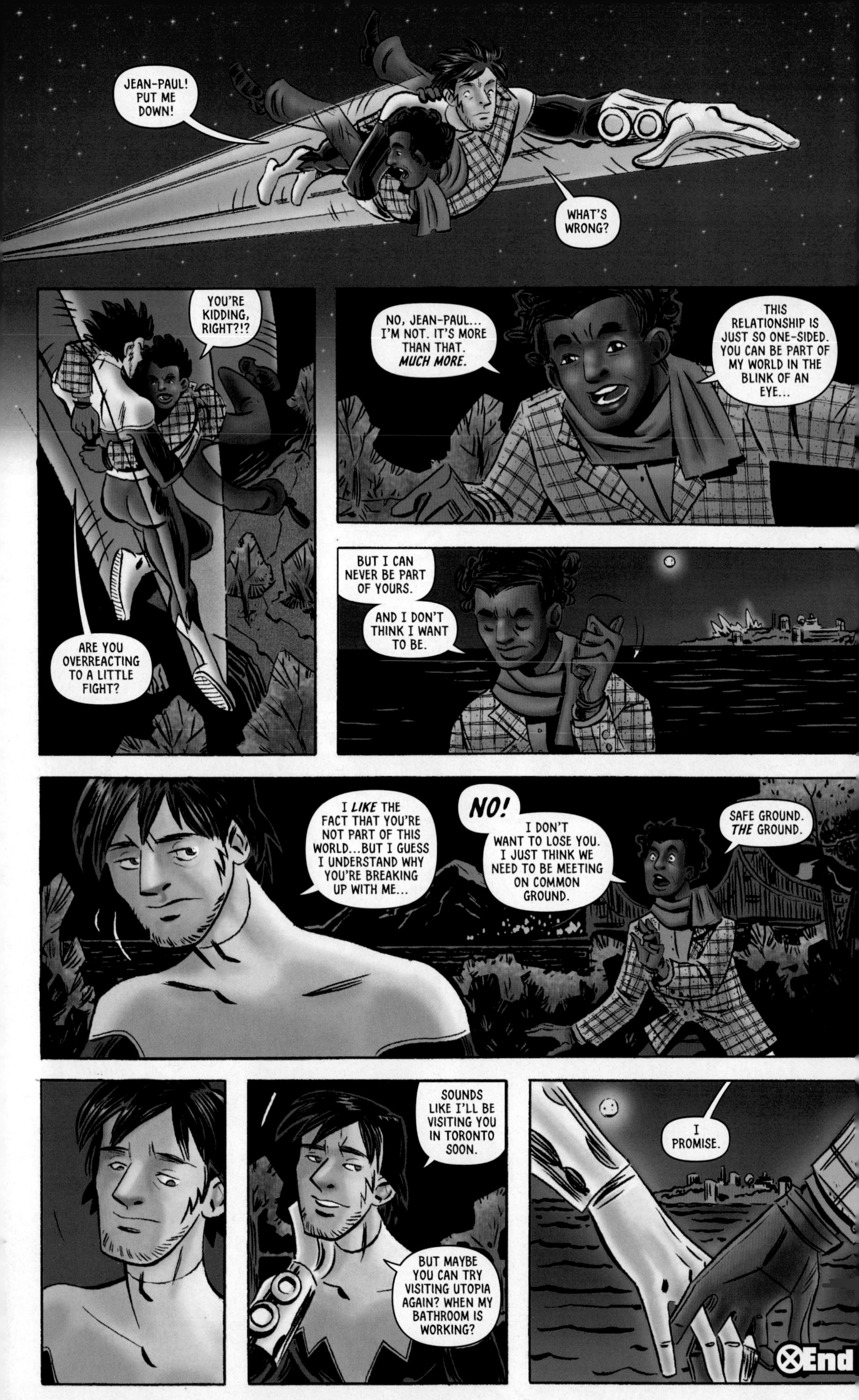
JEAN-PAUL! PUT ME DOWN!
WHAT'S WRONG?
YOU'RE KIDDING, RIGHT?!?
ARE YOU OVERREACTING TO A LITTLE FIGHT?
NO, JEAN-PAUL... I'M NOT. IT'S MORE THAN THAT. MUCH MORE.
THIS RELATIONSHIP IS JUST SO ONE-SIDED. YOU CAN BE PART OF MY WORLD IN THE BLINK OF AN EYE...
BUT I CAN NEVER BE PART OF YOURS.
AND I DON'T THINK I WANT TO BE.
I LIKE THE FACT THAT YOU'RE NOT PART OF THIS WORLD...BUT I GUESS I UNDERSTAND WHY YOU'RE BREAKING UP WITH ME...
NO!
I DON'T WANT TO LOSE YOU. I JUST THINK WE NEED TO BE MEETING ON COMMON GROUND.
SAFE GROUND. THE GROUND.
SOUNDS LIKE I'LL BE VISITING YOU IN TORONTO SOON.
BUT MAYBE YOU CAN TRY VISITING UTOPIA AGAIN? WHEN MY BATHROOM IS WORKING?
I PROMISE.
End

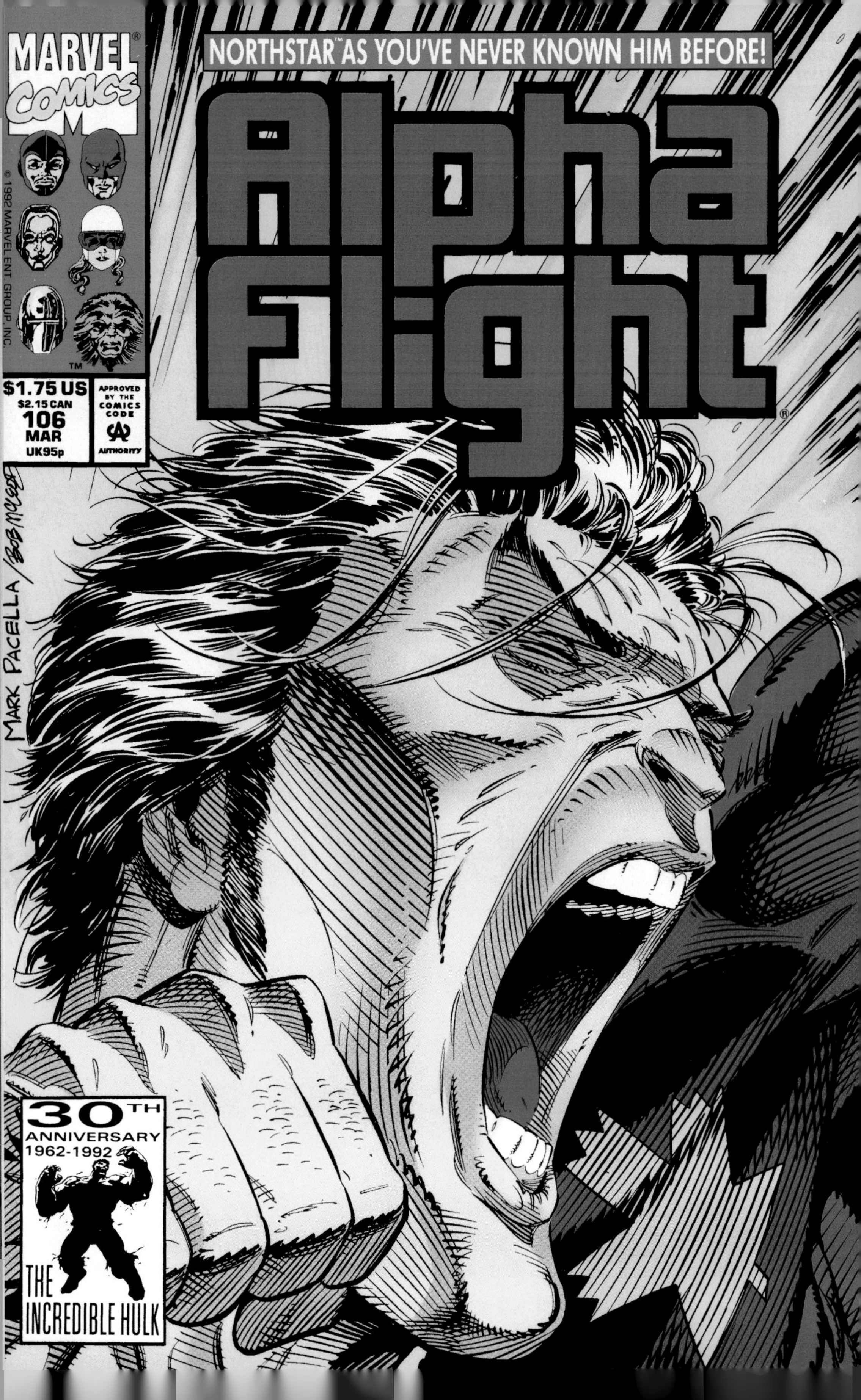
MARVEL®
COMICS
NORTHSTAR™ AS YOU'VE NEVER KNOWN HIM BEFORE!
Alpha Flight®
© 1992 MARVEL ENT. GROUP, INC.
$1.75 US
$2.15 CAN
106
MAR
UK95p
APPROVED BY THE COMICS CODE AUTHORITY
MARK PACELLA / BOB MCLEOD
30TH ANNIVERSARY
1962-1992
THE INCREDIBLE HULK

GUARDIAN! WEAPON OMEGA! SASQUATCH! NORTHSTAR! AURORA! PUCK! WINDSHEAR! THEY ARE CANADA'S OWN SUPER HERO TEAM, DEDICATED TO PROTECTING THEIR NATIVE LAND FROM THREATS BEYOND THE SCOPE OF CONVENTIONAL AUTHORITIES. STAN LEE PRESENTS ALPHA FLIGHT!

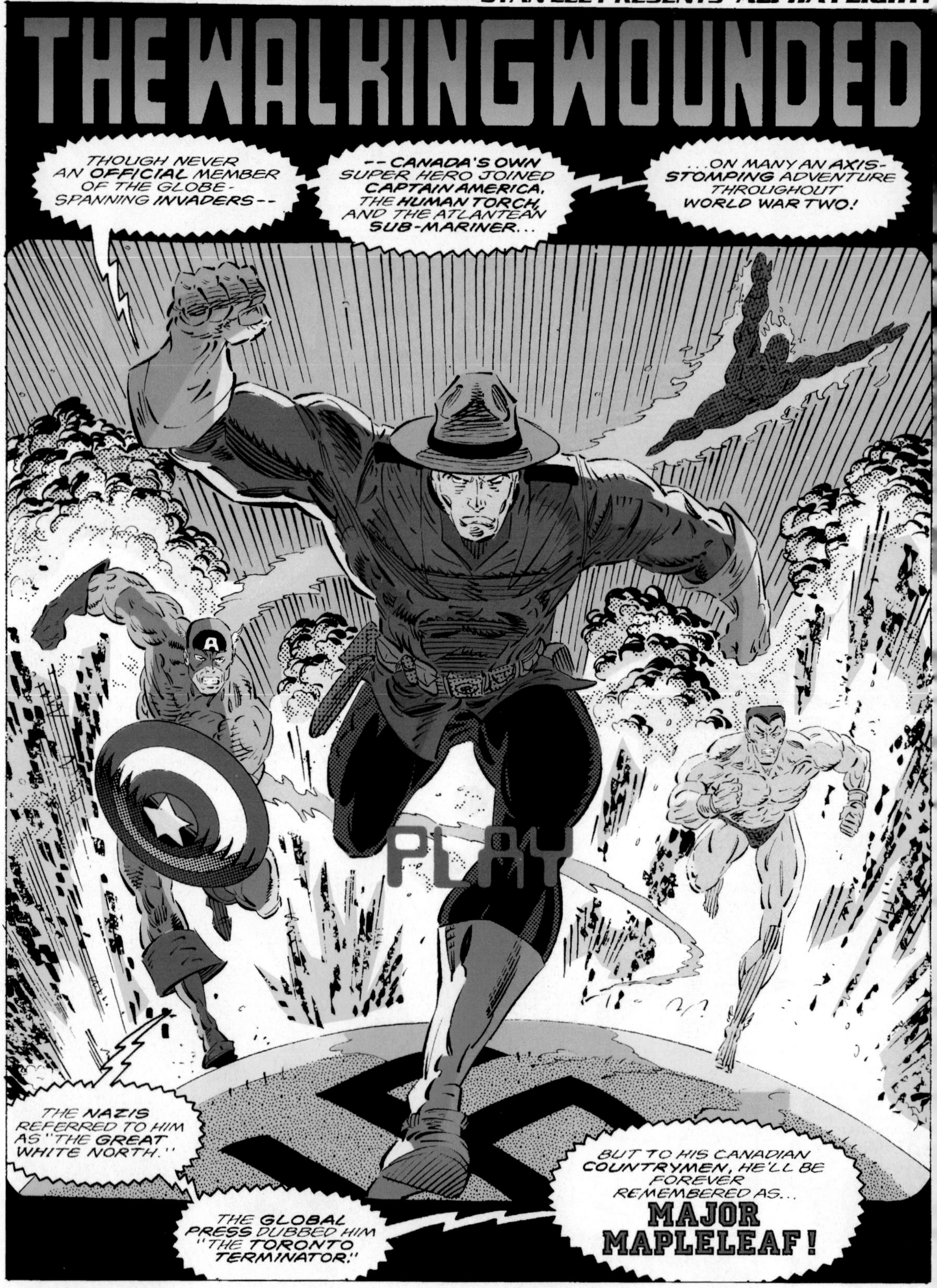
THE WALKING WOUNDED
THOUGH NEVER AN OFFICIAL MEMBER OF THE GLOBE-SPANNING INVADERS--
--CANADA'S OWN SUPER HERO JOINED CAPTAIN AMERICA, THE HUMAN TORCH, AND THE ATLANTEAN SUB-MARINER...
...ON MANY AN AXIS-STOMPING ADVENTURE THROUGHOUT WORLD WAR TWO!
PLAY
THE NAZIS REFERRED TO HIM AS "THE GREAT WHITE NORTH."
THE GLOBAL PRESS DUBBED HIM "THE TORONTO TERMINATOR."
BUT TO HIS CANADIAN COUNTRYMEN, HE'LL BE FOREVER REMEMBERED AS...
MAJOR MAPLELEAF!

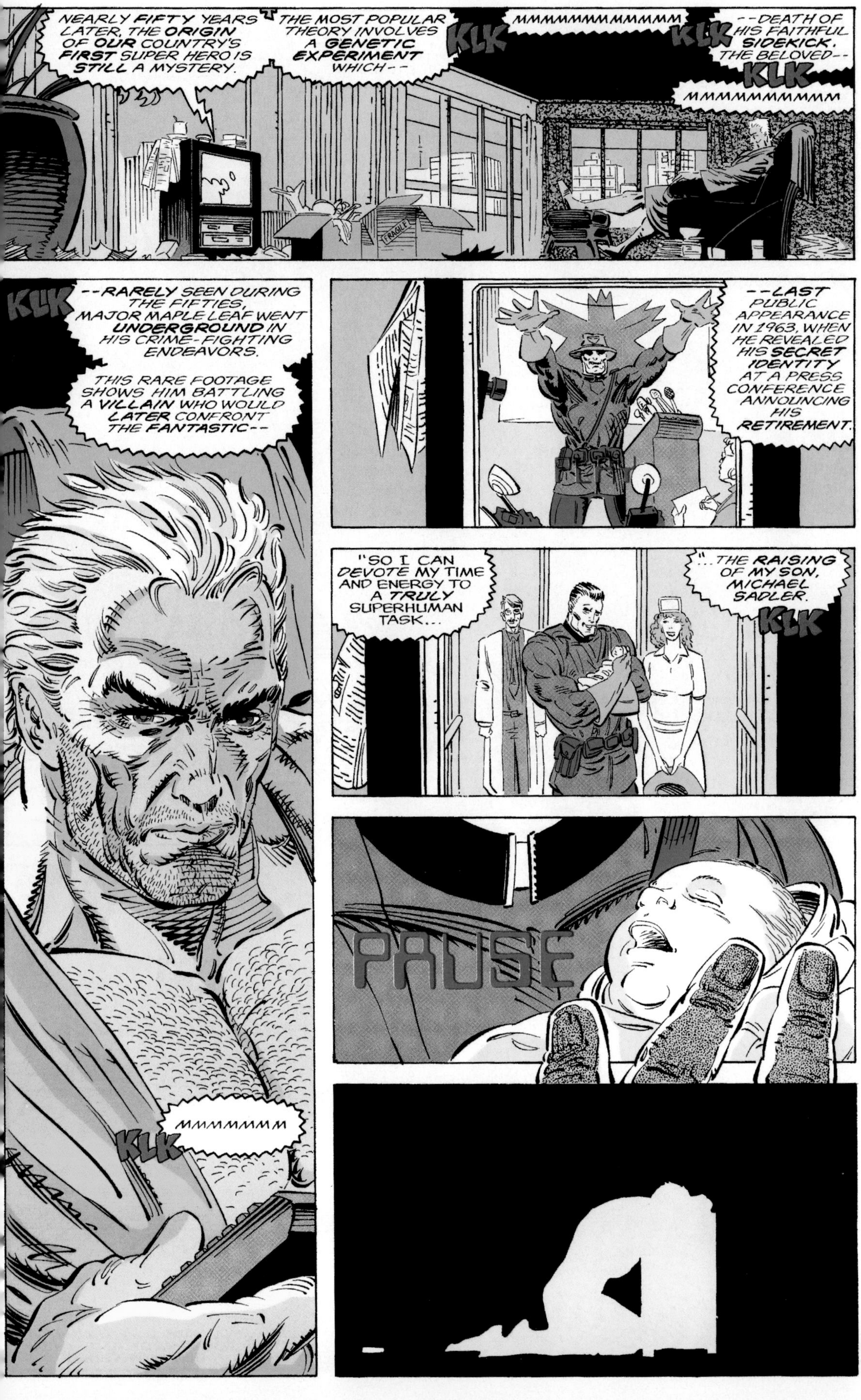
NEARLY FIFTY YEARS LATER, THE ORIGIN OF OUR COUNTRY'S FIRST SUPER HERO IS STILL A MYSTERY.
THE MOST POPULAR THEORY INVOLVES A GENETIC EXPERIMENT WHICH--
KLK
MMMMMMMMMMMMM
KLK
--DEATH OF HIS FAITHFUL SIDEKICK. THE BELOVED--
KLK
MMMMMMMMMMM
KLK
--RARELY SEEN DURING THE FIFTIES, MAJOR MAPLE LEAF WENT UNDERGROUND IN HIS CRIME-FIGHTING ENDEAVORS.
THIS RARE FOOTAGE SHOWS HIM BATTLING A VILLAIN WHO WOULD LATER CONFRONT THE FANTASTIC--
MMMMMMM
KLK
--LAST PUBLIC APPEARANCE IN 1963, WHEN HE REVEALED HIS SECRET IDENTITY AT A PRESS CONFERENCE ANNOUNCING HIS RETIREMENT.
"SO I CAN DEVOTE MY TIME AND ENERGY TO A TRULY SUPERHUMAN TASK...
"...THE RAISING OF MY SON, MICHAEL SADLER.
KLK
PAUSE

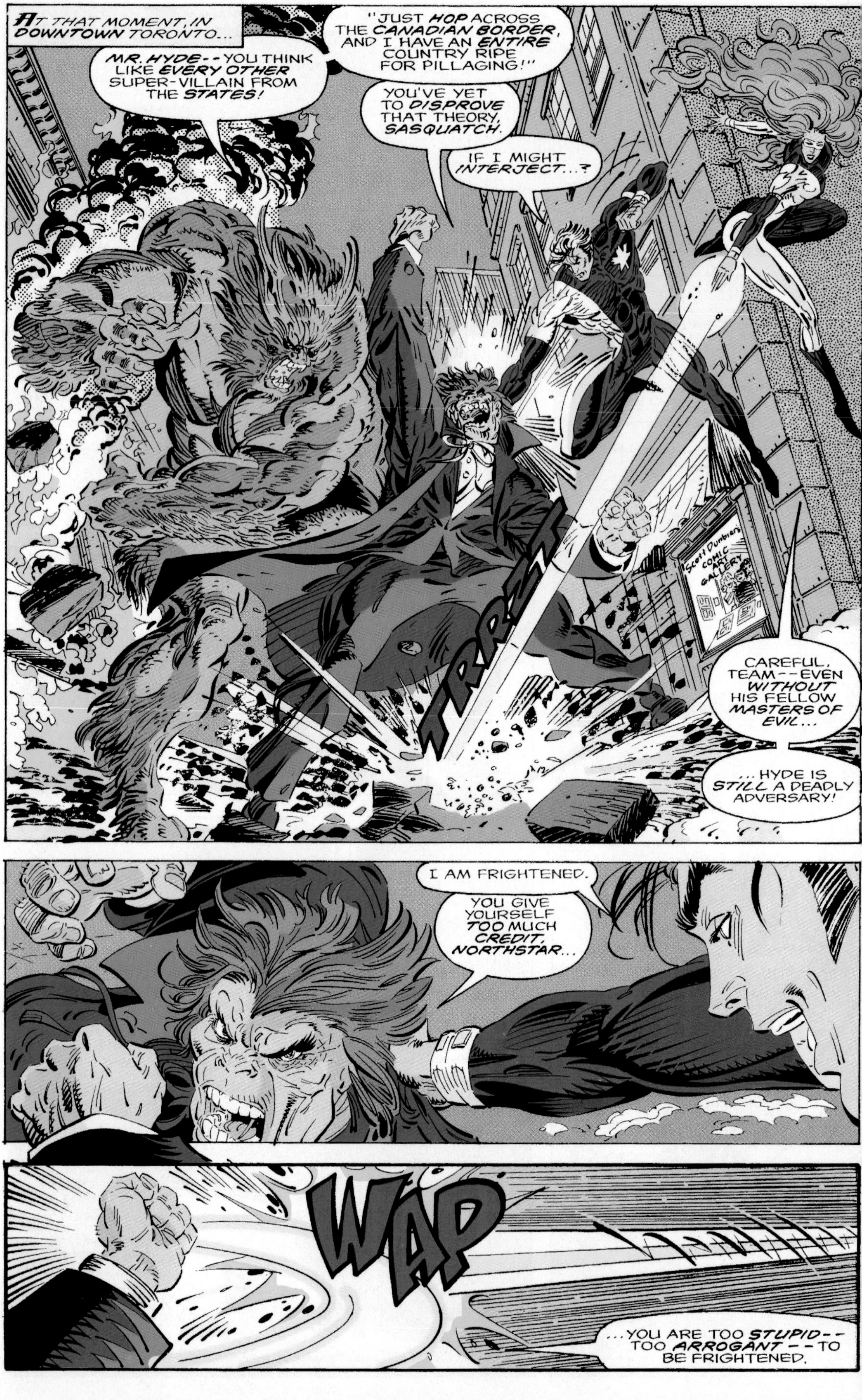
AT THAT MOMENT, IN DOWNTOWN TORONTO...
MR. HYDE--YOU THINK LIKE EVERY OTHER SUPER-VILLAIN FROM THE STATES!
"JUST HOP ACROSS THE CANADIAN BORDER, AND I HAVE AN ENTIRE COUNTRY RIPE FOR PILLAGING!"
YOU'VE YET TO DISPROVE THAT THEORY, SASQUATCH.
IF I MIGHT INTERJECT...?
Scott Dunbier's COMIC ART GALLERY
CAREFUL, TEAM--EVEN WITHOUT HIS FELLOW MASTERS OF EVIL...
...HYDE IS STILL A DEADLY ADVERSARY!
I AM FRIGHTENED.
YOU GIVE YOURSELF TOO MUCH CREDIT, NORTHSTAR...
WAP
...YOU ARE TOO STUPID--TOO ARROGANT--TO BE FRIGHTENED.

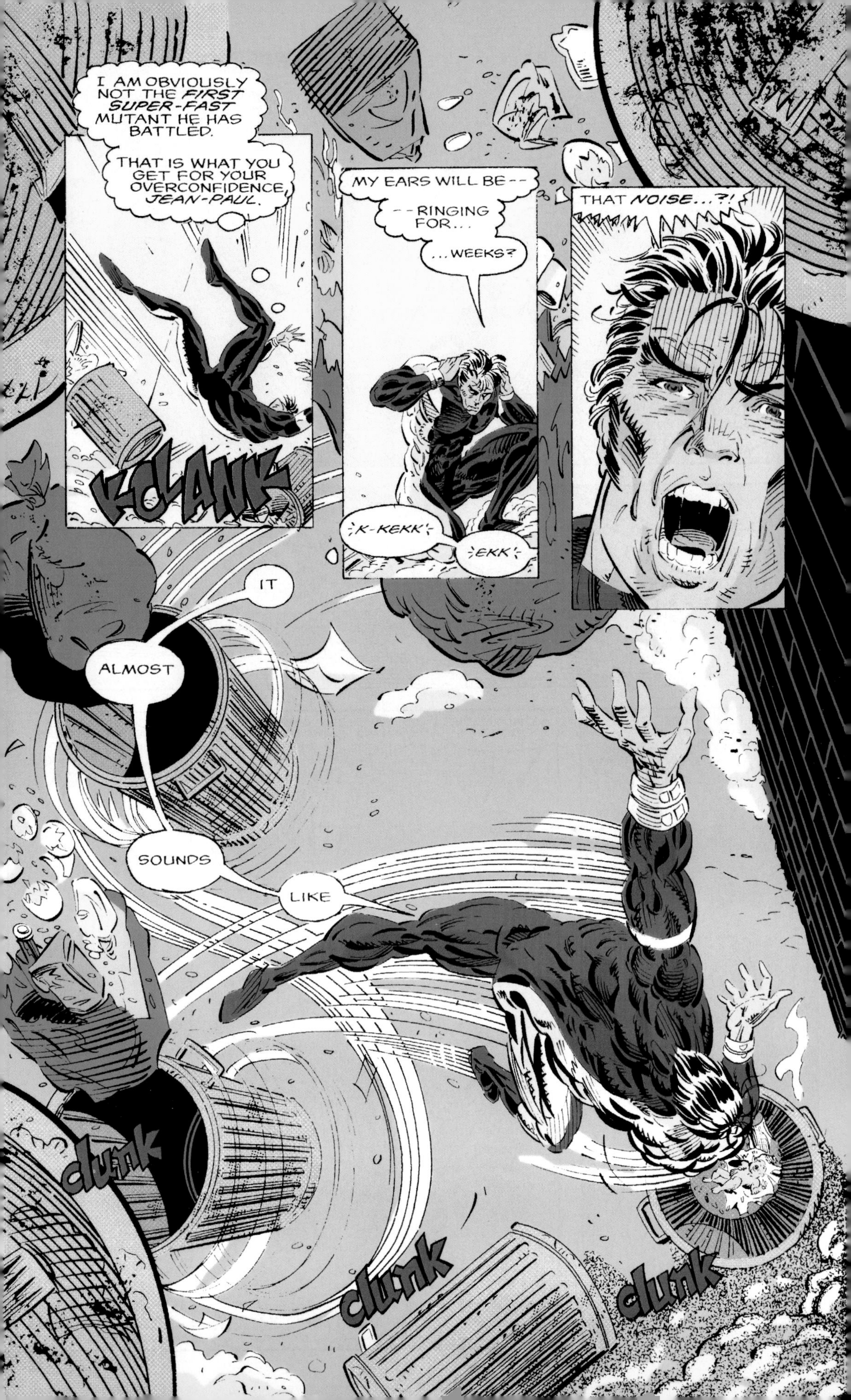
I AM OBVIOUSLY NOT THE FIRST SUPER-FAST MUTANT HE HAS BATTLED.
THAT IS WHAT YOU GET FOR YOUR OVERCONFIDENCE, JEAN-PAUL.
K-CLANK
MY EARS WILL BE--
--RINGING FOR...
...WEEKS?
K-KEKK
EKK
THAT NOISE...?!
IT
ALMOST
SOUNDS
LIKE
clunk
clunk
clunk

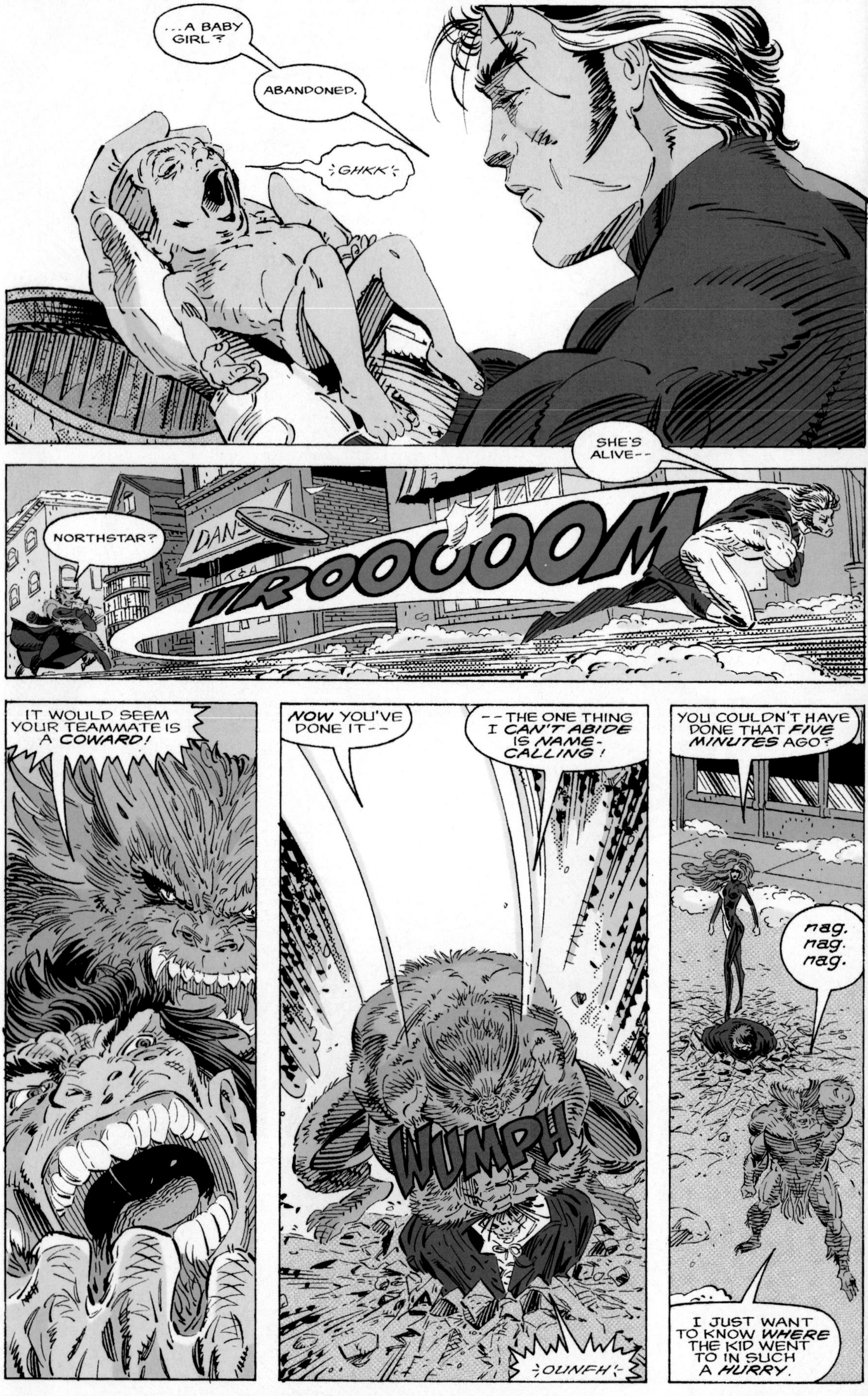
...A BABY GIRL?
ABANDONED.
GHKK
SHE'S ALIVE--
NORTHSTAR?
VROOOOOOM
IT WOULD SEEM YOUR TEAMMATE IS A COWARD!
NOW YOU'VE DONE IT--
--THE ONE THING I CAN'T ABIDE IS NAME-CALLING!
WUMPH
OUNFH
YOU COULDN'T HAVE DONE THAT FIVE MINUTES AGO?
nag. nag. nag.
I JUST WANT TO KNOW WHERE THE KID WENT TO IN SUCH A HURRY.

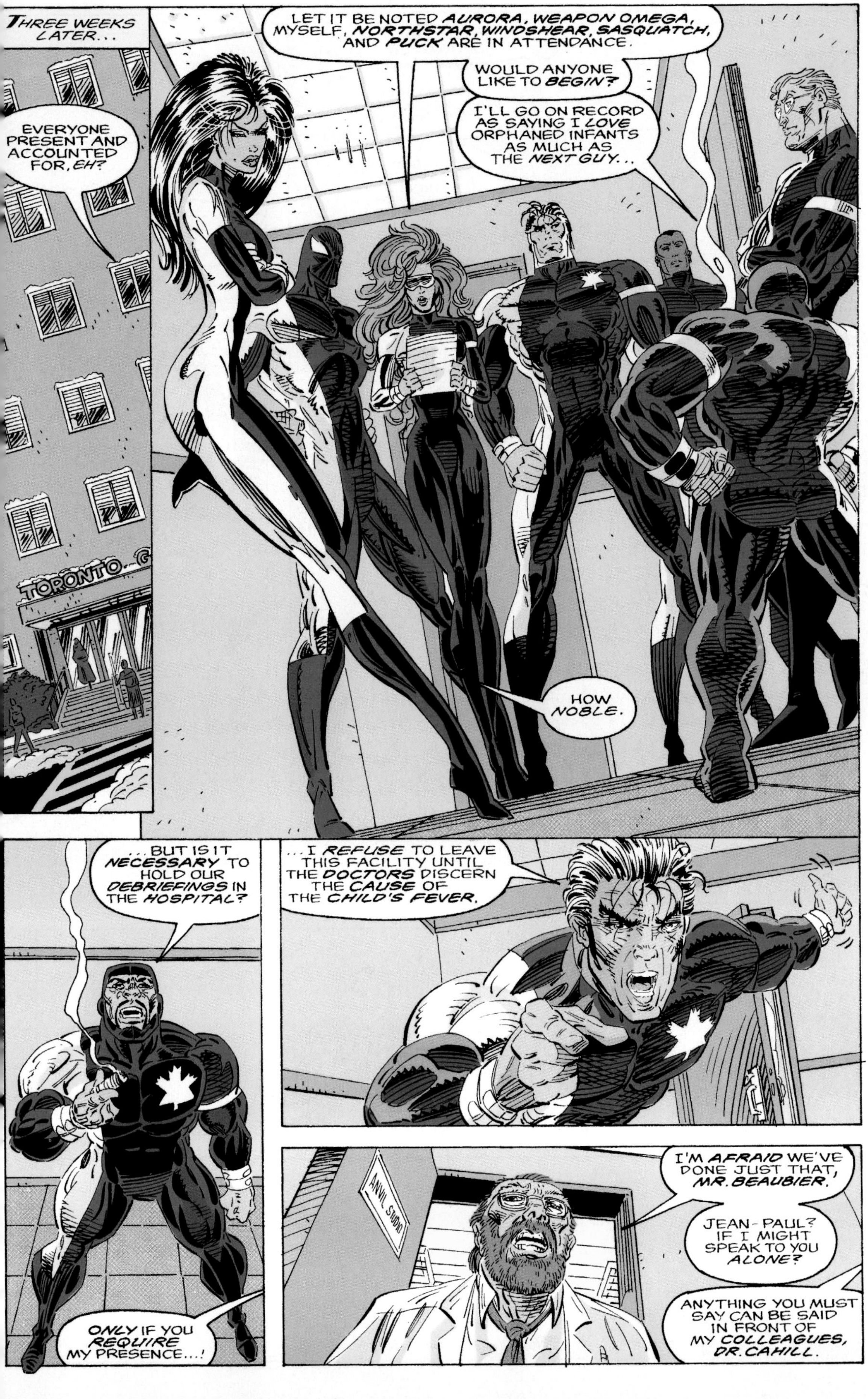
THREE WEEKS LATER...
EVERYONE PRESENT AND ACCOUNTED FOR, EH?
TORONTO G
LET IT BE NOTED AURORA, WEAPON OMEGA, MYSELF, NORTHSTAR, WINDSHEAR, SASQUATCH, AND PUCK ARE IN ATTENDANCE.
WOULD ANYONE LIKE TO BEGIN?
I'LL GO ON RECORD AS SAYING I LOVE ORPHANED INFANTS AS MUCH AS THE NEXT GUY...
HOW NOBLE.
...BUT IS IT NECESSARY TO HOLD OUR DEBRIEFINGS IN THE HOSPITAL?
ONLY IF YOU REQUIRE MY PRESENCE...!
...I REFUSE TO LEAVE THIS FACILITY UNTIL THE DOCTORS DISCERN THE CAUSE OF THE CHILD'S FEVER.
ANVIL STUDIO
I'M AFRAID WE'VE DONE JUST THAT, MR. BEAUBIER.
JEAN-PAUL? IF I MIGHT SPEAK TO YOU ALONE?
ANYTHING YOU MUST SAY CAN BE SAID IN FRONT OF MY COLLEAGUES, DR. CAHILL.

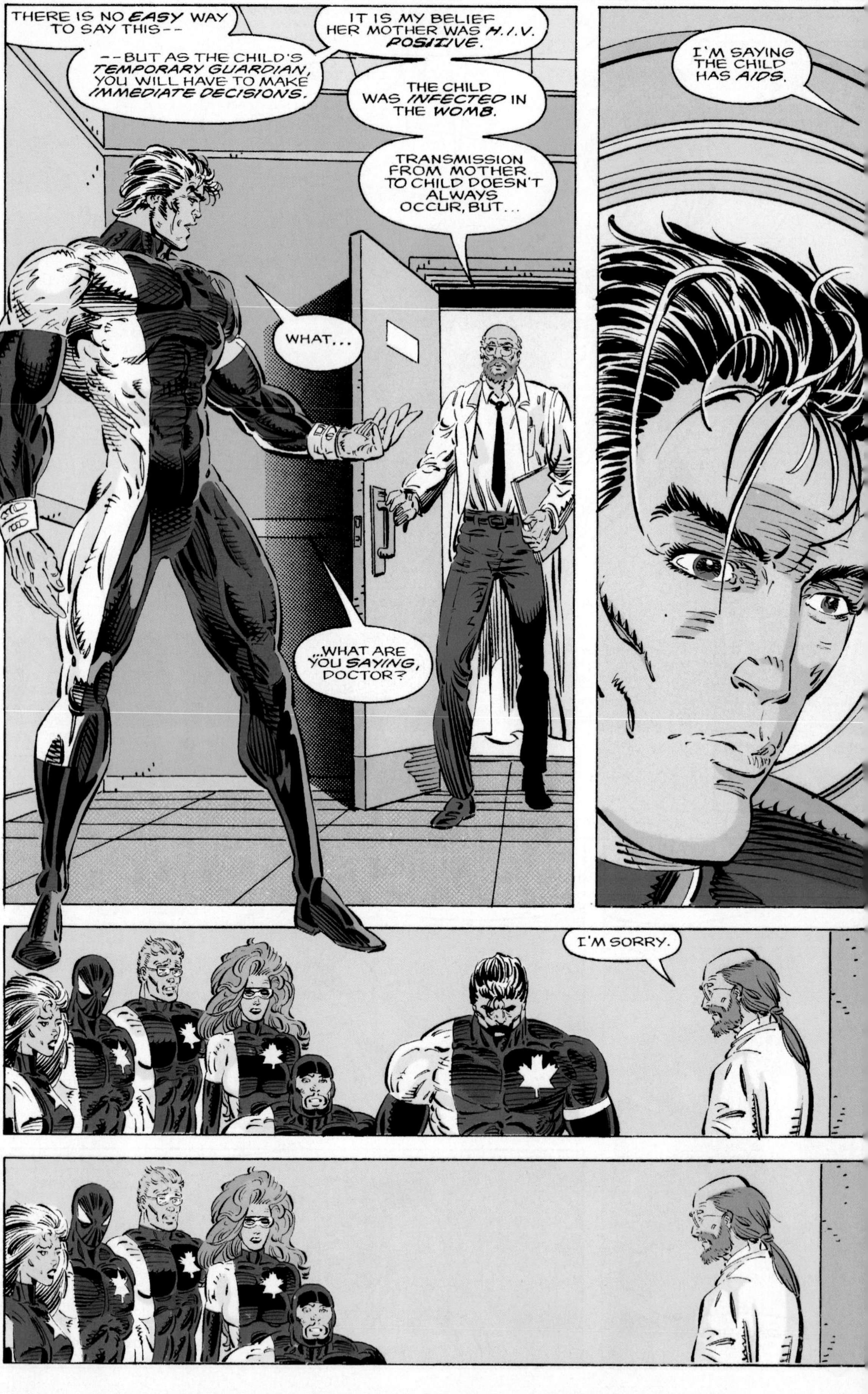
THERE IS NO EASY WAY TO SAY THIS--
--BUT AS THE CHILD'S TEMPORARY GUARDIAN, YOU WILL HAVE TO MAKE IMMEDIATE DECISIONS.
IT IS MY BELIEF HER MOTHER WAS H.I.V. POSITIVE.
THE CHILD WAS INFECTED IN THE WOMB.
TRANSMISSION FROM MOTHER TO CHILD DOESN'T ALWAYS OCCUR, BUT...
WHAT...
...WHAT ARE YOU SAYING, DOCTOR?
I'M SAYING THE CHILD HAS AIDS.
I'M SORRY.

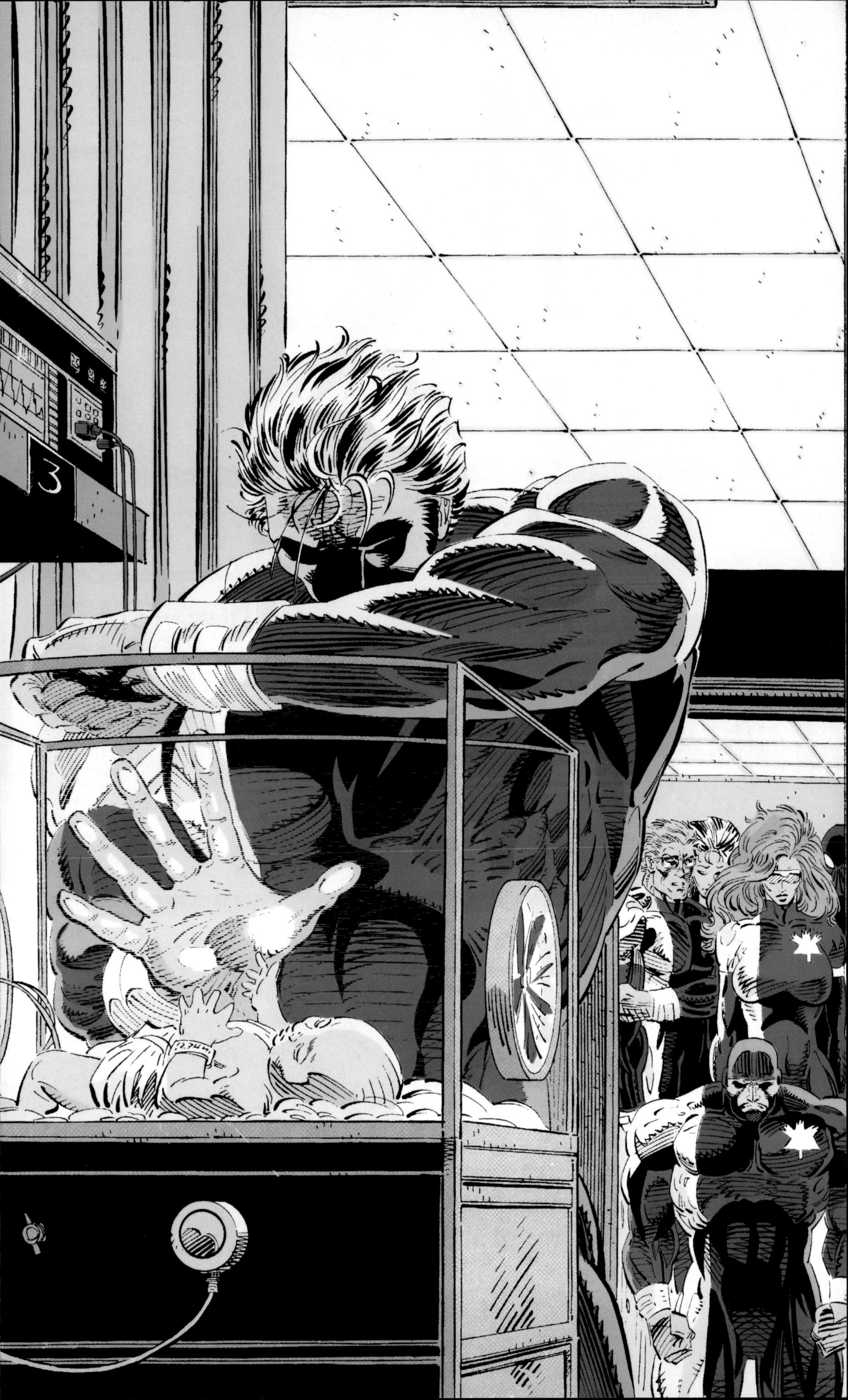
3

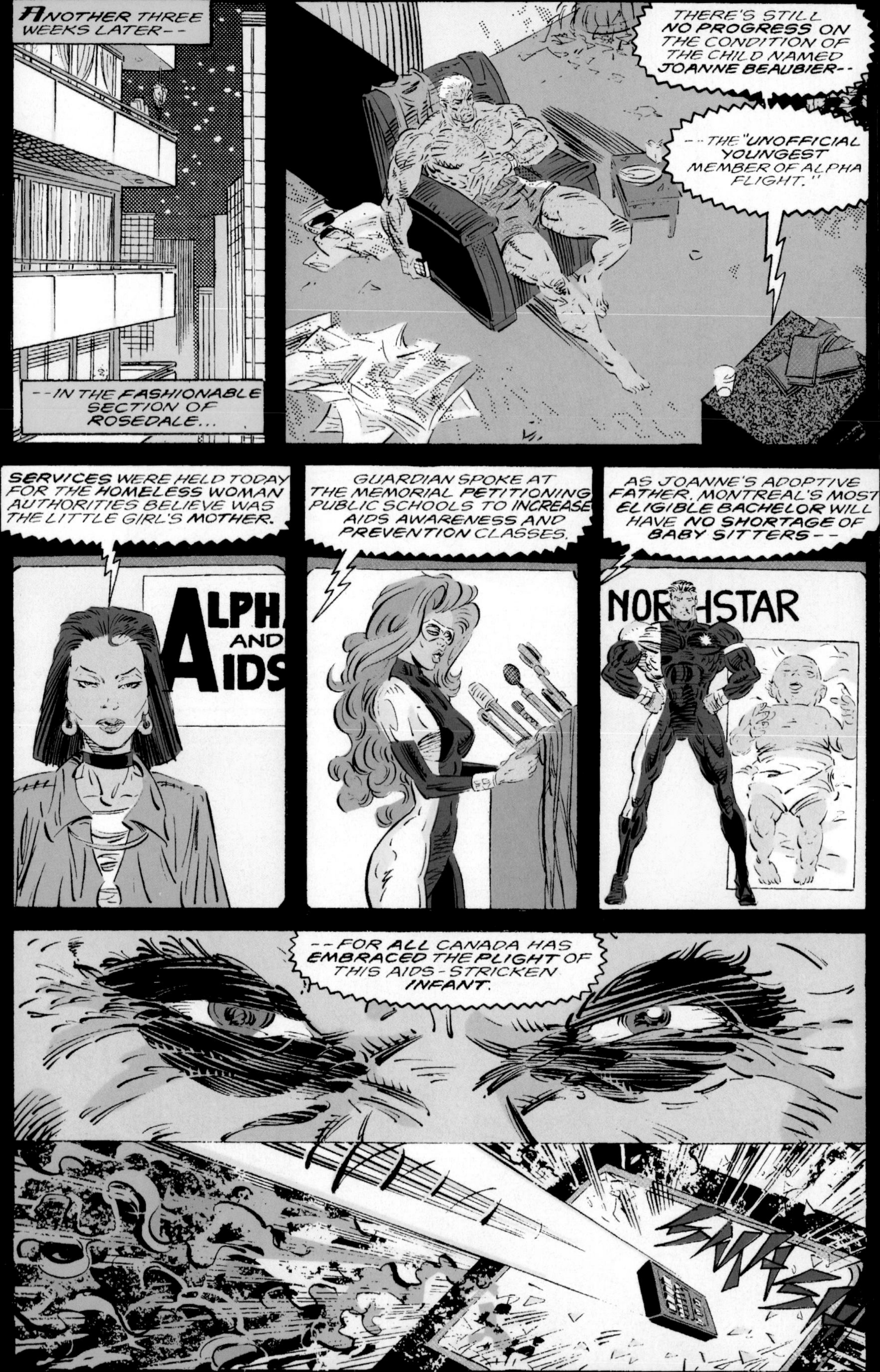
ANOTHER THREE WEEKS LATER--
--IN THE FASHIONABLE SECTION OF ROSEDALE...
THERE'S STILL NO PROGRESS ON THE CONDITION OF THE CHILD NAMED JOANNE BEAUBIER--
--THE "UNOFFICIAL YOUNGEST MEMBER OF ALPHA FLIGHT."
SERVICES WERE HELD TODAY FOR THE HOMELESS WOMAN AUTHORITIES BELIEVE WAS THE LITTLE GIRL'S MOTHER.
ALPH AND AIDS
GUARDIAN SPOKE AT THE MEMORIAL PETITIONING PUBLIC SCHOOLS TO INCREASE AIDS AWARENESS AND PREVENTION CLASSES.
AS JOANNE'S ADOPTIVE FATHER, MONTREAL'S MOST ELIGIBLE BACHELOR WILL HAVE NO SHORTAGE OF BABY SITTERS--
NORHSTAR
--FOR ALL CANADA HAS EMBRACED THE PLIGHT OF THIS AIDS-STRICKEN INFANT.

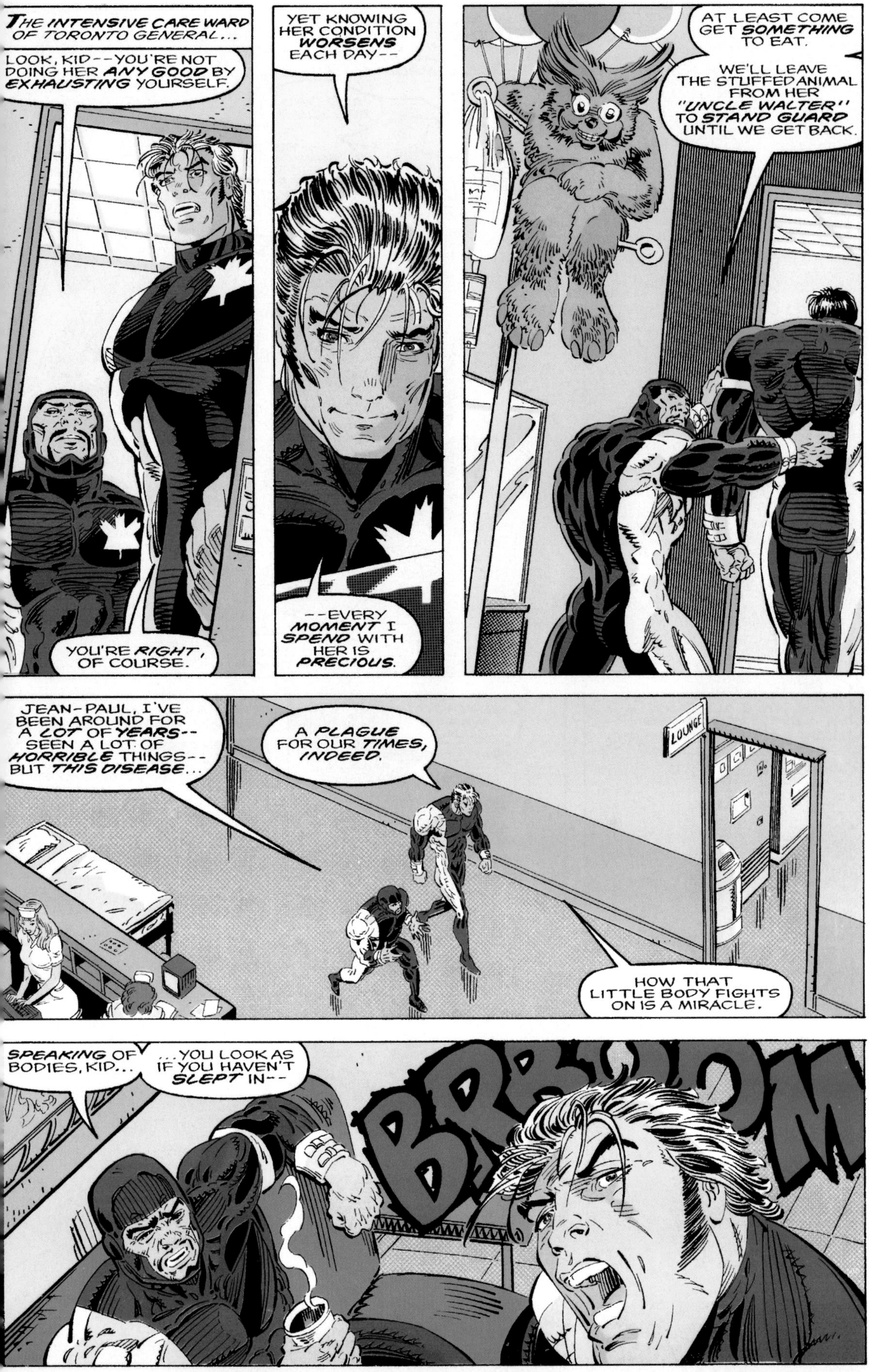
THE INTENSIVE CARE WARD OF TORONTO GENERAL...
LOOK, KID--YOU'RE NOT DOING HER ANY GOOD BY EXHAUSTING YOURSELF.
YOU'RE RIGHT, OF COURSE.
YET KNOWING HER CONDITION WORSENS EACH DAY--
--EVERY MOMENT I SPEND WITH HER IS PRECIOUS.
AT LEAST COME GET SOMETHING TO EAT.
WE'LL LEAVE THE STUFFED ANIMAL FROM HER "UNCLE WALTER" TO STAND GUARD UNTIL WE GET BACK.
JEAN-PAUL, I'VE BEEN AROUND FOR A LOT OF YEARS--SEEN A LOT OF HORRIBLE THINGS--BUT THIS DISEASE...
A PLAGUE FOR OUR TIMES, INDEED.
LOUNGE
HOW THAT LITTLE BODY FIGHTS ON IS A MIRACLE.
SPEAKING OF BODIES, KID...
...YOU LOOK AS IF YOU HAVEN'T SLEPT IN--
BRBOOM

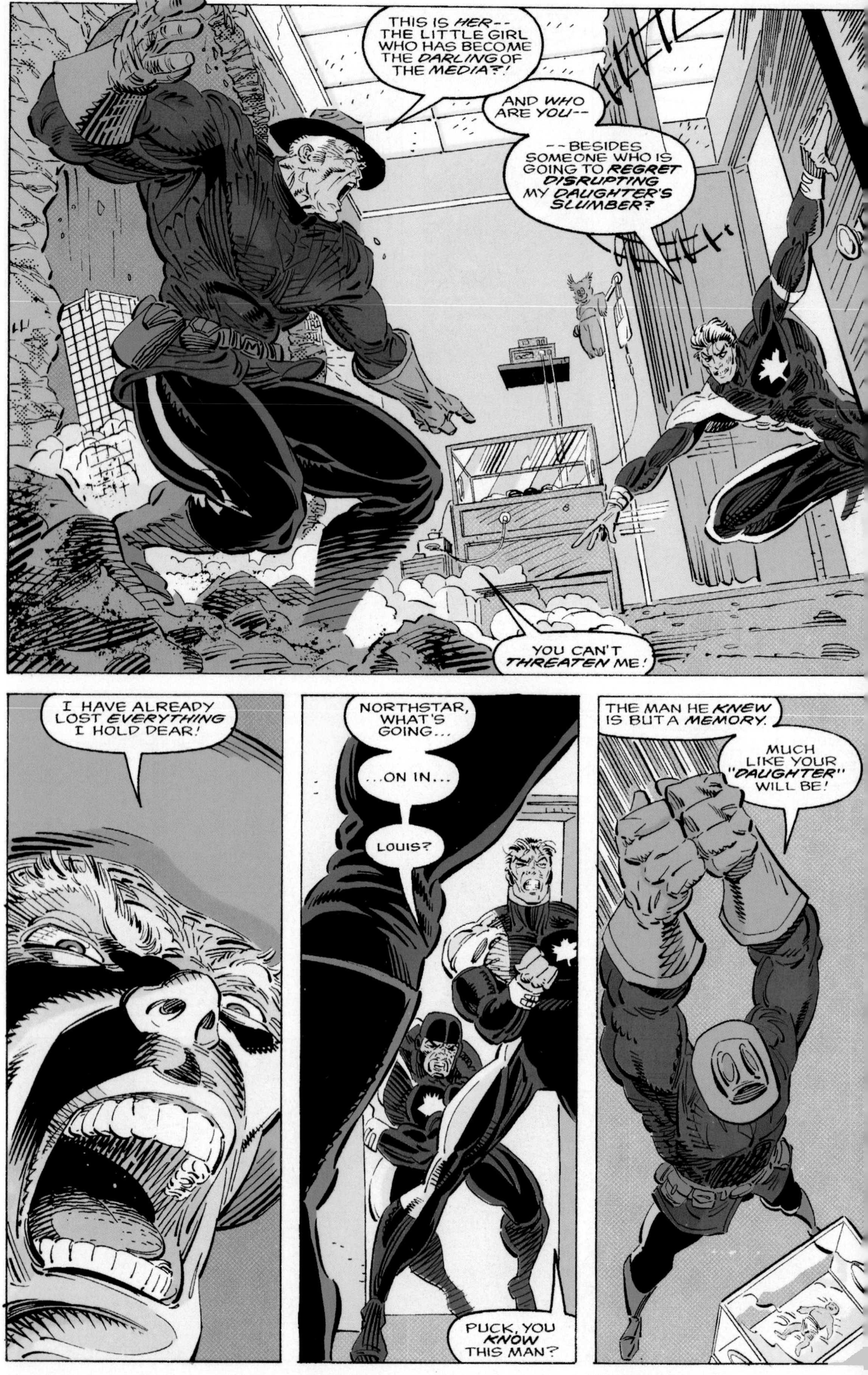
THIS IS *HER*-- THE LITTLE GIRL WHO HAS BECOME THE *DARLING* OF THE *MEDIA*?!
AND *WHO* ARE *YOU*--
--BESIDES SOMEONE WHO IS GOING TO *REGRET DISRUPTING* MY *DAUGHTER'S SLUMBER*?
YOU CAN'T *THREATEN* ME!
I HAVE ALREADY LOST *EVERYTHING* I HOLD DEAR!
NORTHSTAR, WHAT'S GOING...
...ON IN...
LOUIS?
PUCK, YOU *KNOW* THIS MAN?
THE MAN HE *KNEW* IS BUT A *MEMORY*.
MUCH LIKE YOUR "*DAUGHTER*" WILL BE!

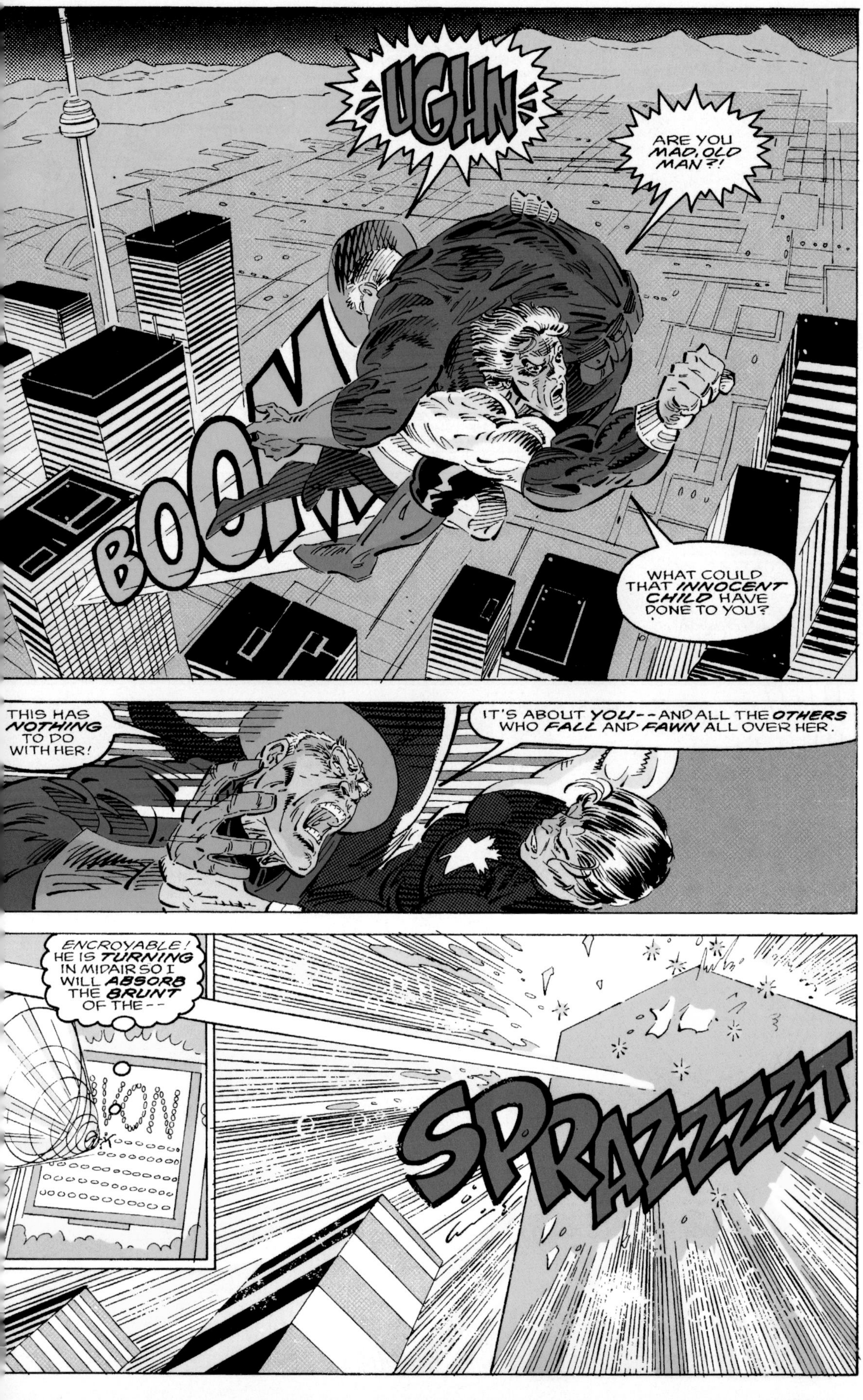
UGHN
ARE YOU MAD, OLD MAN?!
BOOM
WHAT COULD THAT INNOCENT CHILD HAVE DONE TO YOU?
THIS HAS NOTHING TO DO WITH HER!
IT'S ABOUT YOU--AND ALL THE OTHERS WHO FALL AND FAWN ALL OVER HER.
ENCROYABLE! HE IS TURNING IN MIDAIR SO I WILL ABSORB THE BRUNT OF THE--
SPRAZZZZT

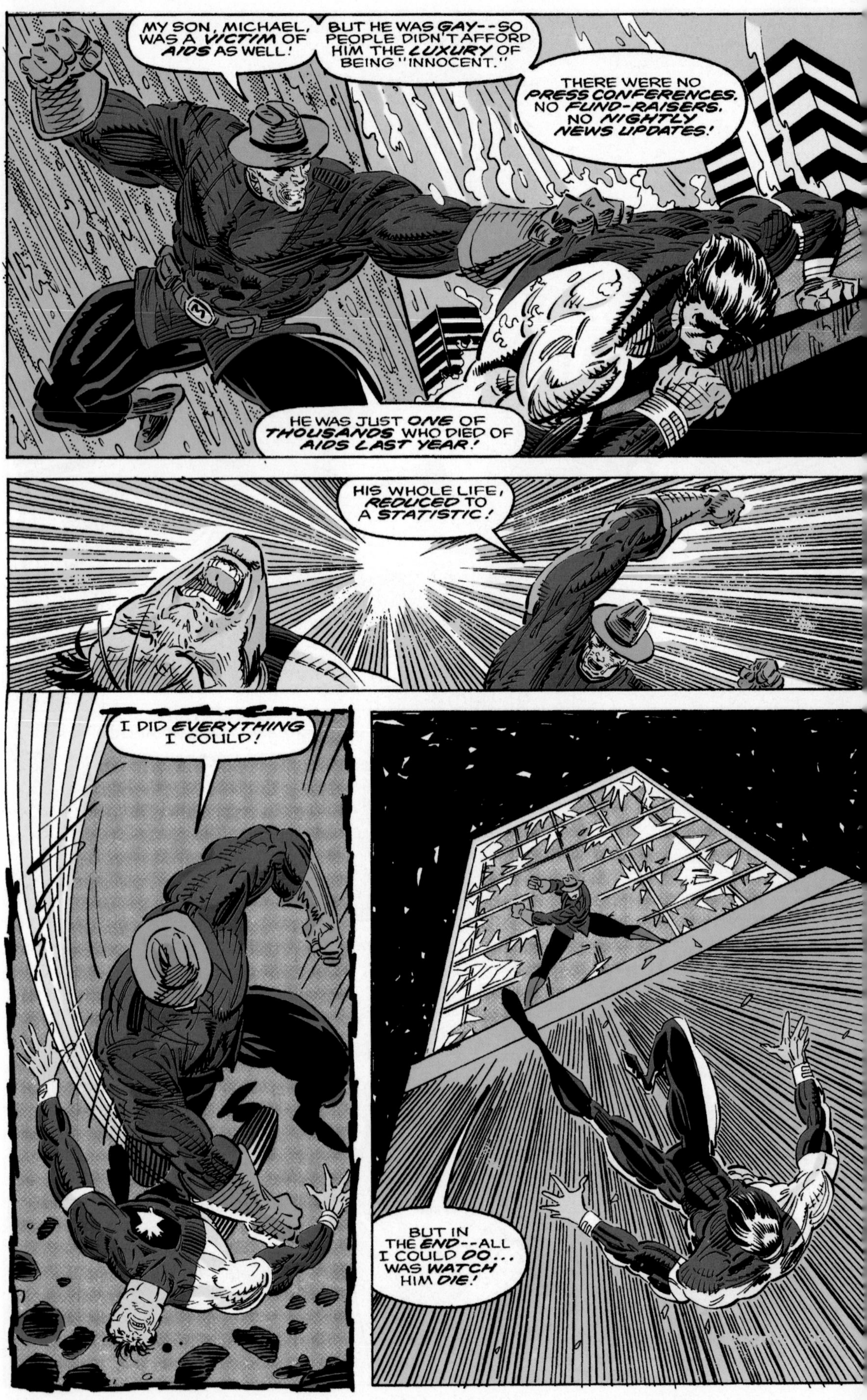
MY SON, MICHAEL, WAS A VICTIM OF AIDS AS WELL!
BUT HE WAS GAY--SO PEOPLE DIDN'T AFFORD HIM THE LUXURY OF BEING "INNOCENT."
THERE WERE NO PRESS CONFERENCES. NO FUND-RAISERS. NO NIGHTLY NEWS UPDATES!
HE WAS JUST ONE OF THOUSANDS WHO DIED OF AIDS LAST YEAR!
HIS WHOLE LIFE, REDUCED TO A STATISTIC!
I DID EVERYTHING I COULD!
BUT IN THE END--ALL I COULD DO... WAS WATCH HIM DIE!

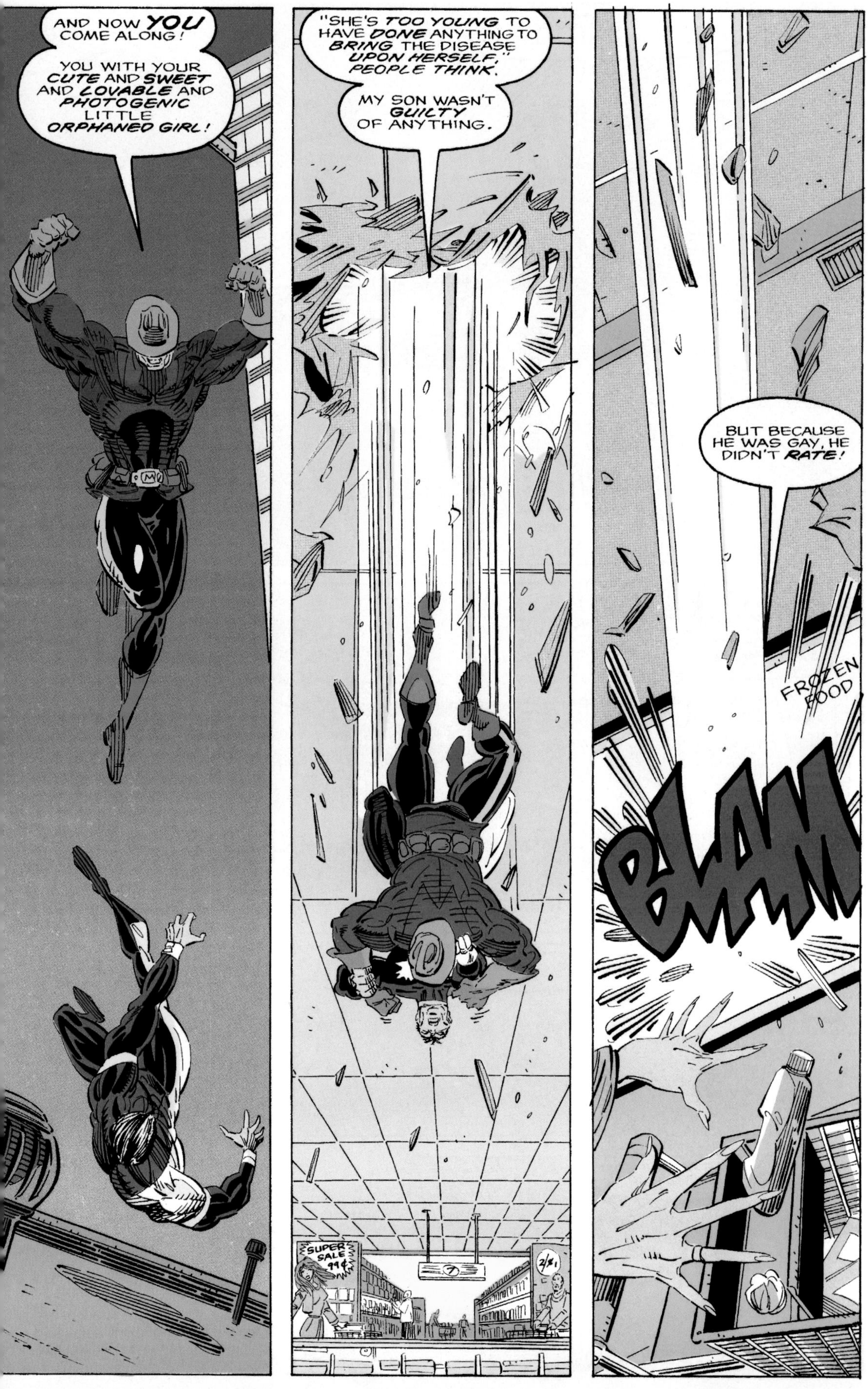
AND NOW **YOU** COME ALONG!
YOU WITH YOUR **CUTE** AND **SWEET** AND **LOVABLE** AND **PHOTOGENIC** LITTLE **ORPHANED GIRL**!
"SHE'S **TOO YOUNG** TO HAVE **DONE** ANYTHING TO **BRING** THE DISEASE **UPON HERSELF**," **PEOPLE THINK**.
MY SON WASN'T **GUILTY** OF ANYTHING.
SUPER SALE 99¢
BUT BECAUSE HE WAS GAY, HE DIDN'T **RATE**!
FROZEN FOOD
BLAM

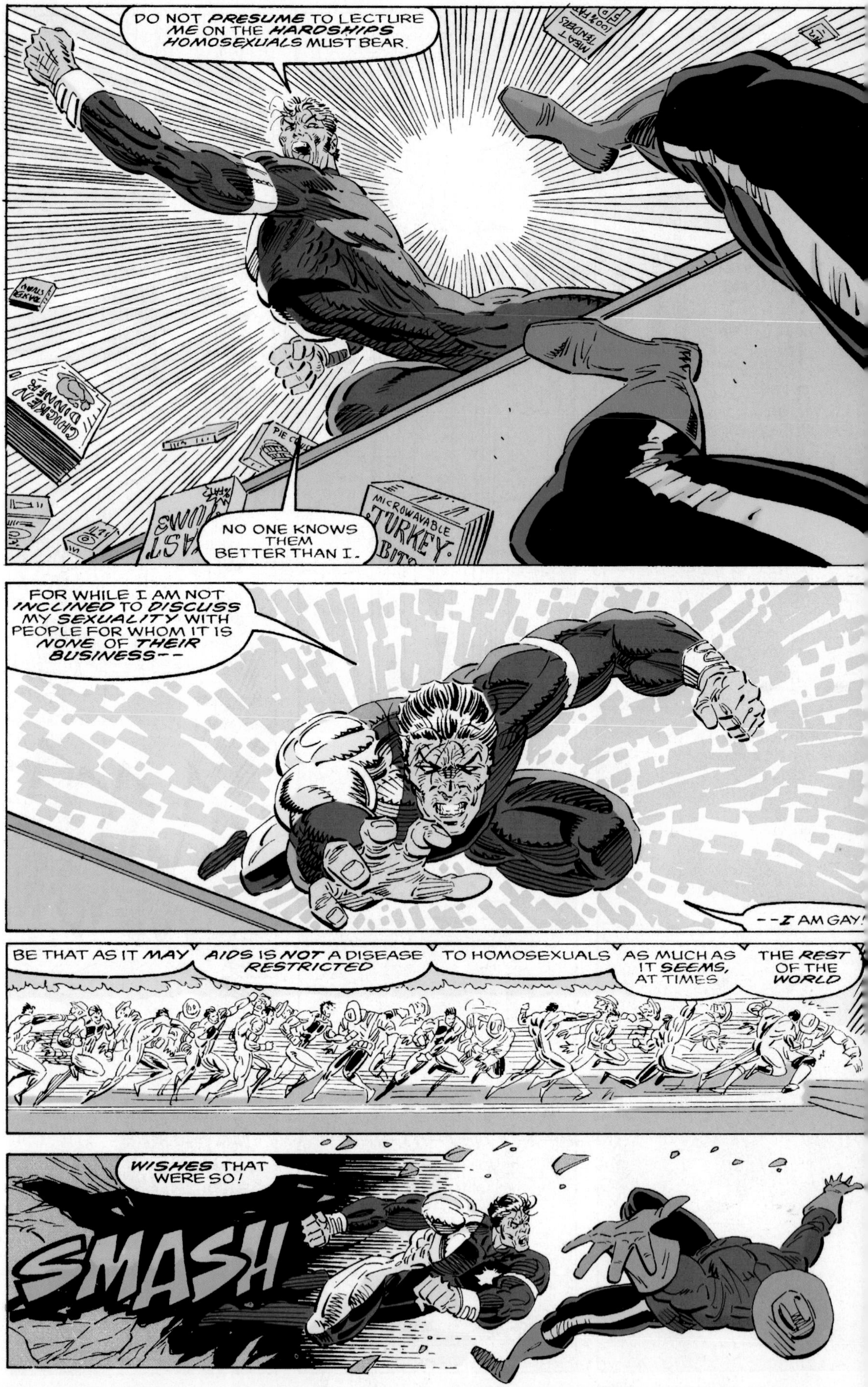
DO NOT PRESUME TO LECTURE ME ON THE HARDSHIPS HOMOSEXUALS MUST BEAR.
NO ONE KNOWS THEM BETTER THAN I.
FOR WHILE I AM NOT INCLINED TO DISCUSS MY SEXUALITY WITH PEOPLE FOR WHOM IT IS NONE OF THEIR BUSINESS--
--I AM GAY!
BE THAT AS IT MAY
AIDS IS NOT A DISEASE RESTRICTED
TO HOMOSEXUALS
AS MUCH AS IT SEEMS, AT TIMES
THE REST OF THE WORLD
WISHES THAT WERE SO!
SMASH

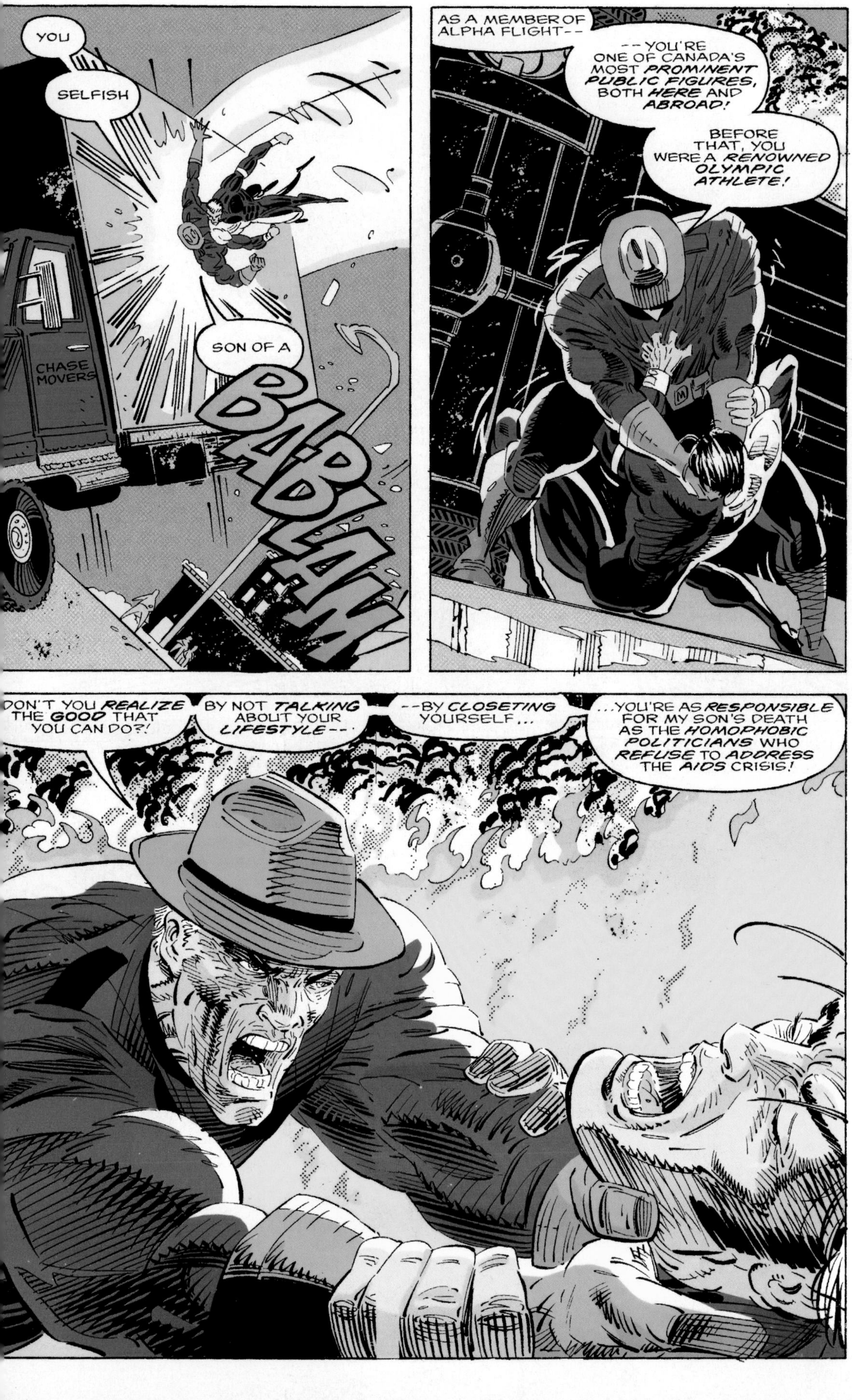
YOU
SELFISH
SON OF A
BABLAM
CHASE MOVERS
AS A MEMBER OF ALPHA FLIGHT--
--YOU'RE ONE OF CANADA'S MOST *PROMINENT PUBLIC FIGURES,* BOTH *HERE* AND *ABROAD!*
BEFORE THAT, YOU WERE A *RENOWNED OLYMPIC ATHLETE!*
DON'T YOU *REALIZE* THE *GOOD* THAT YOU CAN DO?!
BY NOT *TALKING* ABOUT YOUR *LIFESTYLE*--
--BY *CLOSETING* YOURSELF...
...YOU'RE AS *RESPONSIBLE* FOR MY SON'S DEATH AS THE *HOMOPHOBIC POLITICIANS* WHO *REFUSE* TO *ADDRESS* THE *AIDS* CRISIS!

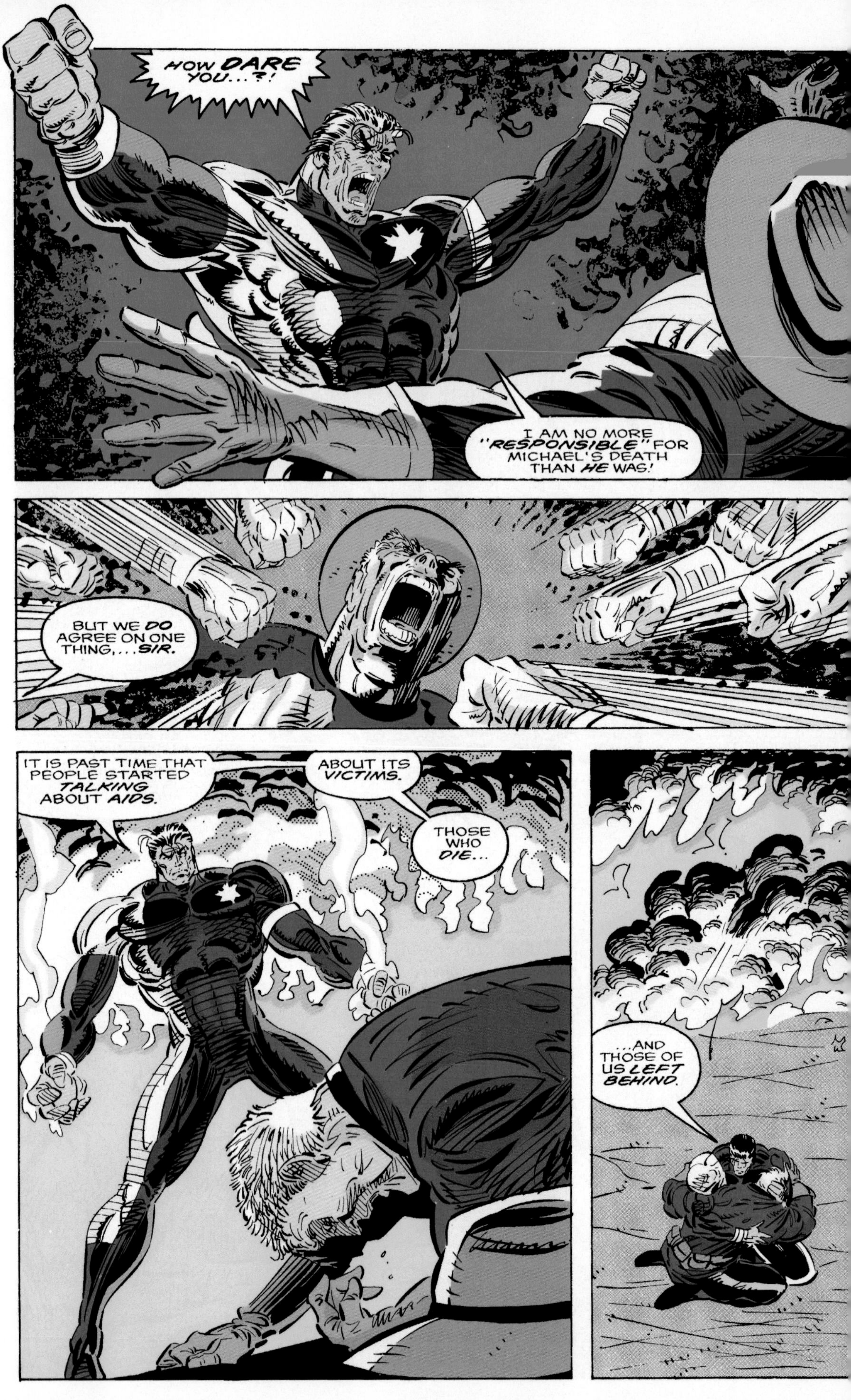
HOW DARE YOU...?!
I AM NO MORE "RESPONSIBLE" FOR MICHAEL'S DEATH THAN HE WAS!
BUT WE DO AGREE ON ONE THING,...SIR.
IT IS PAST TIME THAT PEOPLE STARTED TALKING ABOUT AIDS.
ABOUT ITS VICTIMS.
THOSE WHO DIE...
...AND THOSE OF US LEFT BEHIND.

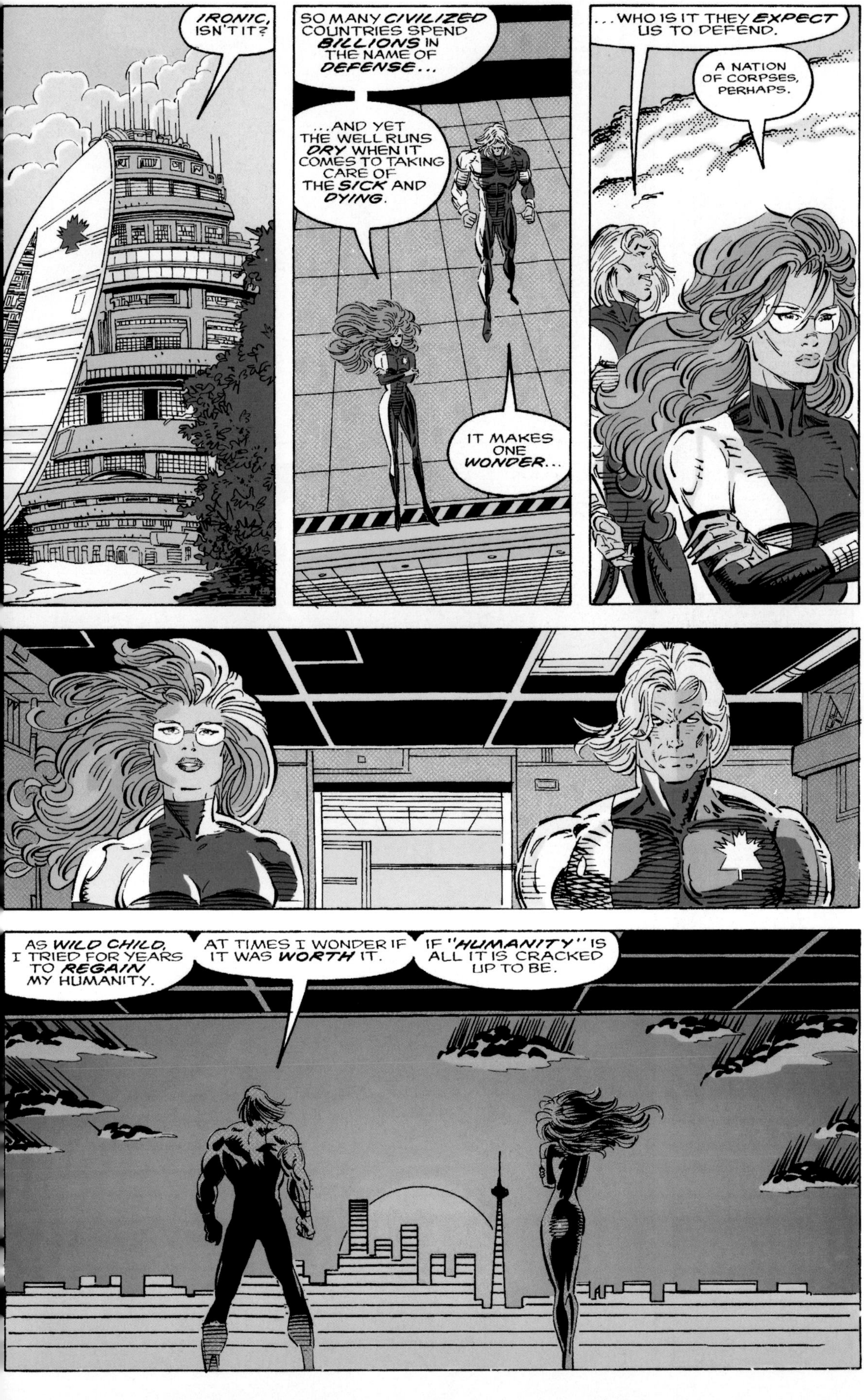

IRONIC, ISN'T IT?
SO MANY CIVILIZED COUNTRIES SPEND BILLIONS IN THE NAME OF DEFENSE...
...AND YET THE WELL RUNS DRY WHEN IT COMES TO TAKING CARE OF THE SICK AND DYING.
IT MAKES ONE WONDER...
...WHO IS IT THEY EXPECT US TO DEFEND.
A NATION OF CORPSES, PERHAPS.
AS WILD CHILD, I TRIED FOR YEARS TO REGAIN MY HUMANITY.
AT TIMES I WONDER IF IT WAS WORTH IT.
IF "HUMANITY" IS ALL IT IS CRACKED UP TO BE.

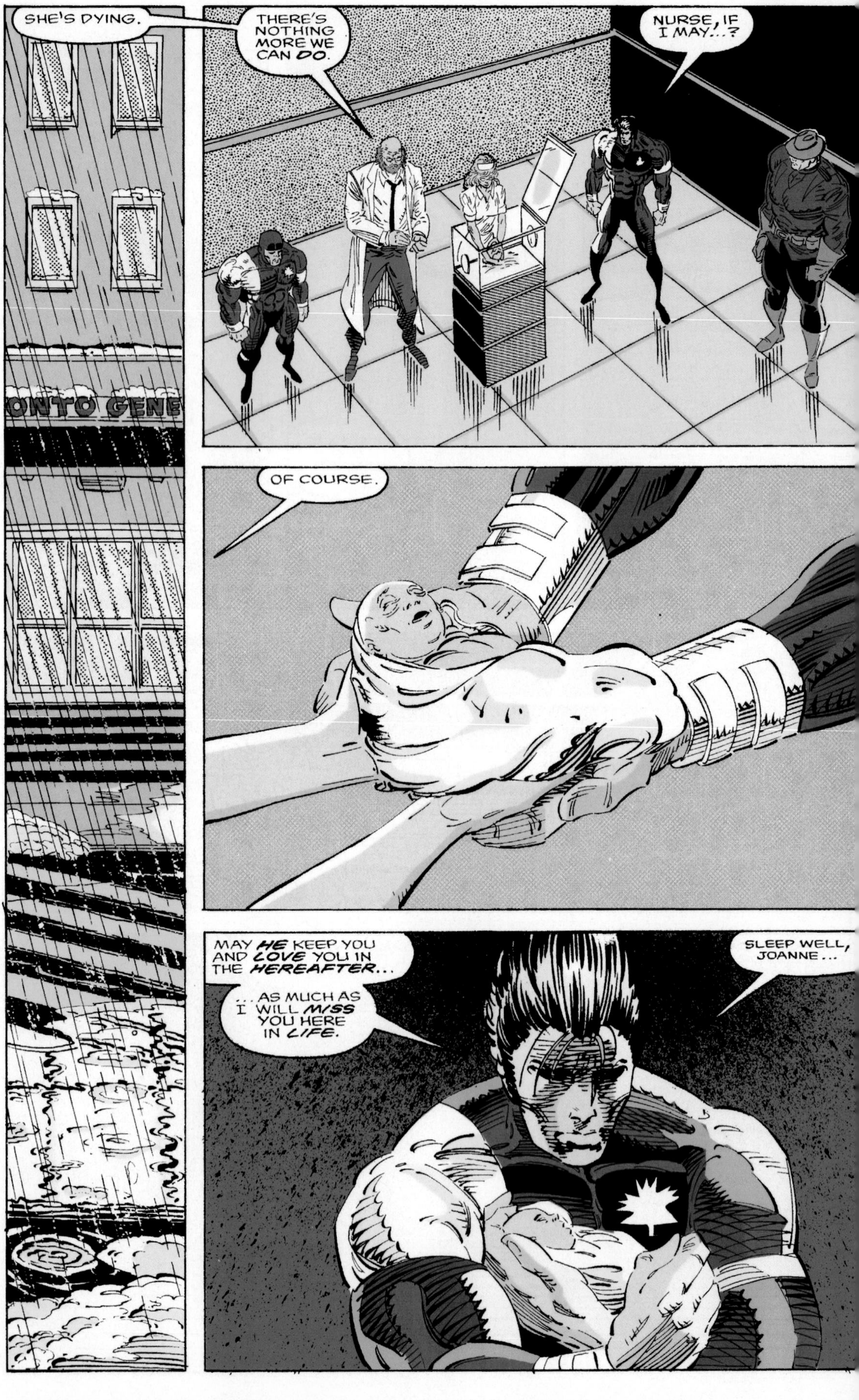
SHE'S DYING.
THERE'S NOTHING MORE WE CAN DO.
NURSE, IF I MAY...?
ONTO GENE
OF COURSE.
MAY HE KEEP YOU AND LOVE YOU IN THE HEREAFTER...
...AS MUCH AS I WILL MISS YOU HERE IN LIFE.
SLEEP WELL, JOANNE...

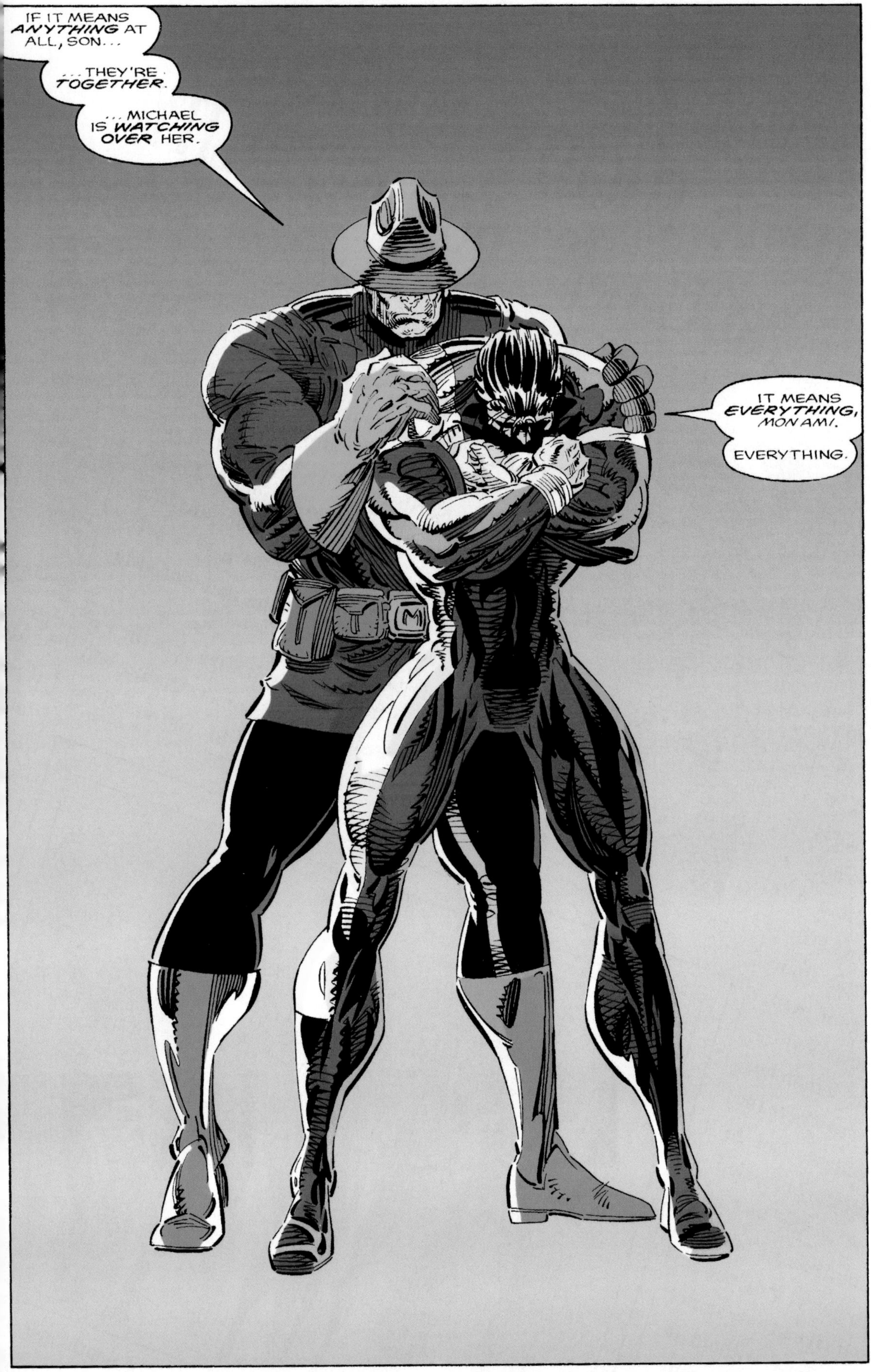

IF IT MEANS ANYTHING AT ALL, SON...
...THEY'RE TOGETHER.
...MICHAEL IS WATCHING OVER HER.
IT MEANS EVERYTHING, MON AMI.
EVERYTHING.

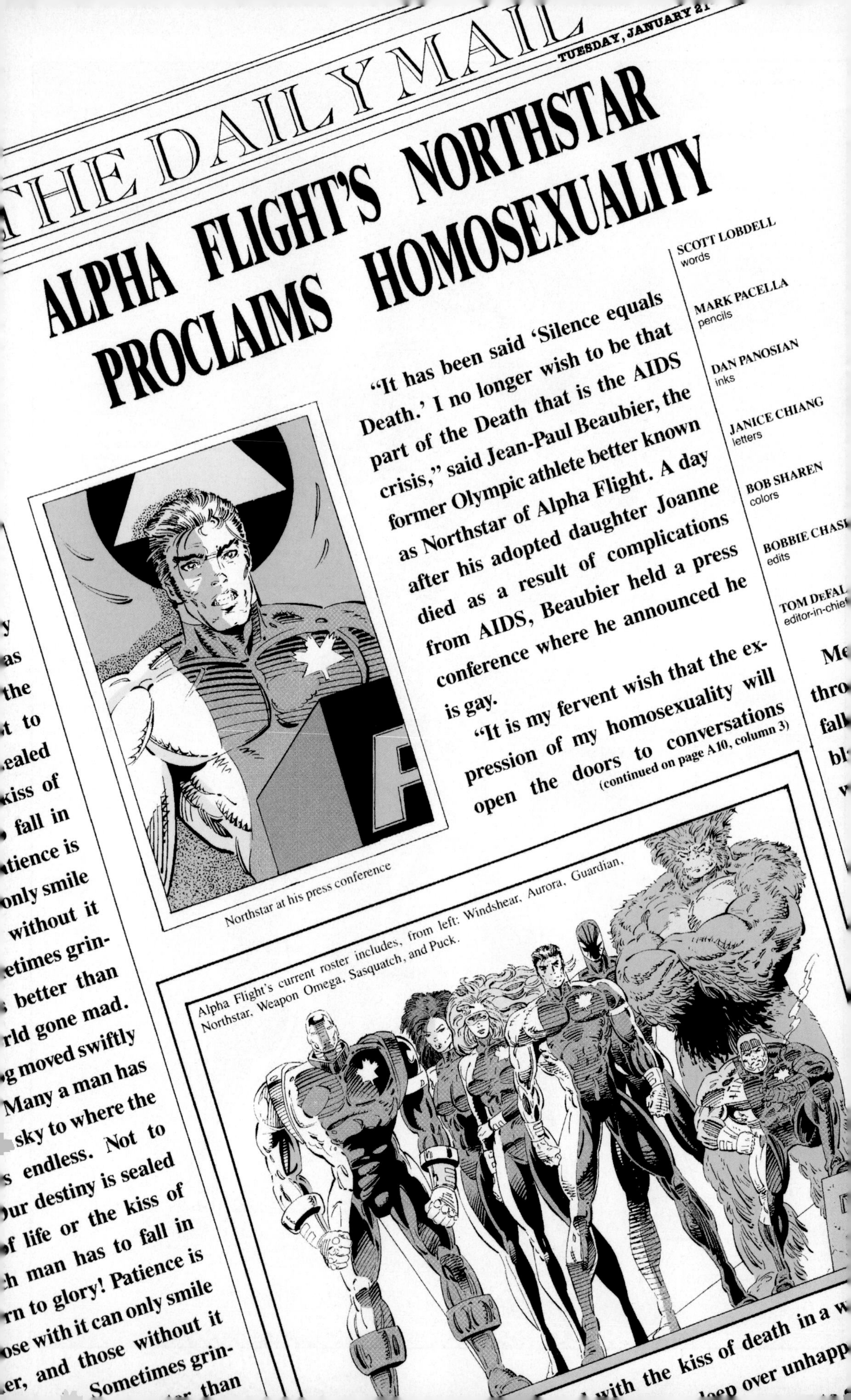

THE DAILY MAIL

TUESDAY, JANUARY 21

ALPHA FLIGHT'S NORTHSTAR PROCLAIMS HOMOSEXUALITY

SCOTT LOBDELL
words

MARK PACELLA
pencils

DAN PANOSIAN
inks

JANICE CHIANG
letters

BOB SHAREN
colors

BOBBIE CHAS
edits

TOM DeFAL
editor-in-chie

"It has been said 'Silence equals Death.' I no longer wish to be that part of the Death that is the AIDS crisis," said Jean-Paul Beaubier, the former Olympic athlete better known as Northstar of Alpha Flight. A day after his adopted daughter Joanne died as a result of complications from AIDS, Beaubier held a press conference where he announced he is gay.

"It is my fervent wish that the expression of my homosexuality will open the doors to conversations

(continued on page A10, column 3)

Northstar at his press conference

Alpha Flight's current roster includes, from left: Windshear, Aurora, Guardian, Northstar, Weapon Omega, Sasquatch, and Puck.

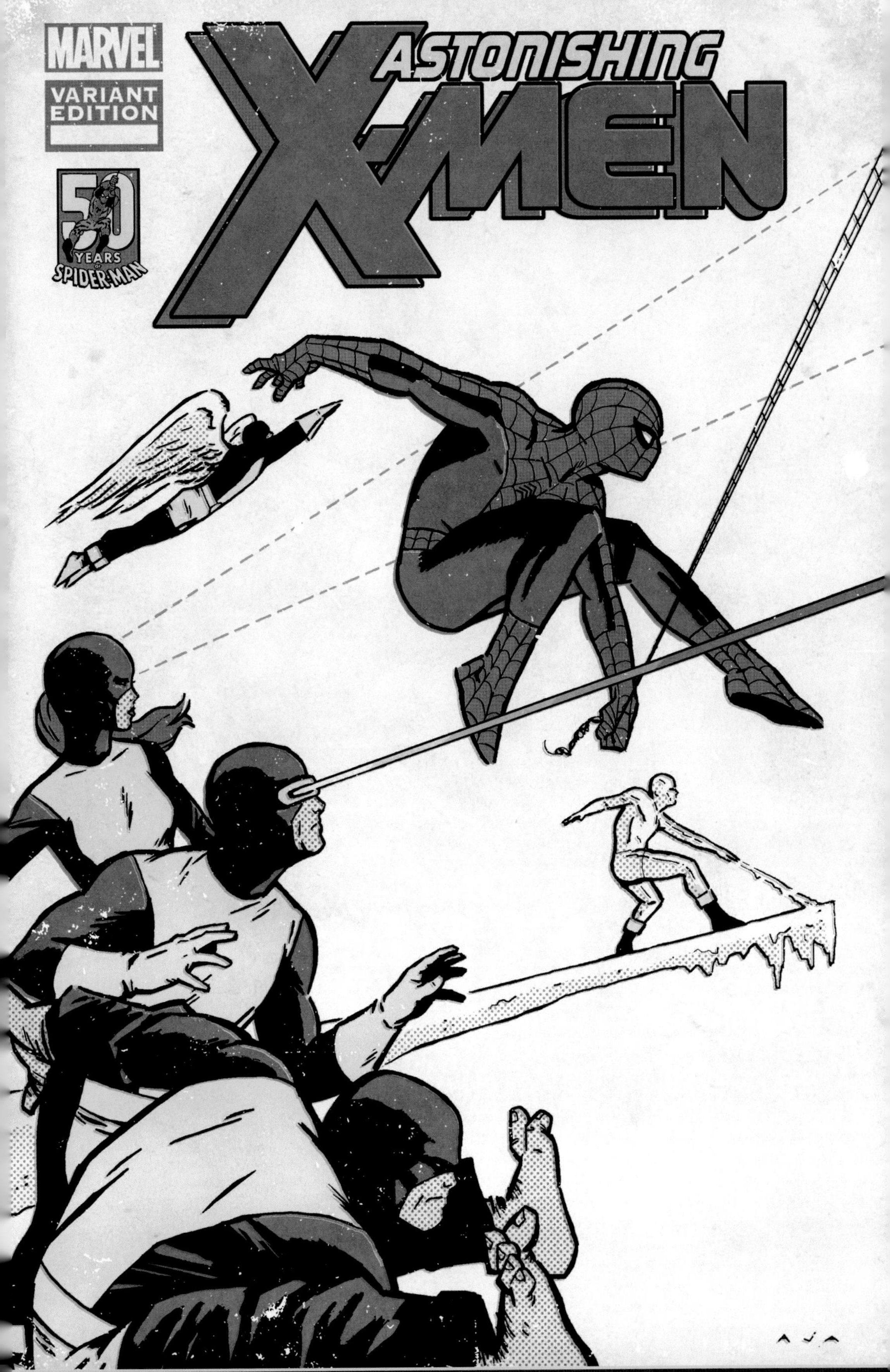
MARVEL
VARIANT EDITION
50 YEARS of SPIDER-MAN
ASTONISHING
X-MEN
AJA

#48 Amazing Spider-Man 50th Anniversary Variant by DAVID AJA

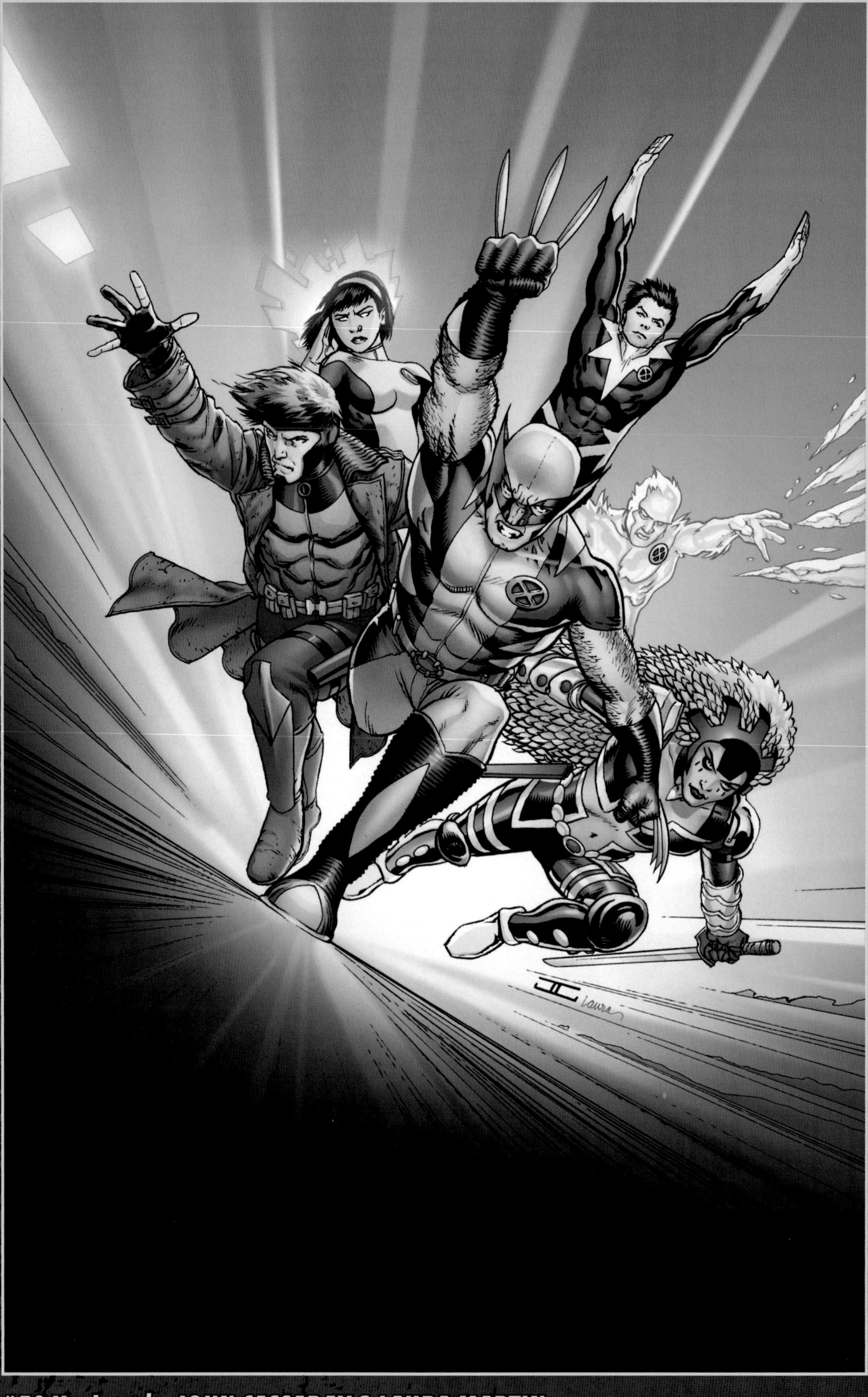

#50 Variant by JOHN CASSADAY & LAURA MARTIN

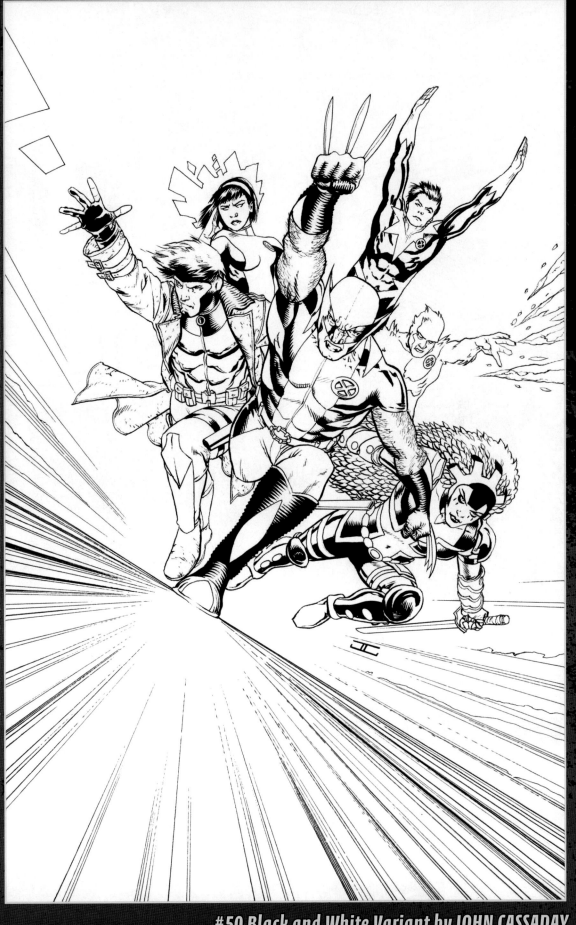

#50 Black and White Variant by JOHN CASSADAY

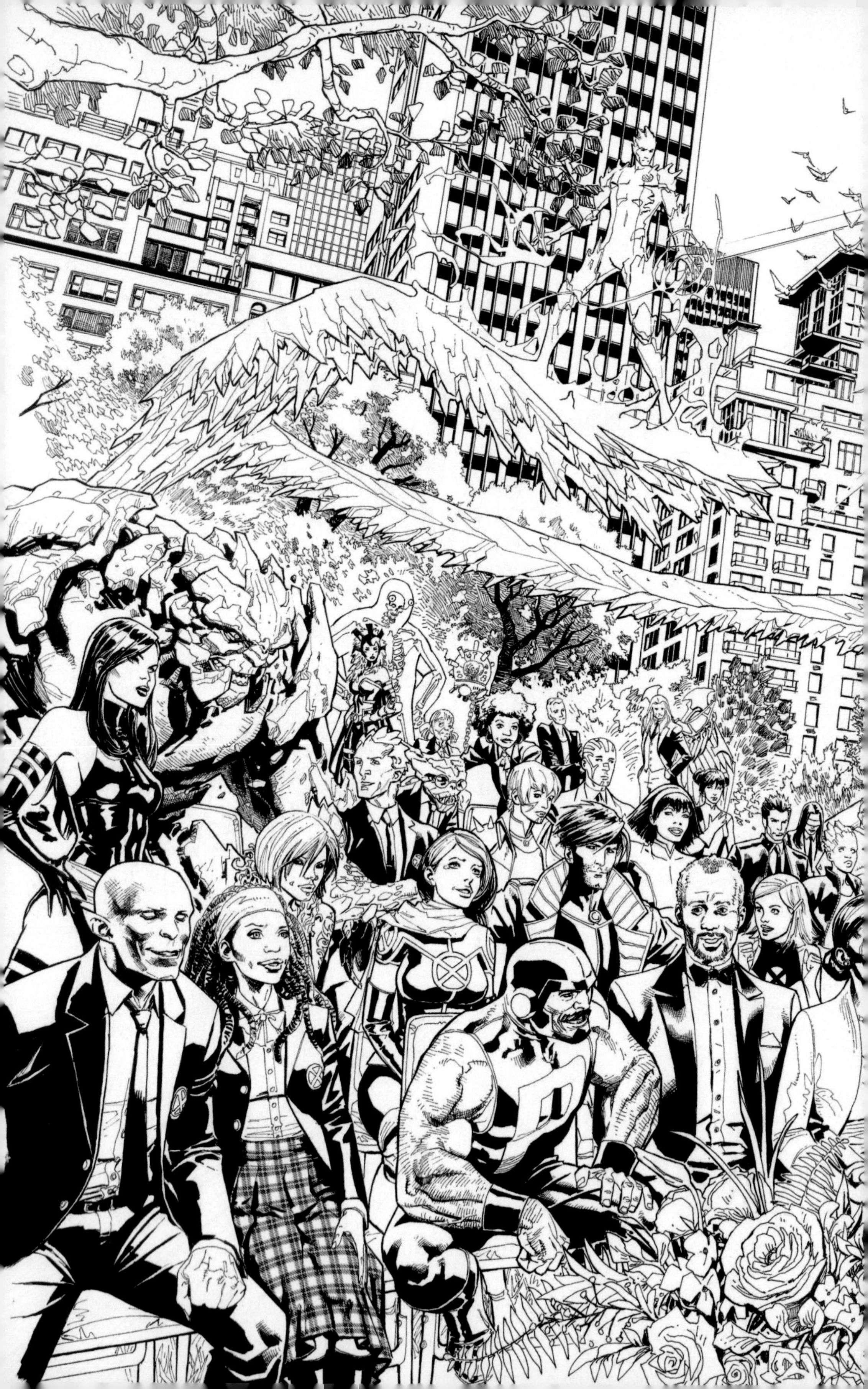

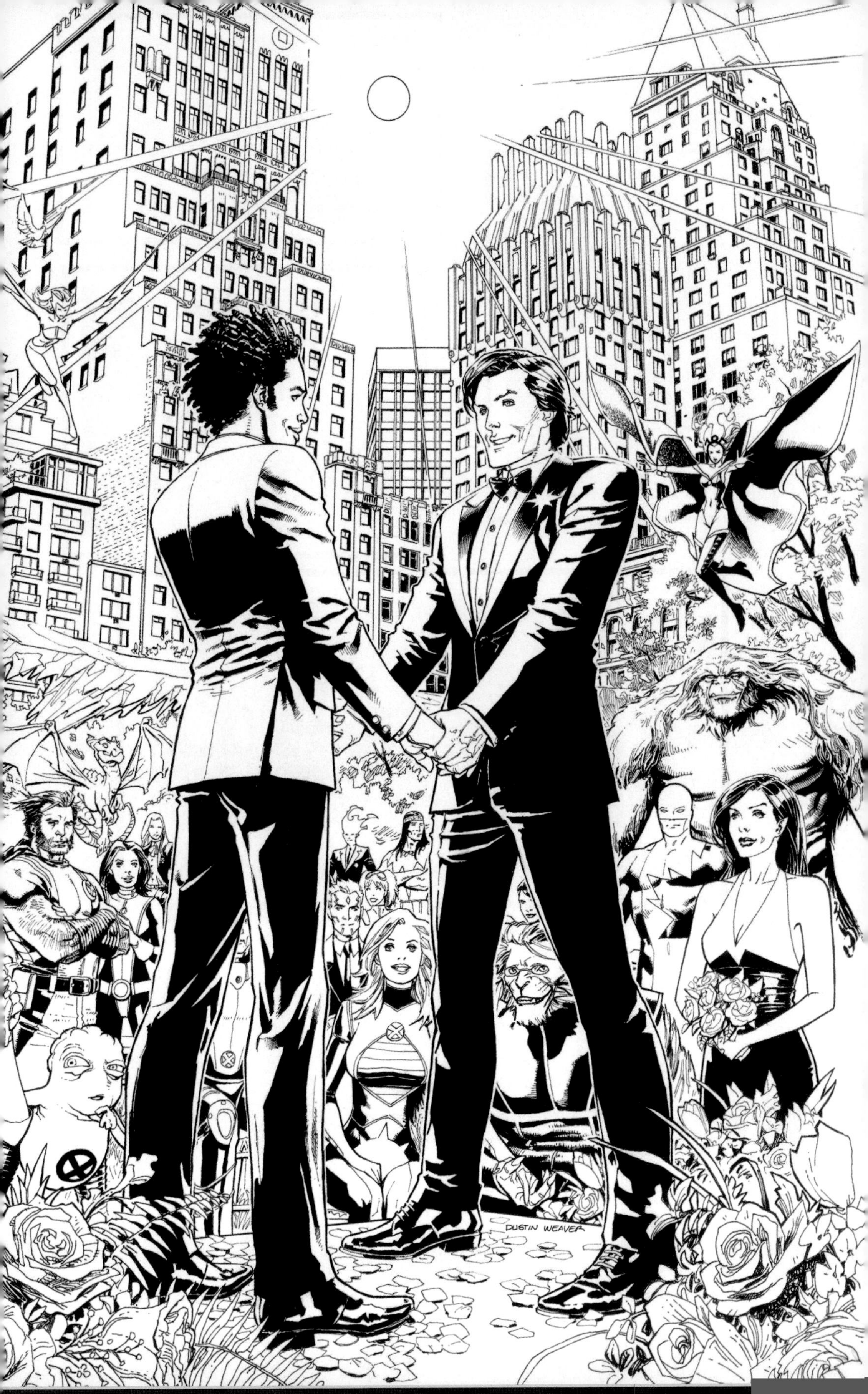
DUSTIN WEAVER

t by DUST

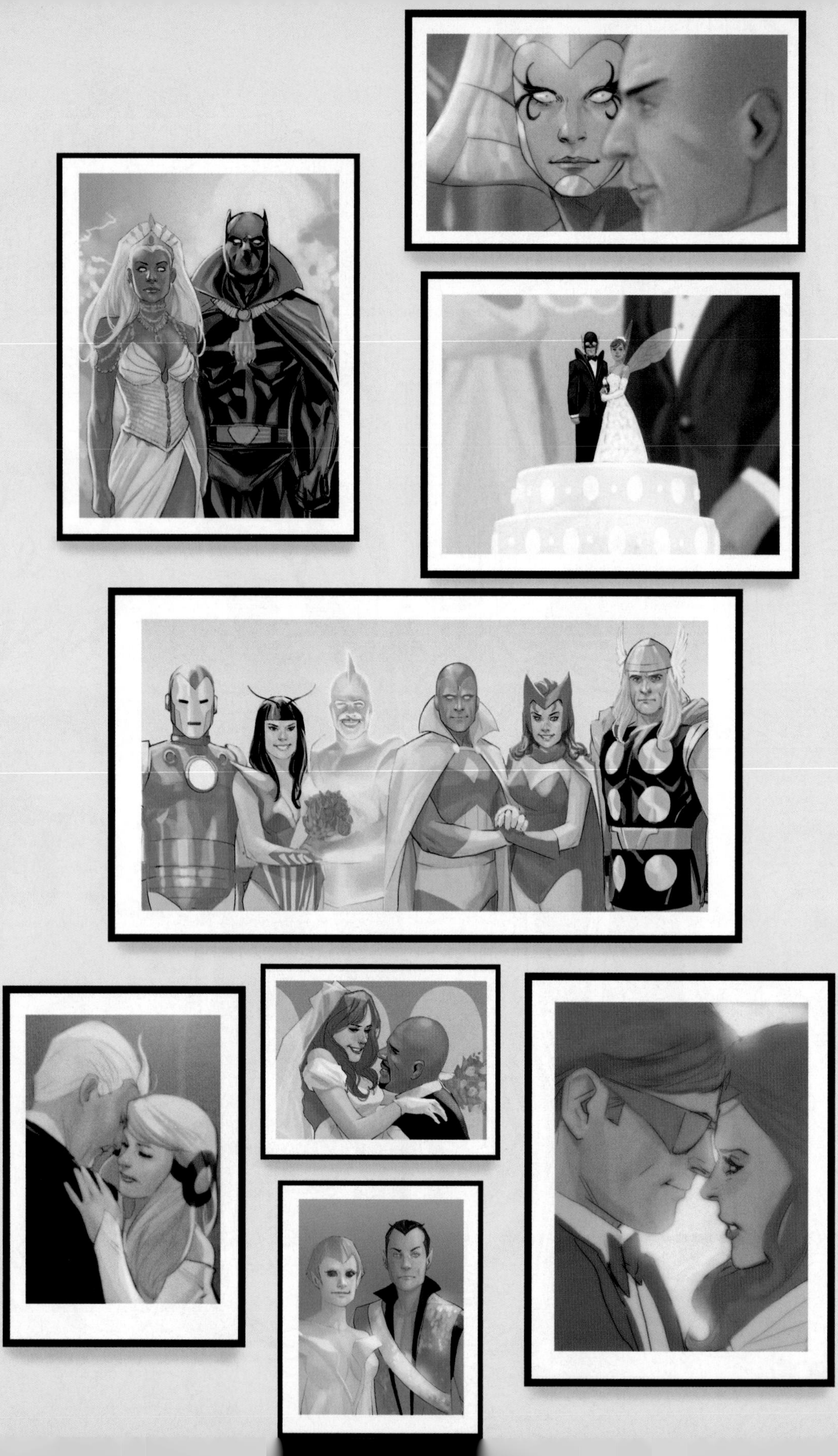

ASTONISHING X-MEN

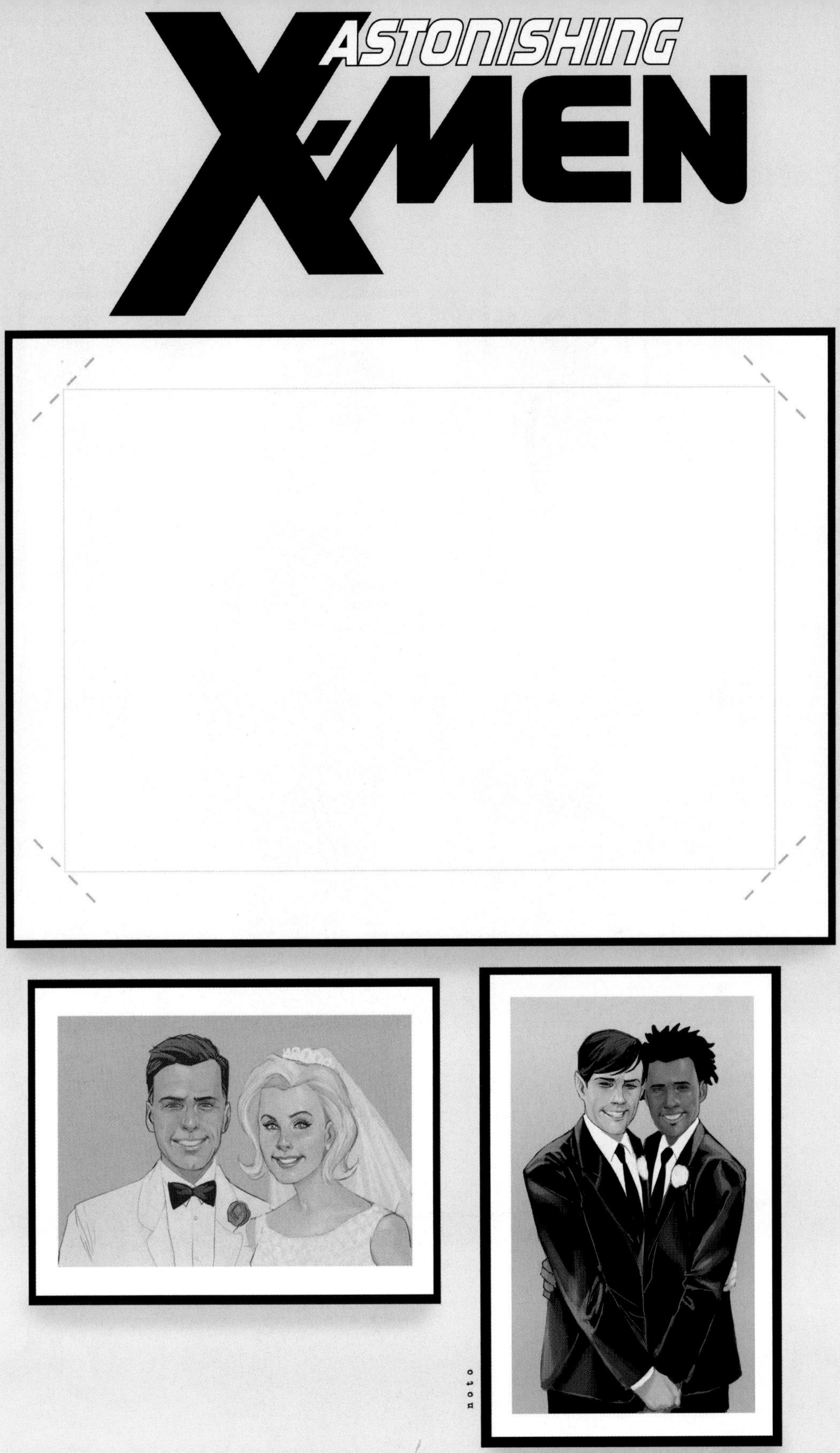

noto

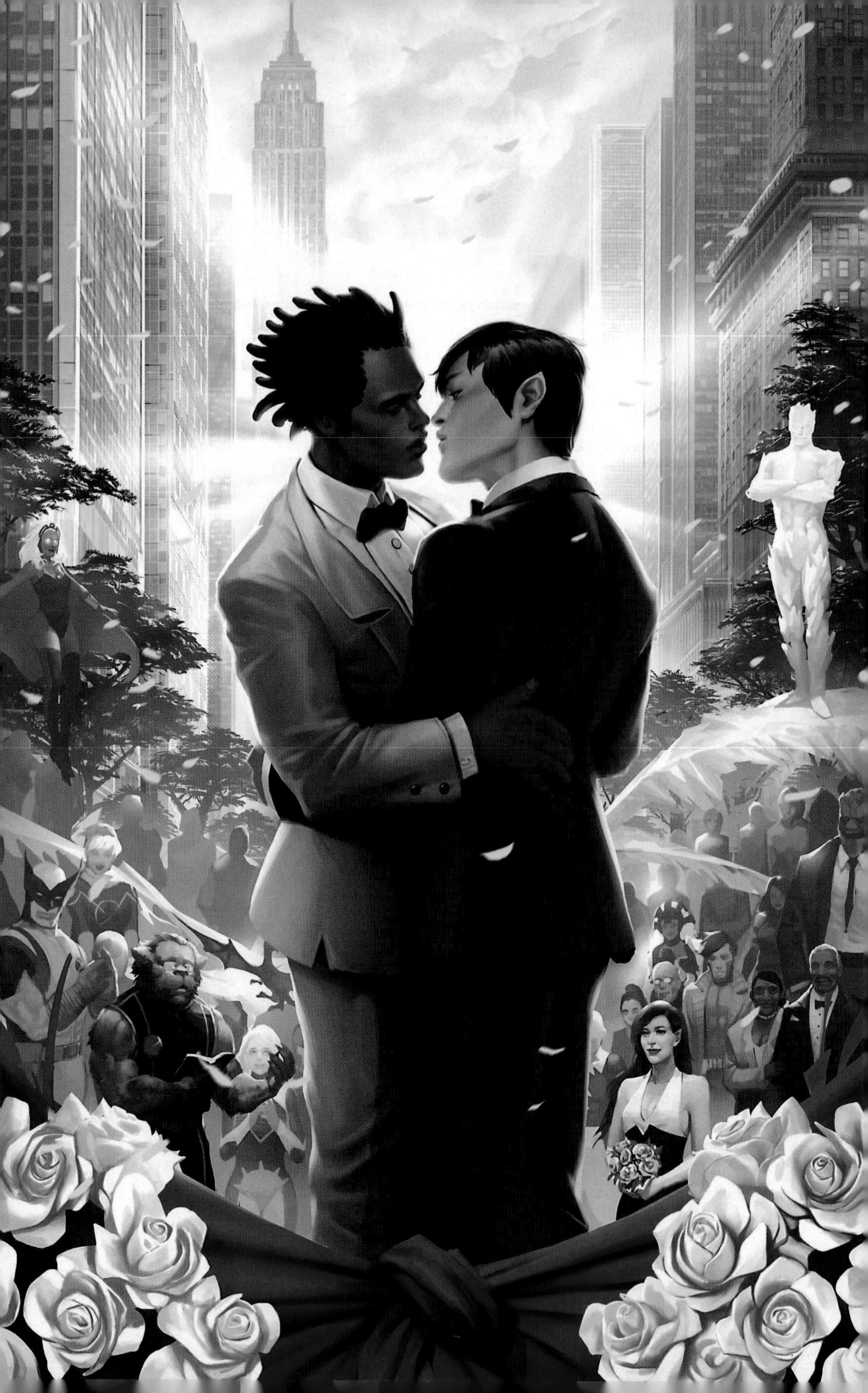